HON. JAMES BRYCE
BRITISH AMBASSADOR TO THE UNITED STATES

Edition de Luxe

THE AMERICAN COMMONWEALTH

by

JAMES BRYCE, M.P.

Abridged and Revised
From First Edition

With a Historical Appendix

Illustrated

John D. Morris and Company
Philadelphia

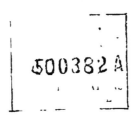

CONTENTS

CONTENTS

APPENDIX

INTRODUCTION

THE United States is a Commonwealth of commonwealths, a Republic of republics, a State which, while one, is nevertheless composed of other States even more essential to its existence than it is to theirs.

This is a point of so much consequence, and so apt to be misapprehended by Europeans, that a few sentences may be given to it.

When within a large political community smaller communities are found existing, the relation of the smaller to the larger usually appears in one or the other of the two following forms: One form is that of a league, in which a number of political bodies, be they monarchies or republics, are bound together so as to constitute for certain purposes, and especially for the purpose of common defense, a single body.

In the second form, the smaller communities are mere subdivisions of that greater one which we call the nation. They have been created, or at any rate they exist, for administrative purposes only. Such powers as they possess are powers delegated by the nation, and can be overridden by its will.

The American Federal Republic corresponds to neither of these two forms, but may be said to stand between them. Its central or national government is not a mere league, for it does not wholly depend on the component communities which we call the States. It is itself a commonwealth as well as a union of commonwealths, because it claims directly the obedience of every citizen, and acts immediately upon him through its courts and executive officers. Still less are the minor communities, the States, mere subdivisions of the Union, mere creatures of the national government, like the counties of England or the departments of France. They have over their citizens an authority which is their own, and not delegated by the central government. They have not been called into being by that government. They existed before it. They could exist without it.

This is the cause of that immense complexity which startles and at first bewilders the student of American institutions, a complexity which makes American history and current American politics so difficult to the European who finds in them phenomena to which his own experience supplies no parallel. There are two loyalties, two patriotisms, two allegiances. There are two governments, two jurisdictions covering the same ground, commanding, with equally direct authority, the obedience of the same citizen.

Let us first consider the Constitution of the United States.[1] The Constitution deserves the veneration with which the Americans have been accustomed to regard it. It is true that many criticisms have been passed upon its arrangement, upon its omissions, upon the artificial character of some of the institutions it creates. Yet, after all deductions, it ranks above every other written constitution for the intrinsic excellence of its scheme, its adaptation to the circumstances of the people, the simplicity, brevity, and precision of its language, its judicious mixture of definiteness in principle with elasticity in details.

There is little in the Constitution that is absolutely new. There is much that is as old as Magna Charta. The men of the Convention had the experience of the English Constitution, and appreciated and turned to excellent account its spirit and methods.

They had for their oracle of political philosophy the treatise of Montesquieu on the Spirit of Laws, which, pub-

[1] For full text see Appendix.

lished anonymously at Geneva forty years before, had won its way to an immense authority on both sides of the ocean. No general principle of politics laid such hold on the Constitution-makers and statesmen of America as his dogma that the separation of the three functions, executive, legislative, judicial, is essential to freedom.

Further, they had the experience of their colonial and State governments, and especially, for this was freshest and most in point, the experience of the working of the State constitutions, framed at or since the date when the colonies threw off their English allegiance.

Lastly, they had one principle of the English common law whose importance deserves special mention, the principle that an act done by any official person or law-making body in excess of his or its legal competence is simply void.

THE AMERICAN
COMMONWEALTH

The

American Commonwealth

Chapter I

NATURE OF THE FEDERAL GOVERNMENT

THE acceptance of the Constitution made the American people a nation. It turned what had been a league of States into a Federal State, by giving it a national government with a direct authority over all citizens. But as this national government was not to supersede the governments of the States, the problem which the Constitution-makers had to solve was twofold. They had to create a central government. They had also to determine the relations of this central government to the States as well as to the individual citizen. An exposition of the Constitution and criticism of its working must therefore deal with it in these two aspects.

It must, however, be remembered that the Constitution does not profess to be a complete scheme of government, creating organs for the discharge of all the functions and duties which a civilized community undertakes. It presupposes the State governments. It assumes their existence, their wide and constant activity. It is a scheme designed to provide for the discharge of such and so many functions of government as the States do not already possess and discharge. It is therefore, so to speak, the complement and crown of the State constitutions, which must be read along with it and into it in order to make it cover the whole field of civil government, as do the Constitutions of such countries as France, Belgium, and Italy.

The administrative, legislative, and judicial functions for which the Federal Constitution provides are those relating to matters which must be deemed common to the whole nation, either because all the parts of the nation are alike interested in them, or because it is only by the nation as a whole that they can be satisfactorily undertaken. The chief of these common or national matters are:

War and peace: treaties and foreign relations generally.

Army and navy.

Federal courts of justice.

Commerce, foreign and domestic.

Currency.

Copyright and patents.

The post office and post roads.

Taxation for the foregoing purposes, and for the general support of the government.

The protection of citizens against unjust or discriminating legislation by any State.

This list includes the subjects upon which the national legislature has the right to legislate, the national executive to enforce the Federal laws and generally to act in defense of national interests, the national judiciary to adjudicate. All other legislation and administration is left to the several States, without power of interference by the Federal legislature or Federal executive.

Such then being the sphere of the national government, let us see in what manner it is constituted, of what departments it consists.

The framers of this government set before themselves four objects as essential to its excellence, *viz.*:

Its vigor and efficiency.

The independence of each of its departments (as being essential to the permanency of its form).

Its dependence on the people.

The security under it of the freedom of the individual.

The first of these objects they sought by creating a strong executive, the second by separating the legislative, executive, and judicial powers from one another, and by the contrivance of various checks and balances, the third by making all authorities elective and elections frequent, the fourth both by the checks and balances aforesaid, so arranged as to restrain any one department from tyranny, and by placing certain rights of the citizen under the protection of the written Constitution.

They had neither the rashness nor the capacity necessary for constructing a Constitution *a priori.* These men, practical statesmen who knew how infinitely difficult a business government is, desired no bold experiments. Accordingly they started from the system on which their own colonial governments, and afterwards their State governments, had been conducted. This system bore a general resemblance to the British constitution; they held England to be the freest and best-governed country in the world, but were resolved to avoid the weak points which had enabled King George III. to play the tyrant. They created a legislature of two houses, Congress, on the model of the two houses of their State legislatures, and of the British Parliament; and following the precedent of the British judges, irremovable except by the crown and Parliament combined, they created a judiciary appointed for life, and irremovable save by impeachment.

In these great matters, however, as well as in many lesser matters, they copied not so much the constitution of England as the constitution of their several States, in which, as was natural, many features of the English constitution had been embodied. One profound difference must be noted here between the United States and British constitutions: the British Parliament had always been, was then, and remains now, a sovereign and constituent assembly. It can make and unmake any and every law, change the form of government or the succession to the throne, interfere with the course of justice, extinguish the most sacred private rights of the citizen.

In the American system there exists no such body. Not merely Congress alone, but also Congress and the President conjoined, are subject to the Constitution, and cannot move a step outside the circle which the Constitution has drawn around them. The only power which is ultimately sovereign, as the British Parliament is always and directly sovereign, is the people of the States, acting in the manner prescribed by the Constitution, and capable in that manner of passing any law whatever in the form of a constitutional amendment.

This fundamental divergence from the British system is commonly said to have been forced upon the men of 1787 by the necessity of safeguarding the rights of the States, and by jealousy and fear of chosen magistrates, so that it led to the creation of a supreme constitution or fundamental instrument of government, placed above and controlling the national legislature itself. They had already such fundamental instruments in the charters of the colonies, which had passed into the constitutions of the several States; and they would certainly have followed, in creating their national constitution, a precedent which they deemed so precious.

The subjection of all the ordinary authorities and organs of government to a supreme instrument expressing the will of the sovereign people, and capable of being altered by them only, has been usually deemed the most remarkable novelty of the American system. But it is merely an application to the wider sphere of the nation, of a plan approved by the experiences of the several States.

Chapter II

THE PRESIDENT

ANYONE who undertakes to describe the American system of government is obliged to follow the American division of it into the three departments —executive, legislative, judicial. I begin with the executive, as the simplest of the three.

The President is the creation of the Constitution of 1789. Under the Confederation there was only a presiding officer of Congress, but no head of the nation.

Why was it thought necessary to have a President at all? The fear of monarchy, of a strong government, of a centralized government, prevailed widely in 1787. George III. was an object of bitter hatred: he remained a bogey to succeeding generations of American children. The Convention found it extremely hard to devise a satisfactory method of choosing the President, nor has the method they adopted proved satisfactory. That a single head is not necessary to a republic might have been suggested to the Americans by those ancient examples to which they loved to recur. Yet it was settled very early in the debates of 1787 that the central executive authority must be vested in one person; and the opponents of the draft Constitution, while quarreling with his powers, did not accuse his existence.

The explanation is to be found not so much in the wish to reproduce the British Constitution as in the familiarity of the Americans, as citizens of the several States, with the office of State governor and in their disgust with the feebleness which Congress had shown under the Confederation

8

in its conduct of the war. Hamilton felt strongly the need for having a vigorous executive who could maintain a continuous policy, and proposed that the head of the State should be appointed for good behavior, *i. e.*, for life, subject to removal by impeachment. The proposal was defeated, but nearly all sensible men admitted that the risks of foreign war required the concentration of executive powers into a single hand.

Assuming that there was to be such a magistrate, the statesmen of the Convention, like the solid practical men they were, did not try to construct him out of their own brains, but looked to some existing models. They, therefore, made an enlarged copy of the State governor, or to put the same thing differently, a reduced and improved copy of the English king—the President. His salary is too small to permit him either to maintain a court or to corrupt the legislature; nor can he seduce the virtue of the citizens by the gift of titles of nobility, for such titles are altogether forbidden. He was to represent the nation as a whole as the governor represented the State commonwealth. The independence of his position, with nothing either to gain or to fear from Congress, would, it was hoped, leave him free to think only of the welfare of the people.

This idea appears in the method provided for the election of a President. To have left the choice of the chief magistrate to a direct popular vote over the whole country would have raised a dangerous excitement, and would have given too much encouragement to candidates of merely popular gifts. To have intrusted it to Congress would have not only subjected the executive to the legislature in violation of the principle which requires these departments to be kept distinct, but have tended to make him the creature of one particular faction instead of the choice of the nation. Hence the device of a double election was adopted.

The Constitution directs each State to choose a number of Presidential electors equal to the number of its representatives in both Houses of Congress. Some weeks later, these electors meet in each State on a day fixed by law, and give their votes in writing for the President and Vice President. The votes are transmitted, sealed up, to the capital and there opened by the president of the Senate in the presence of both Houses and counted. To preserve the electors from the influence of faction, it is provided that they shall not be members of Congress, nor holders of any Federal office. This plan was expected to secure the choice by the best citizens of each State, in a tranquil and deliberate way, of the man whom they in their unfettered discretion should deem fittest to be chief magistrate of the Union. Being themselves chosen electors on account of their personal merits, they would be better qualified than the masses to select an able and honorable man for President.

No part of their scheme seems to have been regarded by the Constitution-makers of 1787 with more complacency than this, although no part had caused them so much perplexity. No part has so utterly belied their expectations. The Presidential electors have become a mere cogwheel in the machine; a mere contrivance for giving effect to the decision of the people. Their personal qualifications are a matter of indifference. They have no discretion, but are chosen under a pledge—a pledge of honor merely, but a pledge which has never, since 1796, been violated—to vote for a particular candidate. In choosing them the people virtually choose the President, and thus the very thing which the men of 1787 sought to prevent has happened—the President is chosen by a popular vote.

In the first two Presidential elections, 1789 and 1792, the independence of the electors did not come into question, because everybody was for Washington, and parties had

ot yet been fully developed. The third election was along
party lines, although there were still some scattering
votes.

The fourth election was a regular party struggle, car-
ied on in obedience to party arrangements. Both Feder-
lists and Republicans put the names of their candidates for
President and Vice President before the country, and round
hese names the battle raged. From that day till now there
as never been any question of reviving the true and original
ntent of the plan of double election, and consequently noth-
ng has ever turned on the personality of the electors. They
ae now so little significant that to enable the voter to know
'or which set of electors his party desires him to vote, it
s found necessary to put the name of the Presidential can-
lidate whose interest they represent at the top of the voting
icket on which their own names are printed.

The completeness and permanence of this change has
een assured by the method which now prevails of choosing
he electors. The Constitution leaves the method to each
State, and in the earlier days many States intrusted the
hoice to their legislatures. But as democratic principles
ecame developed, the practice of choosing the electors by
lirect popular vote spread by degrees through all the States.
In some States the electors were for a time chosen by dis-
ricts, like members of the House of Representatives. But
he plan of choice by a single popular vote over the whole
of the State found increasing favor until all adopted it,
eeing that it was in the interest of the party for the time
eing dominant in the State.

Thus the issue comes directly before the people. The
arties nominate their respective candidates, a tremendous
'campaign" of stump speaking, newspaper writing, street
arades and torchlight processions sets in and rages for
bout four months: the polling for electors takes place

early in November, on the same day over the whole Union, and when the result is known, the contest is over, because the subsequent meeting and voting of the electors in their several States is mere matter of form.

So far the method of choice by electors may seem to be merely a roundabout way of getting the judgment of the people. It is more than this. It has several singular consequences, unforeseen by the framers of the Constitution. It has made the election virtually an election by States, for the present system of choosing electors on a "general ticket" over the whole State causes the whole weight of a State to be thrown into the scale of one candidate, that candidate whose list of electors is carried in the given State. Hence in a Presidential election, the struggle concentrates itself in the doubtful States, where the great parties are pretty equally divided, and is languid in States where a distinct majority either way may be anticipated, because, since it makes no difference whether a minority be large or small, it is not worth while to struggle hard to increase a minority which cannot be turned into a majority. And hence also a man may be, and has been, elected President by a minority of popular votes.

When such has been the fate of the plan of 1787, it need hardly be said that the ideal President, the great and good man above and outside party, whom the judicious and impartial electors were to choose, has not been secured. The ideal was realized once and once only in the person of George Washington. Nearly every subsequent President has been elected as a party leader by a party vote, and has felt bound to carry out the policy of the men who put him in power. Thus America has, despite herself, reproduced the English system of executive government by a party majority, reproduced it in a more extreme form, because in England the titular head of the State in whose name administrative acts are done, stands in isolated dignity outside party politics.

The disadvantages of the American plan are patent; but in practice they are less serious than might be expected, for the responsibility of a great office and the feeling that he represents the whole nation have tended to sober and control the President. Except as regards patronage, he has seldom, at least since the War of Secession, acted as a mere tool of faction, or sought to abuse his administrative powers to the injury of his political adversaries.

The Constitution prescribes no limit for the reëligibility of the President. He may go on being chosen for one four-year period after another for the term of his natural life. But custom has supplied the place of law. Elected in 1789, Washington submitted to be reëlected in 1792. But when he had served this second term he absolutely refused to serve a third, urging the risk to republican institutions of suffering the same man to continue constantly in office. Jefferson, Madison, Monroe, and Jackson obeyed the precedent, and did not seek, nor their friends for them, reëlection after two terms.

The Constitution [1] requires for the choice of a President "a majority of the whole number of electors appointed." If no such majority is obtained by any candidate, i. e., if the votes of the electors are so scattered among different candidates, that out of the total number (which is now 476) no one receives an absolute majority (i. e., at least 239 votes), the choice goes over to the House of Representatives, who are empowered to choose a President from among the three candidates who have received the largest number of electoral votes. In the House the vote is taken by States, a majority of all the States (i. e., at present of twenty-three States out of forty-five) being necessary for a choice.

[1] Amendment xii., which in this point repeats the original Art. xi. sec. 1.

Only twice has the election gone to the House. In 1800, when the rule still prevailed that the candidate with the largest number of votes became President, and the candidate who came second Vice President, Jefferson and Aaron Burr received the same number. After a long struggle the House chose Jefferson.

In 1824 Andrew Jackson had 99 electoral votes, and his three competitors, J. Q. Adams, W. H. Crawford, and Henry Clay, 162 votes between them, so that Jackson wanted 32 of an absolute majority. The House chose J. Q. Adams by a vote of thirteen States against seven for Jackson and four for Crawford.

In this mode of choice the popular will may be still less recognized than it is by the method of voting through Presidential electors, for if the twenty-three smaller States were through their representatives in the House to vote for candidate A, and the twenty-two larger States for candidate B, A would be seated, though the population of the twenty-three smaller States is, of course, very much below that of the twenty-two larger.

In 1876, Mr. Hayes was the Republican candidate for the Presidency, Mr. Tilden the Democratic. The former carried his list of electors in seventeen States, whose aggregate electors numbered 163, and the latter carried his list also in seventeen States whose aggregate electors numbered 184. Four States with 22 votes remained out of the total 38, and in each of these four, two sets of electors had been chosen by popular vote, each basing its claims on complicated grounds. If all were decided for Hayes he would be elected; if any for Tilden, the office was his. The excitement over the whole Union was intense, and the prospect of a peaceful settlement remote, for the Constitution appeared to provide no means of determining the legal questions involved. The Republicans had a majority in the

Senate, and the Democrats in the House of Representatives, so that Congress could not decide. Negotiations between the leaders at last arranged a method of escape. A statute was passed creating an electoral commission of five Senators, five members of the House of Representatives, and five Justices of the Supreme Court, who were to determine all questions as to the admissibility of electoral votes from States sending up double returns. The commission turned out to be divided politically eight to seven for the Republicans. Every vote given by the members of the commission was a strict party vote. They were nearly all lawyers, and had all taken an oath of impartiality. The legal questions were so difficult, and for the most part so novel, that it was possible for a sound lawyer and honest man to take in each case either the view for which the Republicans or that for which the Democrats contended. Mr. Hayes was accordingly declared duly elected, 185 electoral votes against 184.

A President is removable during his term of office only by impeachment, a procedure familiar on both sides of the Atlantic in 1787, when the famous trial of Warren Hastings was still lingering at Westminster. In obedience to State precedents, it is by the House of Representatives that the President is impeached, and by the Senate, sitting as a law court, with the Chief Justice of the Supreme Court, the highest legal official of the country, as presiding officer, that he is tried. A two-thirds vote is necessary for conviction, the effect of which is simply to remove him from and disqualify him for office,[2] leaving him "liable to indictment, trial, judgment, and punishment, according to law."

The impeachable offences are "treason, bribery, or other high crimes and misdemeanors." As yet, Andrew Johnson is the only President who has been impeached. His foolish and headstrong conduct made his removal desirable, but as it was doubtful whether any single offense justified a con-

[2] Constitution, Art. 1. sec. 3, Art. 11. sec. 4.

viction, several of the Senators politically opposed to him voted for acquittal. A two-thirds majority not having been secured upon any one article (the numbers being thirty-five for conviction, nineteen for acquittal) he was declared acquitted.

In case of the removal of a President by his impeachment, or of his death, resignation, or inability to discharge his duties, the Vice President steps into his place. The Vice President is chosen at the same time, by the same electors, and in the same manner as the President. His only functions are to preside in the Senate and to succeed the President. Failing both President and Vice President it was formerly provided by statute, not by the Constitution, that the presiding officer for the time being of the Senate should succeed to the Presidency, and, failing him, the Speaker of the House of Representatives. To this plan there was the obvious objection that it might throw power into the hands of the party opposed to that to which the lately deceased President belonged; and therefore it has now been, by an act in 1886, enacted that on the failure of President and Vice-President, the Secretary of State shall succeed, and after him other officers of the administration, in the order of their rank. Five Presidents (W. H. Harrison, Zachary Taylor, Abraham Lincoln, James A. Garfield, and William McKinley) have died in office, and been succeeded by Vice-Presidents, and in the first and third of these instances the succeeding Vice President has reversed the policy of his predecessor, and become involved in a quarrel with the party which elected him, such as has never yet broken out between a man elected to be President and his party. In practice very little pains are bestowed on the election of a Vice President. The convention which selects the party candidates usually gives the nomination to this post to a man in the second rank, sometimes as a consolation to a disappointed candidate for the Presidential nomination, sometimes to a friend of such a disappointed candidate in order to " placate " his faction, sometimes as a compliment to an elderly leader who is personally popular. If the party carries its candidate for President, it also as a matter of course carries its candidate for Vice President, and thus if the President happens to die, a man of small account may step into the chief magistracy of the nation.

Chapter III

PRESIDENTIAL POWERS AND DUTIES

THE powers and duties of the President as head of the Federal executive are the following:

Command of Federal army and navy and of the militia of the several States when called into service of the United States.

Power to make treaties, but with the advice and consent of the Senate, *i. e.,* consent of two-thirds of Senators present.

Power to appoint ambassadors and consuls, judges of Supreme Court, and all other higher Federal officers, but with the advice and consent of Senate.

Power to grant reprieves and pardons for offenses against the United States, except in cases of impeachment.

Power to convene both Houses on extraordinary occasions.

Power to disagree with (*i. e.,* to send back for reconsideration) any bill or resolution passed by Congress, but subject to the power of Congress to finally pass the same, after reconsideration, by a two-thirds majority in each House.

Duty to inform Congress of the state of the Union, and to recommend measures to Congress.

Duty to receive foreign ambassadors.

Duty to " take care that the laws be faithfully executed."

Duty to commission all the officers of the United States.
These functions group themselves into four classes:

Those which relate to foreign affairs.

Those which relate to domestic administration.

Those which concern legislation.

The power of appointment.

The conduct of foreign policy would be a function of the utmost importance did not America, happy America, stand apart in a world of her own, unassailable by European powers, easily superior to the other republics of her continent, but with no present motive for aggression upon them. The President, however, has not a free hand in foreign policy. He cannot declare war, for that belongs to Congress, though to be sure he may, as President Polk did in 1845-1846, bring affairs to a point at which it is hard for Congress to refrain from the declaration. Treaties require the approval of two-thirds of the Senate; and in order to secure this, it is usually necessary for the Executive to be in constant communication with the Foreign Affairs Committee of that body. The House of Representatives has no legal right to interfere, but it often passes resolutions enjoining or disapproving a particular line of policy.

In all free countries it is most difficult to define the respective spheres of the legislature and Executive in foreign affairs, for while publicity and parliamentary control are needed to protect the people, promptitude and secrecy are the conditions of diplomatic success. But as some treaties, especially commercial treaties, cannot be carried out except by the aid of statutes, and as no war can be entered on without votes of money, the House of Representatives can sometimes indirectly make good its claim to influence. Many delicate questions, some of them not yet decided, have arisen upon these points, which the Constitution has, perhaps unavoidably, left in half-light. Practically, however, and for the purpose of ordinary business, the President is independent of the House, while the Senate, though it can prevent his settling anything, cannot keep him from unsettling everything.

The domestic authority of the President is in time of peace very small, because by far the larger part of law and administration belongs to the State governments, and because Federal administration is regulated by statutes which leave little discretion to the Executive. In war time, however, and especially in a civil war, it extends with portentous speed. Both as commander in chief of the army and navy, and as charged with the "faithful execution of the laws," the President is likely to be led to assume all the powers which the emergency requires. How much he can legally do without the aid of statutes is disputed, for the acts of President Lincoln during the earlier part of the War of Secession, including his proclamation suspending the writ of *habeas corpus,* were subsequently legalized by Congress; but it is at least clear that Congress can make him, as it did make Lincoln, almost a dictator.

It devolves on the Executive as well as on Congress to give effect to the provisions of the Constitution whereby a republican form of government is guaranteed to every State: and a State may, on the application of its legislature, or executive (when the legislature cannot be convened), obtain protection against domestic violence. Fortunately the case has been of rare occurrence, the most notable instances being Louisiana in 1873 and Rhode Island in 1840-1842.

The President has the right of addressing the nation by speech or proclamation, a right not expressly conferred by the Constitution, but inherent in his position. Occasions requiring its exercise are uncommon. On entering office, it is usual for the new magistrate to issue an inaugural address, stating his views on current public questions. Washington also put forth a farewell address, but Jackson's imitation of that famous document was condemned as a piece of vainglory. It is thought bad taste for the President to deliver stump speeches, and Andrew Johnson injured himself by the practice. But he retains that and all other rights of the ordinary citizen, including the right of voting at Federal as well as State elections in his own State. And he has sometimes taken an active, though a covert, share in the councils of his own party.

The position of the President as respects legislation is a peculiar one. He is not a member of the legislature at all. He is an independent and separate power on whom the people, for the sake of checking the legislature and of protecting themselves against it, have specially conferred the function of arresting by his disapproval its acts. He cannot introduce bills, either directly or through his ministers, for they do not sit in Congress. All that the Constitution permits him to do in this direction is to inform Congress of the state of the nation, and to recommend the measures which his experience in administration shows to be necessary. This latter function is discharged by the messages which the President addresses to Congress. The most important is that sent by the hands of his private secretary at the beginning of each session.

George Washington used to deliver his addresses orally, like an English king, and drove in a coach and six to open Congress with something of an English king's state. But Jefferson, when his turn came in 1801, whether from republican simplicity, as he said himself, or because he was a poor speaker, as his critics said, began the practice of sending communications in writing; and this has been followed ever since. The message usually discusses the leading questions of the moment, indicates mischiefs needing a remedy, and suggests the requisite legislation. But as no bills are submitted by the President, and as, even were he to submit them, no one of his ministers sits in either House to explain and defend them, the message is a shot in the air without practical result. It is rather a manifesto, or declaration of opinion and policy, than a step towards legislation. Congress is not moved: members go their own ways and bring in their own bills.

Far more effective is the President's part in the last stage of legislation, for here he finds means provided for carrying out his will. When a bill is presented to him, he may sign it, and his signature makes it law. If, however, he disapproves of it, he returns it within ten days to the House in which it originated, with a statement of his grounds of disapproval. If both Houses take up the bill again and pass it by a two-thirds majority in each House, it becomes law forthwith without requiring the President's signature. If it fails to obtain this majority it drops.

Considering that the arbitrary use, by George III. and his colonial governors, of the power of refusing bills passed by a colonial legislature had been a chief cause of the Revolution of 1776, it is to the credit of the Americans that they inserted this apparently undemocratic provision in the Constitution. It has worked wonderfully well. Most Presidents have used it sparingly, and only where they felt either that there was a cause for delay, or that the country would support them against the majority in Congress. Till the accession of President Cleveland in 1885, the total bills vetoed was only seventy-seven in ninety-six years. Mr. Cleveland vetoed a much larger number, the great majority being private pension bills for Civil War survivors. Though many of these bills had been passed with little or no opposition, scarcely any were repassed against his veto. The only President who used the power in a reckless way was Andrew Johnson. As the majority opposed to him was a large one in both Houses, these bills were promptly passed over his veto.

So far from exciting the displeasure of the people by resisting the will of their representatives, a President generally gains popularity by the bold use of his veto power. It

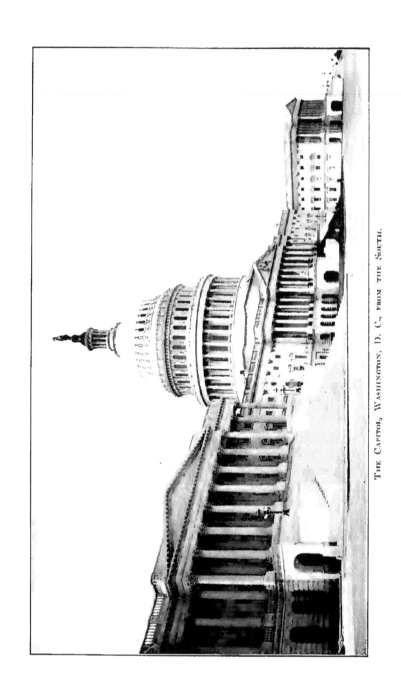

THE CAPITOL, WASHINGTON, D. C., FROM THE SOUTH.

conveys the impression of firmness; it shows that he has a view and does not fear to give effect to it. The people regard him as a check, an indispensable check, not only upon the haste and heedlessness of their representatives, the faults that the framers of the Constitution chiefly feared, but upon their tendency to yield either to pressure from any section of their constituents, or to temptations of a private nature.

As the President is charged with the whole Federal administration, and is responsible for its due conduct, he must of course be allowed to choose his executive subordinates. But as he may abuse this tremendous power the Constitution associates the Senate with him, requiring the "advice and consent" of that body to the appointments he makes. It also permits Congress to vest in the courts of law, or in the heads of departments, the right of appointing to "inferior offices." This last clause has been used to remove many posts from the nomination of the President.

The confirming power intrusted to the Senate has become a political factor of the highest moment. The framers of the Constitution probably meant nothing more than that the Senate should check the President by rejecting nominees who were personally unfit, morally or intellectually, for the post to which he proposed to appoint them. The Senate has always, except in its struggle with President Johnson, left the President free to choose his Cabinet ministers. But it early assumed the right of rejecting a nominee to any other office on any ground which it pleased, as for instance, if it disapproved his political affiliations, or simply if it disliked him, or wished to spite the President. Out of this grew the demands of the Senators from each State to be consulted in regard to Federal appointments in their own States. Each Senator, therefore, supported Senators from other States in opposition to or in favor of confirmation. By this system, which obtained the name of the Courtesy of the Senate, the

President was practically enslaved as regards appointments, because his refusal to be guided by the Senator or Senators within whose State the office lay, exposed him to have his nomination rejected. The Senators, on the other hand, obtained a mass of patronage by means of which they could reward their partisans, control the Federal civil service of their State, and build up a faction devoted to their interests.

Before we quit this subject, it must be remarked that the " Courtesy of the Senate " would never have attained its present strength but for the growth in and since the time of President Jackson, of the so-called spoils system, whereby holders of Federal offices have been turned out at the accession of a new President to make way for the aspirants whose services, past or future, he is expected to requite or secure by the gift of places.

The right of the President to remove from office has given rise to long controversies. In the Constitution there is not a word about removals; and very soon the question arose. When Congress came to settle the matter in the Presidency of Washington it took the freedom-of-removal-without-consent-of-the-Senate view, influenced perhaps by respect for Washington's perfect uprightness. So matters stood till the conflict in 1866 between President Johnson and Congress. In 1867 Congress passed the Tenure of Office Act, which made the consent of the Senate necessary to the removal of officeholders, even the President's (so-called) Cabinet ministers, permitting him only to suspend them from office during the time Congress was not sitting. The constitutionality of this act has been much doubted, and its policy is now generally condemned. It was a blow struck in the heat of passion. When President Grant succeeded in 1869, the act was greatly modified, and it has since been with general approval repealed.

How dangerous it is to leave all offices tenable at the

mere pleasure of a partisan Executive using them for party purposes, has been shown by the fruits of the spoils system. On the other hand a President ought to be free to choose his chief advisers and ministers, and even in the lower ranks of the civil service it is hard to secure efficiency if a specific cause, such as could be proved to a jury, must be assigned for dismissal.

Although Congress has transferred many minor appointments to the courts and the heads of departments, and by the Civil Service Reform Act of 1883 has instituted competitive examinations for a number now estimated at 70,000, many remain in the free gift of the President; and even as regards those which lie with his ministers, he may be invoked if disputes arise between the minister and politicians pressing the claims of their respective friends. The business of nominating is in ordinary times so engrossing as to leave the chief magistrate of the nation little time for his other functions.

Artemus Ward's description of Abraham Lincoln swept along from room to room in the White House by a rising tide of office seekers is hardly an exaggeration. From March 4, when Mr. Garfield came into power, till he was shot in the July following he was engaged almost incessantly in questions of patronage. Yet the President's individual judgment has little scope. He must reckon with the Senate; he must requite the supporters of the men to whom he owes his election; he must so distribute places all over the country as to keep the local wire-pullers in good humor, and generally strengthen the party by " doing something " for those who have worked or will work for it. No one has more to gain from a thorough scheme of civil service reform than the President. The present system makes a wire-puller of him.

In quiet times the power of the President is not great,

He has less influence on legislation,—that is to say, his individual volition makes less difference to the course legislation takes, than that of the Speaker of the House of Representatives. In troublous times it is otherwise, for immense responsibility is then thrown on one who is both the commander in chief and the head of the civil executive.

Setting aside these exceptional moments, the dignity and power of the President have, except in respect to the increase in the quantity of his patronage, been raised but little during the last seventy years, that is, since the time of Andrew Jackson, the last President who, not so much through his office as by his personal ascendency and the vehemence of his character, led and guided his party from the chair. Here, too, one sees how a rigid or supreme Constitution serves to keep things as they were. But for its iron hand, the office would surely, in a country where great events have been crowded on one another and opinion changes rapidly under the teaching of events, have either risen or fallen, have gained strength or lost it.

In no European country is there any personage to whom the President can be said to correspond. It used to be thought that hereditary monarchs were strong because they reigned by a right of their own, not derived from the people. A President is strong for exactly the opposite reason, because his rights come straight from the people. Nowhere is the rule of public opinion so complete as in America, nor so direct, that is to say, so independent of the ordinary machinery of government. Now the President is deemed to represent the people no less than do the members of the legislature. Public opinion governs by and through him no less than by and through them, and makes him powerful even against the legislature. This is a fact to be remembered by those Europeans who seek in the strengthening of the monarchical principle a cure for the faults of

government by assemblies. And it also suggests the risk
that attaches to power vested in the hands of a leader directly chosen by the people.

Although recent Presidents have shown no disposition
to strain their authority, it is still the fashion in America to
be jealous of the President's action, and to warn citizens
against what is called "the one man power." This particular alarm seems to a European groundless. I do not deny
that a really great man might exert very ample authority
from the Presidential chair. But it is hard to imagine a
President overthrowing the existing Constitution. He has
no standing army, and he cannot create one. Congress can
checkmate him by stopping supplies. There is no aristocracy to rally round him. Every State furnishes an independent center of resistance. If he were to attempt a *coup
d'état,* it could only be by appealing to the people against
Congress, and Congress could hardly, considering that it is
reëlected every two years, attempt to oppose the people.
Nothing in the present state of American politics gives
weight to such apprehensions.

Chapter IV

OBSERVATIONS ON THE PRESIDENCY

ALTHOUGH the President has been, not that independent good citizen whom the framers of the Constitution contemplated, but, at least during the last sixty years, a party man, seldom much above the average in character or abilities, the office has attained the main objects for which it was created. Nevertheless certain defects are incidental to the American Presidency. In a country where there is no hereditary throne nor hereditary aristocracy, an office raised far above all other offices offers too great a stimulus to ambition. A second defect is that the Presidential election, occurring once in four years, throws the country for several months into a state of turmoil, for which there may be no occasion. Again these regularly recurring elections produce a discontinuity of policy. Fourthly, the fact that he is reëligible once, but (practically) only once, operates unfavorably on the President. Fifthly, an outgoing President is a weak President during the last four months of his term after his successor has been chosen. Lastly, the result of an election may be doubtful, not from equality of votes, for this is provided against, but from a dispute as to the validity of votes given in or reported from the States.

At this point I will only observe that, even when we allow for the defects last enumerated, the Presidential office, if not one of the conspicuous successes of the American Constitution, is nowise to be deemed a failure. The President

28

has, during one hundred and seventeen years, carried on the internal administrative business of the nation with due efficiency. Socially regarded, the American Presidency deserves nothing but admiration. The President is simply the first citizen of a free nation, depending for his dignity on no title, no official dress, no insignia of state. The head of the ruling President does not appear on coins, nor even on postage stamps. His residence at Washington, called formerly "the Executive Mansion," and nowadays "the White House," is a building with a stucco front and a portico supported by Doric pillars.

The President's salary, which is only $50,000 a year, does not permit display, nor indeed is display expected from him. No President has made the attempt to create a court; and as the earlier career of the chief magistrate and his wife has seldom qualified them to lead the world of fashion, none is likely to make it. There is a great respect for the office, and a corresponding respect for the man as the holder of the office, if he has done nothing to degrade it. There is no servility, no fictitious self-abasement on the part of the citizens, but a simple and hearty deference to one who represents the majesty of the nation, the sort of respect which the proudest Roman paid to the consulship, even if the particular consul was, like Cicero, a "new man."

It begins to be remarked in Europe that monarchy, which used to be deemed politically dangerous but socially useful, has now, since its claws have been cut, become politically valuable, but of more doubtful social utility. In the United States the most suspicious democrat—and there are democrats who complain that the office of President is too monarchical—cannot accuse the chief magistracy of having tended to form a court, much less to create those evils which thrive in the atmosphere of European courts. No President dares to violate social decorum as European sove-

reigns have so often done. If he did, he would be the first
to suffer.

Europeans often ask, and Americans do not always explain, how it happens that this great office, the greatest in
the world, unless we except the Papacy, to which any man
can rise by his own merits, is not more frequently filled by
great and striking men?

Several reasons may be suggested for the fact, which
Americans are themselves the first to admit. One is that
the proportion of first-rate ability drawn into politics is
smaller in America than in most European countries. Another is that the methods and habits of Congress, and indeed
of political life generally, seem to give fewer opportunities
for personal distinction, fewer modes in which a man may
commend himself to his countrymen by eminent capacity
in thought, in speech, or in administration, than is the case
in the free countries of Europe. A third reason is that
eminent men make more enemies, and give those enemies
more assailable points, than obscure men do. They are
therefore in so far less desirable candidates. Where the
choice lies between a brilliant man and a safe man, the safe
man is preferred. Candidates are selected to be run for
nomination by knots of persons who, however expert as
party tacticians, are usually commonplace men; and the
choice between those selected for nomination is made by a
very large body, an assembly of over eight hundred delegates from the local party organizations over the country,
who are certainly no better than ordinary citizens. It must
also be remembered that the merits of a President are one
thing and those of a candidate another thing.

After all, too, and this is a point much less obvious to
Europeans than to Americans, a President need not be a
man of brilliant intellectual gifts. Firmness, common
sense, and most of all, honesty, an honesty above all sus-

picion of personal interest, are the qualities which the
country chiefly needs in its chief magistrate.

So far we have been considering personal merits. But
in the selection of a candidate many considerations have to
be regarded besides personal merits, whether they be the
merits of a candidate, or of a possible President. The chief
of these considerations is the amount of support which can
be secured from different States or from different regions,
or, as Americans say, "sections," of the Union. State
feeling and sectional feeling are powerful factors in a Presidential election. The problem is further complicated by
the fact that some States are already safe for one or other
party, while others are doubtful. It is more important to
gratify a doubtful State than one you have got already,
and hence, *cœteris paribus,* a candidate from a doubtful
State, such as New York or Indiana, is to be preferred.

Other minor disqualifying circumstances require less
explanation. An avowed disbeliever in Christianity would
be an undesirable candidate. Since the close of the Civil
War, anyone who fought, especially if he fought with distinction, in the Northern army, has enjoyed great advantages, for the soldiers of that army, still numerous, rally
to his name. Similarly a person who fought in the Southern
army would be a bad candidate, for he might alienate the
North. These secondary considerations do not always prevail. Intellectual ability and force of character must
influence the choice of a candidate, and their influence is
sometimes decisive. They count for more when times are so
critical that the need for a strong man is felt.

Although several Presidents have survived their departure from office by many years, only one, John Quincy
Adams, has played a part in politics after quitting the
White House. Past greatness is rather an encumbrance
than a help to resuming a political career. I may observe

that the Presidents, regarded historically, fall into three periods, the second inferior to the first, the third rather better than the second.

Down till the election of Andrew Jackson in 1828, all the Presidents had been statesmen in the European sense of the word, men of education, of administrative experience, of a certain largeness of view and dignity of character. All except the first two had served in the great office of Secretary of State; all were well known to the nation from the part they had played. In the second period, from Jackson till the outbreak of the Civil War in 1861, the Presidents were either mere politicians, such as Van Buren, Polk, or Buchanan, or else successful soldiers, such as Harrison or Taylor, whom their party found useful as figure-heads. They were intellectual pigmies beside the real leaders of that generation—Clay, Calhoun, and Webster. A new series begins with Lincoln in 1861. He and General Grant his successor, who cover sixteen years between them, belong to the history of the world. The other less distinguished Presidents of this period contrast favorably with the Polks and Pierces of the days before the war, but they are not, like the early Presidents, the first men of the country.

Chapter V

THE CABINET

ALMOST the only reference in the Constitution to the ministers of the President is that contained in the power given him to " require the opinion in writing of the principal officer in each of the executive departments upon any subject relating to the duties of their respective offices." All these departments have been created by acts of Congress. Washington began in 1789 with four only, at the head of whom were the following four officials:

Secretary of State.
Secretary of the Treasury.
Secretary of War.
Attorney-General.

In 1798 there was added a Secretary of the Navy, in 1829 a Postmaster-General, and in 1849 a Secretary of the Interior. A Secretary of Agriculture was established in 1889, and one of Commerce and Labor in 1903.

These nine now make up what is called the Cabinet. Each receives a salary of $8000. All are appointed by the President, subject to the consent of the Senate (which is practically never refused), and may be removed by the President alone. Nothing marks them off from any other officials who might be placed in charge of a department, except that they are summoned by the President to his private council.

None of them can vote in Congress, Art. xi. sec. 6 of

the Constitution providing that "no person holding any office under the United States shall be a member of either House during his continuance in office."

This restriction was intended to prevent the President not merely from winning over individual members of Congress by the allurements of office, but also from making his ministers agents in corrupting or unduly influencing the representatives of the people, as George III. and his ministers corrupted the English Parliament.

The President has the amplest range of choice for his ministers. He usually forms an entirely new Cabinet when he enters office, even if he belongs to the same party as his predecessor. He may take, he sometimes does take, men who not only have never sat in Congress, but have not figured in politics at all, who may never have sat in a State legislature nor held the humblest office. Generally of course the persons chosen have already made for themselves a position of at least local importance. Often they are those to whom the new President owes his election, or to whose influence with the party he looks for support in his policy. Sometimes they have been his most prominent competitors for the party nominations.

The most dignified place in the Cabinet is that of the Secretary of State. It is the great prize often bestowed on the man to whom the President is chiefly indebted for his election, or at any rate on one of the leaders of the party. In early days, it was regarded as the stepping-stone to the presidency. Jefferson, Madison, Monroe, and J. Q. Adams had all served as secretaries to preceding Presidents. The conduct of foreign affairs is the chief duty of the State Department: its head has therefore a larger stage to play on than any other minister, and more chances of fame. The State Department has also the charge of the great seal of the United States, keeps the archives, publishes the statutes, and of course instructs and controls the diplomatic and consular services.

The Secretary of the Treasury is minister of finance. His function was of the utmost importance at the beginning of the government, when a national system of finance had to be built up and the Federal Government rescued from its grave embarrassments. Hamilton, who then held the office, effected both. During the War of Secession, it became again powerful, owing to the enormous loans contracted and the quantities of paper money issued, and it remains so now because it has the management (so far as Congress permits) of the currency and the national debt. The secretary has, however, nothing directly to do with the imposition of taxes, and very little with the appropriation of revenue to the various burdens of the State.

The Secretary of the Interior has less power than his title would indicate, because most internal functions belong in America to the State governments or to the organs of local government. He is chiefly occupied in the management of the public lands, still of immense value, despite the lavish grants made to railway companies, and with the conduct of Indian affairs, a troublesome and unsatisfactory department, which has always been a reproach to the United States, and will apparently continue so till the Indians themselves disappear or become civilized. Patents and pensions, the latter a source of great expense and abuse, also belong to his province.

The duties of the Secretary of War, the Secretary of the Navy, and the Postmaster-General may be gathered from their names. The Attorney-General is not only public prosecutor and standing counsel for the United States, but also to some extent what is called on the European continent a minister of justice. He has a general oversight— it can hardly be described as a control—of the Federal judicial departments, and especially of the prosecuting officers called district attorneys, and executive court officers, called United States marshals. He is the legal adviser of the President in delicate questions as to the limit of executive power. His opinions are frequently published officially, as a justification of the President's conduct.

The Secretary of Agriculture has charge of all matters relating to the agricultural interests of the country. In his department are the Weather Bureau, the Bureaus of Forestry, of Soils, of Animal Industry, and of Plant Industry. Experiments are constantly being carried on at stations throughout the country.

The Department of Commerce and Labor was recently created, and several bureaus placed under it, as the Census, Immigration, Corporations, Statistics, Fisheries, and Labor, which had been previously independent or under other departments.

It will be observed that from this list of ministerial offices several are wanting which exist in Europe. Thus there is no colonial minister, because no colonies; no minister of education, because that department of business belongs to the several States; no minister of public worship, because the United States Government has nothing to do with any particular form of religion; no minister of public works, because grants made for this purpose come direct from Congress without the intervention of the executive, and are applied as Congress directs. Much of the work which in Europe would devolve on members of the administration falls in America to committees of Congress, especially to committees of the House of Representatives.

The respective positions of the President and his ministers are, as has been already explained, the reverse of those which exist in the constitutional monarchies of Europe. There the sovereign is irresponsible and the minister responsible for the acts which he does in the sovereign's name. In America the President is responsible because the minister is nothing more than his servant, bound to obey him, and independent of Congress. The minister's acts are therefore legally the acts of the President. Nevertheless the minister is also responsible and liable to impeachment for offenses committed in the discharge of his duties.

So much for the ministers taken separately. It remains to consider how an American administration works as a whole, this being in Europe, and particularly in England, the most peculiar and significant feature of the parliamentary or so-called "cabinet" system.

In America the administration does not work as a whole. It is not a whole. It is a group of persons, each individually dependent on and answerable to the President, but with no joint policy, no collective responsibility. Washington chose his Cabinet ministers from both political parties, although dissensions arose before his second term was over. The second President, John Adams, kept five ministers of his predecessor, being in accord with their opinions, for he and they belonged to the now full-grown Federalist party. Jefferson, the third President, was a thorough-going party leader, who naturally chose his ministers from his own political adherents. As all subsequent Presidents have been seated by one or other party, all have felt bound to appoint a party Cabinet. Their party expects it from them; and they naturally prefer to be surrounded and advised by their own friends.

So far, the American Cabinet resembles an English one. It is composed exclusively of members of one party. But now mark the differences in the English system. The head of the executive (be he king or governor) is irresponsible. The ministers are jointly as well as severally liable for their acts.

None of these principles holds true in America. The President is personally responsible for his acts, not indeed to Congress, but to the people, by whom he is chosen. No means exist of enforcing this responsibility, except by impeachment, but as his power lasts for four years only, and is much restricted, this is no serious evil. He cannot avoid responsibility by alleging the advice of his ministers, for he is not bound to follow it, and they are bound to obey him or retire. The ministers do not sit in Congress. They are not accountable to it, but to the President. An adverse vote of Congress does not affect his or their position. And a dozen votes of censure will neither compel them to resign nor oblige the President to pause in any line of conduct which is within his constitutional rights.

In this state of things one cannot properly talk of the Cabinet apart from the President. An American administration resembles not so much the Cabinets of England and France as the group of ministers who surround the Czar or the Sultan, or who executed the bidding of a Roman emperor like Constantine or Justinian. Such ministers are severally responsible to their master, and are severally called in to counsel him, but they have not necessarily any relations with one another, nor any duty of collective action. They are not a government, as Europeans understand the term; they are a group of heads of departments, whose chief, though he usually consults them separately, is sometimes glad to bring them together in one room for a talk about politics.

The so-called Cabinet is unknown to the statutes as well as to the Constitution of the United States. So is the English Cabinet unknown to the law of England. But then the English Cabinet is a part, is, in fact a committee, though no doubt an informal committee, of a body as old as Parliament itself, the Privy Council, or Curia Regis.

Chapter VI

THE SENATE

THE national legislature of the United States, called Congress, consists of two bodies, sufficiently dissimilar in composition, powers, and character to require a separate description. Their respective functions bear some resemblance to those of the two Houses of the English Parliament, which had before 1787 suggested the creation of a double-chambered legislature in all but two of the original thirteen States of the Confederation. Yet the differences between the Senate and the British House of Lords, and in a less degree between the House of Representatives and the British House of Commons, are very considerable.

The Senate consists of two persons from each State, who must be inhabitants of that State, and at least thirty years of age. They are elected by the legislature of their State for six years, and are reëligible. One-third retire every two years, so that the whole body is renewed in a period of six years, the old members being thus at any given moment twice as numerous as the new members elected within the last two years. As there are now forty-five States, the number of Senators, originally twenty-six, is ninety. This great and unforeseen augmentation must be borne in mind when considering the purposes for which the Senate was created, for some of which a small body is fitter than a large one. As there remain only four Territories which can be formed into States, the number of Senators will not (unless, indeed, existing States are divided, or more than one State created out of some of the Territories) rise beyond ninety-eight. This is of course much below the present nominal strength of the English House of Lords (about 560) and below that of the French Senate (300), and the Prussian Herrenhaus (432). No Senator can hold any office under the United States. The Vice President of the Union is *ex officio* president of the Senate, but has no vote, except a casting vote when the numbers are equally divided. Failing him (if, for instance, he dies, or falls sick, or succeeds to the presidency), the Senate chooses one of its number to be president *pro tempore*. His authority in questions of order is very limited, the decision of such questions being held to belong to the Senate itself.

The functions of the Senate fall into three classes—legislative, executive, and judicial. Its legislative function is to pass, along with the House of Representatives, bills which become acts of Congress on the assent of the President, or even without his consent if passed a second time by a two-thirds majority of each House, after he has returned them for reconsideration. Its executive functions are: (*a*) To approve or disapprove the President's nominations of Federal officers, including judges, ministers of state, and ambassadors. (*b*) To approve, by a majority of two-thirds of those present, of treaties made by the President—*i. e.* if less than two-thirds approve, the treaty falls to the ground. Its judicial function is to sit as a court for the trial of impeachments preferred by the House of Representatives.

The most conspicuous, and what was at one time deemed the most important feature of the Senate, is that it represents the several States of the Union as separate commonwealths, and is thus an essential part of the Federal scheme. Every State, be it as great as New York or as small as Delaware, sends two Senators, no more and no less. This

arrangement was long resisted by the delegates of the larger
States in the Convention of 1787, and ultimately adopted
because nothing less would reassure the smaller States, who
feared to be overborne by the larger. It is now the provision of the Constitution most difficult to change, for " no
State can be deprived of its equal suffrage in the Senate
without its consent," a consent most unlikely to be given.
There has never in point of fact been any division of interests or consequent contests between the great States and
the small ones.

The plan of giving representatives to the States as commonwealths has had several useful results. It has provided
a basis for the Senate unlike that on which the other House
of Congress is chosen. It also constitutes, as Hamilton
anticipated, a link between the State Governments and the
National Government. It is a part of the latter, but its
members derive their title to sit in it from their choice by
State legislatures. The method of choice in these bodies
was formerly left to be fixed by the laws of each State, but
as this gave rise to much uncertainty and intrigue, a Federal
statute was passed in 1866 providing that each House of a
State legislature shall first vote separately for the election
of a Federal Senator, and that if the choice of both Houses
shall not fall on the same person, both Houses in joint meeting shall proceed to a joint vote, a majority of each House
being present.

The method of choosing the Senate by indirect election
has in substance almost ceased to be indirect. They are still
nominally chosen, as under the letter of the Constitution
they must be chosen, by the State legislatures. The State
legislature means, of course, the party for the time dominant, which holds a party meeting (caucus) and decides on
the candidate, who is thereupon elected, the party going
solid for whomsoever the majority has approved. Now the

determination of the caucus has almost always been arranged beforehand. Sometimes the aspirants put themselves before the people of the State at the State party convention. Sometimes the aspirant goes on the stump in the interest of those candidates for the legislature who are prepared to support him.

Members of the Senate vote as individuals, that is to say, the vote a Senator gives is his own and not that of his State. It was otherwise in the Congress of the old Confederation before 1789. Accordingly, in the American Senate, the two Senators from a State may belong to opposite parties; and this often happens in the case of Senators from States in which the two great parties are pretty equally balanced, and the majority oscillates between them. This fact has contributed to render the Senators independent of the State legislatures, for as these latter bodies sit for short terms (the larger of the two houses usually for two years only), a Senator has during the greater part of his six years' term to look for reëlection not to the present but to a future State legislature.

The length of the senatorial term was one of the provisions of the Constitution which were most warmly attacked and defended in 1788. A six years' tenure, it was urged, would turn the Senators into dangerous aristocrats, forgetful of the legislature which had appointed them; and some went so far as to demand that the legislature of a State should have the right to recall its Senators. Experience has shown that the term is by no means too long; and its length is one among the causes which have made it easier for Senators than for members of the House to procure reëlection, a result which, though it offends the doctrinaires of democracy, has worked well for the country.

The average age of the Senate is less than might be expected. Three-fourths of its members are under sixty.

The importance of the State he represents makes no great difference to the influence which a Senator enjoys; this depends on his talents, experience, and character; and as the small State Senators have often the advantage of long service and a safe seat, they are often among the most influential.

The Senate does not change all at once, as do bodies created by a single popular election, but undergoes an unceasing process of gradual change and renewal. This provision was designed to give the Senate that permanency of composition which might qualify it to conduct or control the foreign policy of the nation. An incidental and more valuable result has been the creation of a set of traditions and a corporate spirit which have tended to form habits of dignity and self-respect.

The legislative powers of the Senate are, except in one point, the same as those of the House of Representatives. That one point is a restriction as regards money bills. On the ground that it is only by the direct representatives of the people that taxes ought to be levied, and in obvious imitation of the venerable English doctrine, which had already found a place in several State constitutions, the Constitution (Art. i. sec. 7) provides that " All bills for raising revenue shall originate in the House of Representatives, but the Senate may propose or concur with amendments, as on other bills." In practice, while the House strictly guards its right of origination, the Senate largely exerts its power of amendment, and wrangles with the House over taxes, and still more keenly over appropriations.

Among the rules of the Senate there is none providing for closure of debate, or limiting the length either of a debate or of a speech. The Senate is proud of having conducted its business without the aid of such regulations, and this has been due, not merely to the small size of the as-

sembly, but to the sense of its dignity which has usually
pervaded its members, and to the power which the opinion
of the whole body has exercised on each.   Till recently,
systematic obstruction, or, as it is called in America, " filibustering," familiar to the House, was almost unknown to
the Senate.

Divisions are taken, not by separating the Senators into
lobbies and counting them, as in the British Parliament, but
by calling the names of the Senators alphabetically.   The
Constitution provides that one-fifth of those present may
demand that the yeas and nays be entered in the journal.
Every Senator answers to his name with aye or no.   He
may, however, ask the leave of the Senate to abstain from
voting; and if he is paired, he states, when his name is called,
that he has paired with such and such another Senator, and
is therefore excused.   No one is permitted to speak more
than twice to the same question on the same day.

When the Senate goes into executive session, the galleries are cleared and the doors closed, and the obligation
of secrecy is supposed to be enforced by the penalty of ex-
pulsion to which a Senator, disclosing confidential proceedings, makes himself liable.   Practically, however, newspaper
men find little difficulty in ascertaining what passes in secret
session.

Chapter VII

THE SENATE AS AN EXECUTIVE AND JUDICIAL BODY

THE Senate is not only a legislative, but also an executive chamber; in fact in its early days the executive functions seem to have been thought the more important. These executive functions are two, the power of approving treaties, and that of confirming nominations to office submitted by the President.

To what has already been said regarding the functions of the President and Senate as regards treaties I need only add that the Senate through its right of confirming or rejecting engagements with foreign powers, secures a general control over foreign policy. It is in the discretion of the President whether he will communicate current negotiations to it and take its advice upon them, or will say nothing till he lays a completed treaty before it. One or other course is from time to time followed, according to the nature of the case, or the degree of friendliness existing between the President and the majority of the Senate. But in general, the President's best policy is to keep the leaders of the senatorial majority, and in particular the Committee on Foreign Relations, informed of the progress of any pending negotiation. He thus feels the pulse of the Senate, and foresees what kind of arrangement he can induce it to sanction, while at the same time a good understanding between himself and his coadjutors is promoted. The right of going into secret session enables the whole Senate to consider dispatches communicated by the President; and the more important ones, having first been submitted to the

Foreign Relations Committee, are thus occasionally discussed without the disadvantage of publicity.

This control of foreign policy by the Senate goes far to meet that terrible difficulty which a democracy, or indeed any free government, finds in dealing with foreign powers. If every step to be taken must be previously submitted to the governing assembly, the nation is forced to show its whole hand, and precious opportunities of winning an ally or striking a bargain may be lost. If on the other hand the executive is permitted to conduct negotiations in secret, there is always the risk, either that the governing assembly may disavow what has been done, a risk which makes foreign states legitimately suspicious and unwilling to negotiate, or that the nation may have to ratify, because it feels bound in honor by the act of its executive agents, arrangements which its judgment condemns. Nor, is it the least of the merits of the system of senatorial control that it has tended, by discouraging the executive from schemes which may prove resultless, to diminish the taste for foreign enterprises, and to save the country from being entangled with alliances, protectorates, responsibilities of all sorts beyond its own frontiers. Yet it must be remembered that many of the most important acts done in the sphere of foreign relations are purely executive acts (as for instance, the movement of troops and ships) which the Senate cannot control. The Senate may, and occasionally does, amend a treaty, and return it amended to the President. There is nothing to prevent it proposing a draft treaty to him, or asking him to prepare one, but this is not the practice. For ratification, a vote of two-thirds the Senators present is required. This gives great power to a vexatious minority, and increases the danger, evidenced by several incidents in the history of the Union, that the Senate or a faction in it may deal with foreign policy in a narrow, sectional, electioneering spirit indifferent to foreign affairs, and so little skilled in judging of them, that offenses of the kind I have described may be committed with practical impunity. It is harder to fix responsibility on a body of Senators than on the Executive.

The other executive function of the Senate, that of confirming nominations submitted by the President, has been discussed in the chapter on the powers of that officer. It is there explained how Senators have used their right of confirmation to secure for themselves a huge mass of Federal patronage, and how by means of this right, a majority hostile to the President can thwart and annoy him.

Does the control of the Senate operate to prevent abuse of the patronage by the President? To some extent it does, yet less completely than could be wished. When the majority belongs to the same party as the President, appointments are usually arranged, or to use a familiar expression, "squared," between them, with a view primarily to party interests. When the majority is opposed to the President, they are tempted to agree to his worst appointments, because such appointments discredit him and his party with the country, and become a theme of hostile comment in the next electioneering campaign. As the initiative is his, it is the nominating President, and not the confirming Senate, whom public opinion will condemn.

It must be admitted that the participation of the Senate causes in practice less friction and delay than might have been expected from a dual control. The appointments to the Cabinet offices are confirmed as a matter of course. Those of diplomatic officers are seldom rejected. The machinery, if it does not work smoothly, works well enough to carry on the ordinary business of the country.

The judicial function of the Senate is to sit as a High Court for the trial of persons impeached by the House of

Representatives. The Chief Justice of the United States presides, and a vote of two-thirds of the Senators voting is needed for a conviction. Rare as this method of proceeding is, it could not be dispensed with, and it is better that the Senate should try cases in which a political element is usually present, than that the impartiality of the Supreme Court should be exposed to the criticism it would have to bear, did political questions come before it. Most Senators are or have been lawyers of eminence, so that so far as legal knowledge goes they are competent members of a court.

Americans consider the Senate one of the successes of their Constitution, a worthy monument of the wisdom and foresight of its founders. Foreign observers have repeated this praise, and have perhaps, in their less perfect knowledge, sounded it even more loudly.

The aim with which the Senate was created, the purposes it was to fulfill, are set forth under the form of answers to objections, in five letters, all by Alexander Hamilton, in the *Federalist*. These aims were the five following:

To conciliate the spirit of independence in the several States, by giving each, however small, equal representation with every other, however large, in one branch of the national government.

To create a council qualified, by its moderate size and the experience of its members, to advise and check the President in the exercise of his powers of appointing to office and concluding treaties.

To restrain the impetuosity and fickleness of the popular House, and so guard against the effects of gusts of passion or sudden changes of opinion in the people.

To provide a body of men whose greater experience, longer term of membership, and comparative independence of popular election, would make them an element of stability

THE SENATE OF THE UNITED STATES, CAPITOL BUILDING, WASHINGTON, D. C.

in the government of the nation, enabling it to maintain its character in the eyes of foreign states, and to preserve a continuity of policy at home and abroad.

To establish a court proper for the trial of impeachments, a remedy deemed necessary to prevent abuse of power by the Executive.

All of these five objects have been more or less perfectly attained; and the Senate has acquired a position in the government of the nation which Hamilton scarcely ventured to hope. It may be doubted whether the Senate has excelled the House in attachment to the public good; but it has certainly shown greater capacity for managing the public business, and has won the respect, if not the affections, of the people, by its sustained intellectual power.

The *Federalist* did not think it necessary to state, nor have Americans generally realized, that this masterpiece of the Constitution-makers was in fact a happy accident. The concession of equal representation in the Senate induced the small States to accept the principle of representation according to population in the House of Representatives; and a series of compromises between the advocates of popular power, as embodied in the House, and those of monarchical power, as embodied in the President, led to the allotment of attributes and functions which have made the Senate what it is. The framers thought of the Senate as first and foremost a body with executive functions. And this, at first, it was. It was a small body, originally of twenty-six, and not ill-fitted for executive work. For the first five years of its existence, the Senate sat with closed doors, occupying itself chiefly with the confidential business of appointments and treaties, and conferring in private with the ministers of the President. Not until 1816 did it create, in imitation of the House, standing committees. Its present character as a legislative body, not less active and powerful than the other branch of Congress, is the result of a long process of evolution.

What is meant by saying that the Senate has proved a success?

It has succeeded by effecting that chief object of the Fathers of the Constitution, the creation of a center of gravity in the government, an authority able to correct and check on the one hand the " democratic recklessness " of the House, on the other the " monarchical ambition " of the President, and it has made itself eminent and respected. To what is this to be ascribed? The Senate, albeit not chosen by direct popular election, does represent the people; and what it may lose through not standing in immediate contact with the masses, it gains in representing such ancient and powerful commonwealths as the States. A Senator from New York or Pennsylvania speaks for, and is responsible to, millions of men.

This is the first reason for the strength of the Senate, as compared with the upper chambers of other countries. A second cause is to be found in its small size. A small body educates its members better than a large one, because each member is of more consequence, has more to do, sooner masters the business not only of its committee, but of the whole body, feels a livelier sense of the significance of his own action in bringing about collective action.

Its comparative permanence has also worked for good. Six years, which seems a short term in Europe, is in America a long term when compared with the two years for which the House of Representatives and the Assemblies of nearly all the States are elected, long also when compared with the swiftness of change in American politics. A Senator has the opportunity of thoroughly learning his work, and of proving that he has learned it.

The smallness and the permanence of the Senate have,

however, another important influence on its character. They contribute to one main cause of its success, the superior intellectual quality of its members. A Senator has more power than a member of the House, more dignity, a longer term of service, a more independent position. Hence every Federal politician aims at a senatorship, and looks on the place of Representative as a stepping-stone to what is in this sense an Upper House, that is it is the House to which Representatives seek to mount. What is more, the Senate so trains its members as to improve their political efficiency.

Most of the leading men of the last eighty years have sat in the Senate, and in it were delivered most of the famous speeches which illumine, though too rarely, the wearisome debates over State rights and slavery from 1825 till 1860. As might be expected from the small number of the audience, as well as from its character, discussions in the Senate are apt to be sensible and practical. Speeches are shorter and less fervid than those made in the House of Representatives, for the larger an assembly the more prone is it to declamation. On "show-days" the speeches are made not to convince the assembly, for that no one dreams of doing, but to keep a man's opinions before the public and sustain his fame.

The Senate now contains many men of great wealth. Some, an increasing number, are Senators because they are rich; a few are rich because they are Senators, while in the remaining cases the same talents which have won success in law or commerce have brought their possessor to the top in politics also. The great majority are or have been lawyers; some regularly practice before the Supreme Court. The Senators indulge some social pretensions and are the nearest approach to an official aristocracy that has yet been seen in America, but as the office is temporary, and the rank vanishes with the office, these pretensions are harmless; it is only the universal social equality of the country that makes them noteworthy. Apart from such petty advantages, the position of a Senator who can count on reëlection is the most desirable in the political world of America. It gives as much power and influence as a man need desire.

The Senate should not be idealized. Actually it is a company of shrewd and vigorous men who have fought their way to the front by the ordinary methods of American politics, and on many of whom the battle has left its stains. There are abundant opportunities for intrigue in the Senate, there are opportunities for misusing senatorial powers, scandals have sometimes arisen from their employment as counsel before the Supreme Court, there are opportunities for corruption and blackmailing, of which unscrupulous men are well known to take advantage. Such men are, however, fortunately few.

The place which the Senate holds in the constitutional system of America cannot be fully appreciated till the remaining parts of that system have been described. This much, however, may be claimed for it, that it has been and is, on the whole, a steadying and moderating power. Each of the great historic parties has in turn commanded a majority in it. But on none of the great issues that have divided the nation has the Senate been, for any long period, decidedly opposed to the other House of Congress. It showed no more capacity than the House for grappling with the problems of slavery extension. It was scarcely less ready than the House to strain the Constitution by supporting Lincoln in the exercise of the so-called war powers, or subsequently by cutting down Presidential authority in the struggle between Congress and Andrew Johnson. All the fluctuations of public opinion tell upon it, although less energetically than on the House of Representatives.

The Senate has been a stouter bulwark against agitation, not merely because a majority of the Senators have always four years membership before them, within which period public feeling may change, but also because the Senators have been individually stronger men than the Representatives. The Senate has usually, therefore, kept its head better than the House of Representatives. In this sense it does constitute a "check and balance" in the Federal government. Of the three great functions which the Fathers of the Constitution meant it to perform, the first, that of securing the rights of the smaller States, is no longer important, because the extent of State rights has been now well settled; while the second, that of advising or controlling the Executive in appointments as well as in treaties, has given rise to evils almost commensurate with its benefits. But the third duty is still well discharged, for "the propensity of a single and numerous assembly to yield to the impulse of sudden and violent passions" is restrained.

Chapter VIII

THE HOUSE OF REPRESENTATIVES

THE House of Representatives, usually called for shortness the House, represents the nation on the basis of population, as the Senate represents the States.

But even in the composition of the House the States play an important part. The Constitution provides that "Representatives and direct taxes shall be apportioned among the several States according to their respective numbers," and under this provision Congress allots so many members of the House to each State in proportion to its population at the last preceding decennial census, leaving the State to determine the districts within its own area for and by which the members shall be chosen. These districts are now equal or nearly equal in size, but in laying them out there is ample scope for the process called "gerrymandering" (or laying out to political advantage), which the dominant party in a State rarely fails to apply for its own advantage. Where a State legislature has failed to redistribute the State into congressional districts, after the State has received an increase of Representatives, the additional member or members are elected by the voters of the whole State on a general ticket, and are called "Representatives at large." Each district, of course, lies wholly within the limits of one State. When a seat becomes vacant the governor of the State issues a writ for a new election, and when a member desires to resign his seat he does so by letter to the governor.

The original House which met in 1789 contained only sixty-five members, the idea being that there should be one member to every 30,000 persons. As population grew and new States were added, the number of members was increased. Originally Congress fixed the ratio of members to population, and the House accordingly grew; but latterly, fearing a too rapid increase, it has fixed the number of members with no regard for any precise ratio of members to population. At present the total number of representatives is 386, being, according to the census of 1900, one member to 194,182 souls. Besides these full members there are also four territorial delegates, from each of the Territories, regions in the southwest, enjoying a species of self-government, but not yet formed into States, and a commissioner from Porto Rico. These delegates sit and speak, but have no right to vote, being unrecognized by the Constitution. They are, in fact, merely persons whom the House under a statute admits to its floor and permits to address it.

The electoral franchise on which the House is elected is for each State the same as that by which the members of the more numerous branch of the State legislature are chosen. Originally electoral franchises varied very much in different States: now a suffrage practically all but universal prevails everywhere. A State, however, has a right of limiting the suffrage as it pleases, and many States do exclude paupers, illiterates, and persons convicted of crime. By the fifteenth amendment to the Constitution (passed in 1870) "the right of citizens of the United States to vote shall not be denied or abridged by any State on account of race, color, or previous condition of servitude," while by the fourteenth amendment (passed in 1868) "the basis of representation in any State is reduced in respect of any male citizens excluded from the suffrage, save for participation in rebellion or other crimes." Each State has therefore a strong motive for keeping its suffrage wide, but the fact remains that the franchise by which the Federal legislature is chosen may differ vastly, and does in some points actually differ in different parts of the Union.

Members are elected for two years, and the election always takes place in the even years. Thus the election of every second Congress coincides with that of a President; and admirers of the Constitution find in this arrangement another of their favorite " checks," because while it gives the incoming President a Congress presumably, though by no means necessarily, of the same political complexion as his own, it enables the people within two years to express their approval or disapproval of his conduct by sending up another House of Representatives which may support or oppose the policy he has followed. The House does not in the regular course of things meet until a year has elapsed from the time when it has been elected, though the President may convoke it sooner, *i. e.,* a House elected in November, 1906, will not meet till December, 1907, unless the President summons it in " extraordinary session " sometime after March, 1907, when the previous House expires. It is a singular result of the present arrangement that the old House continues to sit for nearly four months after the members of the new House have been elected.

The expense of an election varies greatly from district to district. Sometimes, especially in great cities, where illegitimate expenditure is more frequent and less detectible than in rural districts, it rises high: sometimes it is trifling. Most of the expenditures are legitimate, that is to say, are made for meetings. for printing, for advertisements, and for agency. All the official expenses, such as for clerks, polling booths, etc., are paid by the public. Bribery is not rare in some of the urban districts, nor in some of the country districts; but elections are seldom impeached on that ground, for the difficulty of proof is increased by the circumstance that the House, which is of course the investigating and deciding authority, does not meet till a year after the election.

Among the members of the House there are few young men, and still fewer old men. The immense majority are between forty and sixty. Lawyers are the most numerous class in the House, generally about two-thirds being of that profession. No military or naval officer, and no person in the civil service of the United States can sit. The absence of railroad men by no means implies the absence of railroad influence, for it is as easy for a company to influence legislation from without Congress as from within.

Most members, including nearly all western men, have received their early education in the common schools, but generally one-half or more of the whole number have also graduated from a university or college. A good many, but apparently not the majority, have served in the legislature of their own State. Comparatively few are wealthy, and few are very poor, while scarcely any were at the time of their election workingmen.

A member of the House enjoys the title of Honorable. As he shares it with members of State senates, all the higher officials, both Federal and State, and judges, the distinction is not deemed a high one.

As regards the powers of the House, it is enough to say that they are in theory purely legislative. The House has no share in the executive functions of the Senate, nothing to do with confirming appointments or approving treaties. On the other hand, it has the exclusive right of initiating revenue bills and of impeaching officials, features borrowed, through the State constitutions, from the English House of Commons, and of choosing a President in case there should be no absolute majority of Presidential electors 'for any one candidate. This very important power it exercised in 1801 and 1825.

Setting extraordinary sessions aside, every Congress has two sessions, distinguished as the First or Long, and the Second or Short. The long session begins in December of the year after the election of Congress, and continues, with a recess at Christmas, till the July or August following. The short session begins in the December after the July adjournment, and lasts till the following March 4. The whole working life of a House is thus from ten to twelve months. Bills do not, as in the English Parliament, expire at the end of each session; they run on from the long session to the short one. All, however, that have not been passed when the fatal March 4 arrives perish forthwith, for the session being fixed by statute cannot be extended at pleasure. There is consequently a terrible scramble to get business pushed through in the last week or two of a Congress.

The usages and rules of procedure of the House, which differ in many respects from those of the Senate, are too numerous to be described here. It is said that an industrious member needs one whole session to learn them.

An oath or affirmation of fidelity to the Constitution of the United States is (as prescribed by the Constitution) taken by all members; also by the clerk, the sergeant-at-arms, the doorkeeper, and the postmaster.

The sergeant-at-arms is the treasurer of the House, and pays to each member his salary and mileage (traveling expenses). He has the custody of the mace, and the duty of keeping order, which in extreme cases he performs by carrying the mace into a throng of disorderly members. The clerk of the last preceding House acts as a sort of temporary chairman till a Speaker is chosen; members then address him, and he decides questions of order.

The proceedings each day begin with prayers, which

are conducted by a chaplain who is appointed by the House, not as in England by the Speaker, and who may, of course, be selected from any religious denomination. Lots are drawn for seats at the beginning of the session, each member selecting the place he pleases according as his turn arrives. By courtesy the senior member is allowed to retain the seat he has appropriated before the drawing by putting his hat upon it.

Every member addresses the Speaker and the Speaker only, and refers to another member not by name, but as the "gentleman from Pennsylvania," or as the case may be, without any particular indication of the district which the person referred to represents. On a division members rise and are counted by the Speaker; if one-fifth of a quorum demand it, a count is taken by tellers. If one-fifth of a quorum demand a call of yeas and nays, this is taken; the clerk calls the full roll of the House, and each member answers aye or no to his name, or says " no vote."

When the question is an important one, it is obviously necessary that the names of members voting should be put on record. But the call is sometimes demanded in order to give people time to consider how they should vote. A process which consumes so much time, for it takes an hour and a half to call through the three hundred and eighty-six names, is an obvious and effective engine of obstruction.

The great remedy against prolix or obstructive debate is the so-called previous question, which is moved in the form, " Shall the main question be now put?" and when ordered closes forthwith all debate, and brings the House to a direct vote on that main question. On the motion for the putting of the main question no debate is allowed.

Closure by previous question is in almost daily use, and is considered so essential to the progress of business that I never found any member or official who thought it could be dispensed with. It is not abused, owing to the fear entertained of the disapproval of the people, and to the sentiment within the House itself in favor of full and fair discussion.

Notwithstanding this powerful engine for expediting business, obstruction, or, as Americans call it, filibustering, is by no means unknown. It is usually practiced by making repeated motions for the adjournment of a debate, or for " taking a recess " (suspending the sitting), or for calling the yeas and nays. Between one such motion and another some business must intervene, but as the making of a speech is " business," there is no difficulty in complying with this requirement.

The rules of the House (including that of " previous question " to check obstruction) are, however, generally acquiesced in, because the House of Representatives is a legislating, not a debating, body. It rules through and by its committees, in which discussion is unchecked by any closing power; and the whole House does little more than register by its votes the conclusions which the committees submit. One subject alone, the subject of revenue, that is to say, taxation and appropriation, receives genuine discussion by the House at large. And although the " previous question " is often applied to expedite appropriation bills, it is seldom applied till opportunity has been given for the expression of all relevant views.

The number of bills brought into the House every year is very large, averaging over 15000. By far the larger number of bills in Congress are what would be called in England " private " or " local and personal " bills, i. e., they establish no general rule of law, but are directed to particular cases. Such are the numerous bills for satisfying persons with claims against the Federal Government, and for giving or restoring pensions to individuals who served in the Northern

armies or navy during the War of Secession. It is only to
a very small extent that bills can attempt to deal with ordinary private law, since nearly the whole of that topic belongs
to State legislation. It is needless to say that the proportion
of bills that pass to bills that fail is a very small one, not one-
thirtieth. As in England so even more in America, bills are
lost less by direct rejection than by failing to reach their third
reading.

The title and attributions of the Speaker of the House
are taken from his famous English original. But the character of the office has greatly altered from that original.
The note of the Speaker of the British House of Commons
is his impartiality. In America the Speaker has immense
political power, and is permitted, nay expected, to use it in
the interests of his party. In calling upon members to
speak he prefers those of his own side. He decides in their
favor such points of order as are not distinctly covered by
the rules. His authority over the arrangement of business
is so large that he can frequently advance or postpone particular bills or motions in a way which determines their
fate. He is usually the most eminent member of the party
who has a seat in the House, and is really, so far as the
confidential direction of its policy goes, almost its leader.

His most important privilege is, however, the nomination of the numerous standing committees. Not only does
he, at the beginning of each Congress, select all the members of these committees, but he even chooses the chairman of each, and thereby vests the direction of its business
in hands approved by himself. The chairman is of course
always selected from the party which commands the House,
and the committee is so composed as to give that party a
majority. Since legislation, and so much of the control of
current administration as the House has been able to bring
within its grasp, belong to these committees, their composi-

tion practically determines the action of the House on all questions of moment.

The Speaker is, of course, far from free in disposing of these places. He must redeem pledges and placate various sections and interests. These conditions surround the exercise of his power with trouble and anxiety. Yet after all it is power, power which in the hands of a capable and ambitious man becomes so far-reaching that it is no exaggeration to call him the second, if not the first political figure in the United States, with an influence upon the fortunes of men and the course of domestic events superior, in ordinary times, to the President's, although shorter in its duration and less patent to the world. The Speaker's distribution of members among the committees is, next to his own election, the most critical point in the history of a Congress, and that watched with most interest.

Although expected to serve his party in all possible directions, he must not resort to all possible means. Both in the conduct of debate and in the formation of committees a certain measure of fairness to opponents is required from him. The dignity of the Speaker's office is high. He receives a salary of $8000 a year, which is a large salary for America. In rank he stands next after the President and on a level with the Justices of the Supreme Court.

Chapter IX

THE HOUSE OF REPRESENTATIVES: ITS WORK AND COMMITTEES

THE seats in the House are arranged in curved concentric rows looking towards the Speaker, whose handsome marble chair is placed on a raised marble platform. Each member has a revolving armchair with a roomy desk in front of it, where he writes and keeps his papers. When you enter, your first impression is of noise and turmoil. The raising and dropping of desk lids, the scratching of pens, the clapping of hands to call the pages, keen little boys who race along the gangways, the pattering of many feet, the hum of talking on the floor and in the galleries, make up a din over which the Speaker with the sharp taps of his hammer, or the orators straining shrill throats, find it hard to make themselves audible. Nor is it only the noise that gives the impression of disorder. Often three or four members are on their feet at once, each shouting to catch the Speaker's attention. Less favorable conditions for oratory cannot be imagined. It is hard to talk calm, good sense at the top of your voice, hard to unfold a complicated measure. So, too, the huge galleries add to the area the voice has to fill; but the public likes them, and might resent a removal to a smaller room.

The method of taking a division by calling on each party to stand up, first the ayes and then the noes, is more expeditious than the English plan of sending men into opposite lobbies, but the calling of the roll, which one-fifth of half the House can and frequently does demand, is slower.

There is little good speaking. Speeches are often but partly spoken and then printed in full in the Congressional Record, which can be sent out to constituents.

That there is not much good business debating, by which I mean a succession of comparatively short speeches addressed to a practical question, and hammering it out by the collision of mind with mind, arises not from any want of ability among the members, but from the unfavorable conditions under which the House acts. Most of the practical work is done in the standing committees, while much of the House's time is consumed in pointless discussions, where member after member delivers himself upon large questions, not likely to be brought to a definite issue. Many of the speeches thus called forth have a value as repertories of facts, but the debate as a whole is unprofitable and languid. On the other hand the five-minute debates which take place, when the House imposes that limit of time, in Committee of the Whole on the consideration of a bill reported from a standing committee, are often lively, pointed, and effective. The topics which excite most interest and are best discussed are those of taxation and the appropriation of money, more particularly to public works, the improvement of rivers and harbors, erection of Federal buildings, and so forth.

As a theater or school either of political eloquence or political wisdom, the House has been inferior not only to the Senate, but to most European assemblies. Nor does it enjoy much consideration at home. Its debates are very shortly reported in the Washington papers, as well as in those in Philadelphia and New York. They are not widely read, and do little to instruct or influence public opinion.

This is of course only one part of a legislature's functions. An assembly may dispatch its business successfully and yet shine with few lights of genius. But the legislation on public matters which the House turns out is scanty in quantity and generally mediocre in quality. The House frequently plays to the people with bills or resolutions not meant seriously, but to make impressions. This is especially the case with foreign affairs in which the House has no responsibility.

In the composition of the House one finds much character, shrewdness, and keen, though limited, intelligence among the Representatives. Yet in respect of width of view, of capacity for penetrating thought on political problems, Representatives are scarcely above the class from which they came, that of second-rate lawyers or farmers, less often merchants or petty manufacturers. They do not pretend to be statesmen in the European sense of the word, for their careers, which have made them smart and active, have given them little opportunity for acquiring such capacities. As regards manners they are not polished, because they have not lived among polished people; yet neither are they rude, for to get on in American politics one must be civil and pleasant. The standard of parliamentary language, and of courtesy generally, has steadily risen during the last few decades.

On the whole the most striking difference between the House of Representatives and European popular assemblies is its greater homogeneity. The type is marked; the individuals vary little from the type. The American people, though composed of immigrants from every country and occupying a whole continent, tend to become more uniform than most of the great European peoples; and this characteristic is palpable in its legislature.

Uneasy lies the head of an ambitious Congressman, for the chances are about even that he will lose his seat at the next election. Anyone can see how much influence this constant change in the composition of the American House must have upon its legislative efficiency.

I have kept to the last the feature of the House which
an Englishman finds the strangest. It has parties, but they
are headless. There is neither Government nor Opposition;
neither leaders nor whips. No minister, no person holding
any Federal office or receiving any Federal salary, can be
a member of it. That the majority may be and often is
opposed to the President and his Cabinet, does not strike
Americans as odd, because they proceed on the theory that
the legislative ought to be distinct from the executive authority. Since no minister sits, there is no official representative of the party which for the time being holds the reins
of the executive government. Neither is there any un-
official representative. And as there are no persons whose
opinions expressed in debate are followed, so there are none
whose duty it is to bring up members to vote, to secure a
quorum, to see that people know which way the bulk of the
party is going.

So far as the majority has a chief, that chief is the
Speaker, but he seldom joins in debate. The chairman of
the most important committee, that of Ways and Means,
enjoys a sort of eminence, and comes nearer than anyone
else to the position of leader of the House. The minority
do not formally choose a leader, nor is there usually anyone among them whose career marks him out as practically
the first man, but the person whom they have put forward
as their party candidate for the Speakership has a sort of
vague claim to be so regarded. This honor amounts to
very little.

How then does the House work? If it were a chamber, like those of France or Germany, divided into four
or five sections of opinion, none of which commanded a steady
majority, it would not work at all. But parties are few in
the United States, and their cohesion tight. There are usually two only, so nearly equal in strength that the majority

cannot afford to divide into groups like those of France. Hence upon all large national issues, whereon the general sentiment of the party has been declared, both the majority and the minority know how to vote, and vote solid.

Neither is the House an executive body, but merely legislative. It neither creates nor controls nor destroys the administration, which depends on the President, himself the offspring of a direct popular mandate.

Yet the House, since it is without leaders or organization, often makes mistakes. It votes the necessary supplies, but not wisely, and for many years it has fumbled over both the tariff problem and the currency problem. It produces few useful laws, and neglects grave practical questions. An Englishman is disposed to ascribe these failures to the fact that there are no leaders responsible for neglect, miscarriage of bills, and unwise appropriations. Americans reply, "It is not for want of leaders, but because the division of opinion in the country has been faithfully reflected in Congress. It is not for Congress to go faster than the people. When the country knows and speaks its mind, Congress will not fail to act." This shows the different conceptions in America and Europe.

Europeans have thought of a legislature as belonging to the governing class. In America there is no such class. Europeans think that the legislature ought to consist of the best men in the country, Americans that it should be a fair average sample of the country. Europeans think that it ought to lead the nation, Americans that it ought to follow the nation.

Without some sort of organization, an assembly of three hundred and ninety men would be a mob, so necessity has provided in the system of committees a substitute for the European party organization. It is enough to observe that when a matter which has been (as all bills are) referred to a committee, comes up in the House to be dealt with there, the chairman of the particular committee is treated as a leader *pro hac vice,* and members who knew nothing of the matter are apt to be guided by his speech or his advice given privately. When a debate arises unexpectedly on a question of importance, members are often puzzled how to vote. If the issue is one of serious consequence to the party, a recess is demanded by the majority, say for two hours. The House then adjourns, each party "goes into caucus" (the Speaker possibly announcing the fact), and debates the matter with closed doors. Then the House resumes, and each party votes solid according to the determination arrived at in caucus. In spite of these expedients, surprises and scratch votes are not uncommon.

I have spoken of the din of the House of Representatives, of its air of restlessness and confusion, contrasting with the staid gravity of the Senate, of the absence of dignity both in its proceedings and in the bearing and aspect of individual members. All these things notwithstanding, there is something impressive about it, something not unworthy of the continent for which it legislates.

This huge gray hall, filled with perpetual clamor, this multitude of keen and eager faces, this ceaseless coming and going of many feet, this irreverent public, watching from the galleries and forcing its way onto the floor, all speak to the beholder's mind of the mighty democracy, destined in another century to form one-half of civilized mankind, whose affairs are here debated.

The most abiding difficulty of free government is to get large assemblies to work promptly and smoothly either for legislative or executive purposes. We perceive this difficulty in primary assemblies of thousands of citizens, like those of ancient Athens or Syracuse; we see it again in the smaller representative assemblies of modern countries.

Three methods of overcoming it have been tried. One is to leave very few and comparatively simple questions to the assembly, reserving all others for a smaller and more permanent body, or for executive officers. Another method is to organize the assemblies into well-defined parties, voting generally according to the guidance of leaders. This has been the English system since about the time of Queen Anne. The third method, which admits of being more or less combined with the second, is to divide the assembly into a number of smaller bodies to which legislative and administrative questions may be referred, either for final determination, or to be examined and reported on to the whole body. This is the system of committees, applied to some small extent in England, to a larger extent in France under the name of *bureaux,* and most of all in the United States.

When Congress first met in 1789, both Houses found themselves, as the State legislatures had theretofore been and still are, without official members and without leaders. The Senate occupied itself chiefly with executive business, and appointed no standing committees until 1816. The House, however, had bills to discuss, plans of taxation to frame, difficult questions of expenditure, and particularly of the national debt, to consider. For want of persons whose official duty required them, like English ministers, to run the machine by drafting schemes and bringing the raw material of its work into shape, it was forced to appoint committees. At first there were few; even in 1802 we find only five. As the numbers of the House increased and more business flowed in, additional committees were appointed; and as the House became more and more occupied by large political questions, minor matters were more and more left to be settled by these select bodies. The men on the committees were workers and desired to be occupied. It was impossible for them all to speak in the House; but all could talk in a committee. This arrangement recognized republican equality. It, therefore, prevailed, and the present elaborate system grew slowly to maturity.

There are few differences between the Senate and the House committees, although the system is more fully developed in the House. But a very few words on the Senate may serve to prevent misconceptions.

There are about forty standing Senate committees, appointed for two years, being the period of a Congress. They and their chairmen are chosen not by the presiding officer, but by the Senate itself, voting by ballot. Practically they are selected by a caucus of the majority party meeting in secret conclave, and then carried wholesale by vote in the Senate. Each consists of from three to eleven members, the most common numbers being seven and nine, and all Senators sit on more than one committee, some upon four or more. The chairman is appointed by the Senate, and not by the committees themselves. There are also select committees appointed for a special purpose. Every bill introduced goes after its first and second readings (which are granted as a matter of course) to a standing committee, which examines and amends it, and reports it back to the Senate.

There are about fifty standing committees of the House, *i. e.,* committees appointed under standing regulations, and therefore regularly formed at the beginning of every Congress. Each committee consists of from three to sixteen members, eleven and thirteen being the commonest numbers. Every member of the House is placed on some one committee, and few on more than one. Besides these, select committees on particular subjects of current interest are appointed from time to time. The most important standing committees are the following: Ways and Means; Appropriations; Elections; Banking and Currency; Accounts; Rivers and Harbors; Judiciary (including changes in private law as well as in courts of justice); Railroads and Canals; Foreign Affairs; Naval Affairs; Military Affairs; Public Lands; Agriculture; Claims; and the several committees on the expenditures of the various departments of the administration (war, navy, etc.).

The members of every standing committee are nominated by the Speaker at the beginning of each Congress, and sit through its two sessions; those of a select committee also by the Speaker, after the committee has been ordered by the House. A select committee lasts only for the session. In pursuance of the rule that the member first named shall be chairman, the Speaker has also the selection of all the chairmen.

To some one of these standing committees each and every bill is referred. Its second, as well as its first, reading is granted as a matter of course, and without debate, since there would be no time to discuss the immense number of bills presented. Sometimes a dispute arises as to what committee a bill should be referred. Such disputes are determined by the vote of the House itself.

Not having been discussed, much less affirmed in principle, by the House, a bill comes before its committee with no presumption in its favor. It is one of many, and for the most a sad fate is reserved. The committee may take evidence regarding it and members who are interested approach the committee and state their case there. The committee can amend the bill as they please, and although they cannot formally extinguish it, they can practically do so by reporting adversely, or by delaying to report it till late in the session, or by not reporting it at all.

In one or other of these ways nineteen-twentieths of the bills introduced meet their death, a death which the majority doubtless deserve, and the prospect of which tends to make members reckless as regards both the form and the substance of their proposals.

The deliberations of committees are usually secret, or if not, are not generally reported. Some committees, such as those on naval and military affairs, and those on the expenditure of the several departments, deal with administration rather than legislation. It is through these committees chiefly that the executive and legislative branches of government touch one another. Yet although executive officials are forced to take time to explain affairs, and to make reports, the committees on the one hand do not follow out recommendations, and on the other, do not always detect abuses and peculation.

After a bill has been debated and amended by the committee it is reported back to the House, and is taken up when that committee is called in its order. One hour is allowed to the member whom his fellow committeemen have appointed to report. He seldom uses the whole of this hour, but allots part of it to other members, opponents as well as friends, and usually concludes by moving the previous question. This precludes subsequent amendments and leaves only an hour before the vote is taken. As on an average each committee (excluding the two or three great ones) has only two hours out of the whole ten months of Congress allotted to it to present and have discussed all its bills, it is plain that few measures can be considered, and each but shortly, in the House. The best chance of pressing one through is under the rule which permits the suspension of standing orders by a two-thirds majority during the last six days of the session.

What are the results of this system?

It destroys the unity of the House as a legislative body, and the interest of members centers in the committees.

It prevents the capacity of the best members from being brought to bear upon any one piece of legislation, however important, for the men of most ability and experience are scattered over various committees. The defect is not supplied by discussion in the House, for there is no time for such discussion.

It cramps debate, because the center of gravity has shifted from the House to the committees.

It lessens the cohesion and harmony of legislation, for each committee goes on its own way with its own bills, and other committees with theirs.

It gives facilities for the exercise of underhand, and even corrupt, influence, for the committees are small enough for members to be secured, and numerous enough not to be watched thoroughly. But I do not think that corruption, in its grosser forms, is rife at Washington. When it appears, it appears chiefly in the milder form of reciprocal jobbing or (as it is called) "log-rolling."

It reduces responsibility. There is no ministry to be blamed, for the Cabinet officers do not sit in Congress; the House cannot be blamed because it has only followed the decision of its committee; the committee is a comparatively obscure body, whose members are usually too insignificant to be worth blaming. The chairman is often a man of note, but the people have no leisure to watch fifty chairmen. No discredit attaches to the dominant party; and thus public displeasure rarely finds a victim. Only when a scandal has arisen so serious as to demand investigation is the responsibility of the member to his constitutents and the country brought duly home.

It lowers the interest of the nation in the proceedings of Congress. Except in exciting times, when large questions have to be settled, the bulk of real business is done not in the great hall of the House, but in this labyrinth of committee rooms and the lobbies that surround them. Hence people cease to watch Congress with that sharp eye which every principal ought to keep fixed on his agent.

It throws power into the hands of the chairmen of committees, especially, of course, of those which deal with finance and with great material interests, but this power is not necessarily accompanied by responsibility.

On the other hand, it enables the House to deal with a far greater number of measures and subjects than could otherwise be undertaken; and has the advantage of enabling evidence to be taken by those whose duty it is to re-shape or amend a bill.

It sets the members of the House to work for which their previous business training has fitted them much better than for either legislating or debating " in the grand style."

On the whole, it may be said that under this system the House dispatches a vast amount of work and does the negative part of it, the killing off of worthless bills, in a thorough way.

But why, if mischiefs exist, is the system of committee legislation maintained?

It is maintained because none better has been, or, as most people think, can be devised. " We have," say Americans, " three hundred and eighty-six members in the House. The bills brought in are very numerous. If even the twentieth reported were discussed, no time would remain for supervision of the Departments of State. That supervision itself must, since it involves the taking of evidence, be conducted by committees and not by the whole House." The Americans say: " We cannot have a committee, such as the English Cabinet, because no officeholder sits in Congress. Neither can we organize the House under leaders, because prominent men have among us little authority. Neither can we create a ruling committee of the majority, because this would be disliked as an undemocratic and tyrannical institution. Hence our only course is to divide the unwieldy multitude into small bodies capable of dealing with particular subjects. This may give patchwork legislation, but it gives all that is necessary, as nearly the whole field of ordinary private law lies outside the province of Congress. Be our present system bad or good, it is the only system possible under our Constitution, and the fact that it was not directly created by that instrument, but has been evolved by the experience of a hundred years, shows how strong must be the tendencies whose natural working has produced it."

Chapter X

CONGRESSIONAL LEGISLATION AND FINANCE

IN order to judge of the excellence of Congress as a working machine, we must examine the quality of the legislation which it turns out.

Acts of Congress are of two kinds, public and private. Public acts are of two kinds, those which deal with the law or its administration, and those which deal with finance, that is to say, provide for the raising and application of revenue.

There are many points of view from which one may regard the work of legislation. I suggest a few only, in respect of which the excellence of the work may be tested; and propose to ask: What security do the legislative methods and habits of Congress offer for the attainment of the following desirable objects? *viz.:*

1. The excellence of the substance of a bill, *i. e.*, its tendency to improve the law and promote the public welfare.

2. The excellence of the form of a bill. *i. e.*, its arrangement and the scientific precision of its language.

3. The harmony and consistency of an act with the other acts of the same session.

4. The due examination and sifting in debate of a bill.

5. The publicity of a bill, *i. e.*, the bringing it to the knowledge of the country at large, so that public opinion may be fully expressed regarding it.

6. The honesty and courage of the legislative assembly in rejecting a bill, however likely to be popular, which their judgment disapproves.

7. The responsibility of some person or body of persons for the enactment of a measure, *i. e.*, the fixing on the right shoulders of the praise for passing a good, the blame for passing a bad, act.

As to these points we may take them up one by one.

1. The excellence of the substance of a bill introduced in Congress depends entirely on the wisdom and care of its introducer. The officials of the government cannot submit bills, and if they find a congressman willing to do so for them, must leave the advocacy and conduct of the measure entirely in his hands.

2. The drafting of a measure depends on the pains taken and skill exerted by its author. Senate bills are usually well drafted, because many Senators are experienced lawyers: House bills are often crude and obscure.

3. The only security for the consistency of the various measures of the same session is to be found in the fact that those which affect the same matter ought to be referred to the same committee. That mischief from this cause is not serious arises from the fact that out of the multitude of bills introduced, few are reported and still fewer become law.

4. The function of a committee of either House of Congress extends not merely to the sifting and amending of the bills referred to it, but to practically re-drawing them, if the committee desires any legislation, or rejecting them by omitting to report them till near the end of the session if it thinks no legislation needed. In the Senate there is a better chance of discussion, for the Senate, having more time and fewer speakers, can review to some real purpose the findings of its committees.

5. As there is no debate on the introduction or on the second reading of a bill, the public is not necessarily apprised of the measures which are before Congress.

6. The general good-nature of Americans, and the tendency of members of their legislatures to oblige one another by doing reciprocal good turns, dispose people to let any bill go through which does not injure the interest of a party or of a person.

7. What has been said already will have shown that except as regards bills of great importance, or directly involving party issues, there can be little effective responsibility for legislation.

The best defense that can be advanced for this system is that it has been naturally evolved as a means of avoiding worse mischiefs. Hence, as Henry Wilson observes: " The legislation of a session is simply an aggregate of the bills recommended by committees, and these are compromise conclusions bearing some shade or tinge of each of the variously colored opinions and wishes of the committeemen of both parties."

Add to the conditions above described the fact that the House in its few months of life has not time to deal with one-twentieth of the many thousand bills which are thrown upon it, that it therefore drops the enormous majority unconsidered, though some of the best may be in this majority, and passes many of those which it does pass by a suspension of the rules which leaves everything to a single vote, and the marvel comes to be, not that legislation is faulty, but that an intensely practical people tolerates such defective machinery. Some reasons may be suggested tending to explain this phenomenon.

Americans surpass all other nations in their power of making the best of bad conditions, getting the largest results out of scanty materials or rough methods. Many things in this country work better than they ought to work, so to speak, or could work in any other country, because the people are shrewdly alert in minimizing such mischiefs as arise from their own haste or heedlessness, and have a great capacity for self-help.

Aware that they have this gift, Americans are content to leave their political machinery unreformed. The want of legislation on topics where legislation is needed breeds fewer evils than if Congress were the only law-making body. The powers of Congress are limited to comparatively few subjects: its failures do not touch the general well-being of the people, nor the healthful administration of the ordinary law.

The faults of bills passed by the House are often cured by the Senate, where discussion is more leisurely and thorough. The President's veto kills off some vicious measures. He does not trouble himself about defects of form; but when a bill seems to him opposed to sound policy, it is his constitutional duty to disapprove it, and to throw on Congress the responsibility of passing it "over his veto" by a two-thirds vote. A good President accepts this responsibility.

No legislature devotes a larger proportion of its time than does Congress to the consideration of financial bills. These are of two kinds: those which raise revenue by taxation, and those which direct the application of the public funds to the various expenses of the government. At present Congress raises all the revenue it requires by indirect taxation, and chiefly by duties of customs and excise; so taxing bills are practically tariff bills, the excise duties being comparatively little varied from year to year.

The method of passing both kinds of bills is unlike that of most European countries. In England, with which, of course, America can be most easily compared, although both the levying and the spending of money are absolutely under the control of the House of Commons, the House of Commons originates no proposal for either. The Chan-

cellor of the Exchequer bases his budget on estimates prepared by the several administrative departments.   The
House of Commons debates and may decrease, but never
increases the amounts.   The ministry is as careful not to
overestimate as it is not to underestimate the revenue needed.

   In the United States the Secretary of the Treasury
sends annually to Congress a report containing a statement
of the national income and expenditure, and of the condition of the public debt, together with remarks on the system
of taxation and suggestions for its improvement.   He also
sends what is called his Annual Letter, enclosing the estimates, framed by the various departments, of the sums
needed for the public services of the United States during
the coming year.   So far the Secretary is like a European
finance minister, except that he communicates with the
chamber on paper instead of making his statement and proposals orally.   But here the resemblance stops.   Everything
that remains in the way of financial legislation is done solely
by Congress and its committees, the Executive having no
further hand in the matter.

   The business of raising money belongs to one committee only, the standing Committee of Ways and Means, consisting of eleven members.   Its chairman is always a leading
man in the party which commands a majority in the House.
This committee prepares and reports to the House the bills
needed for imposing or continuing the various customs
duties, excise duties, etc.   The report of the Secretary has
been referred by the House to this committee, but the latter
does not necessarily base its bills upon or in any way regard
that report.   Neither does it in preparing them start from
an estimate of the sums needed to support the public service.   It does not, because it cannot; for it does not know
what grants for the public service will be proposed by the
spending committees, since the estimates submitted in the

Secretary's letter furnish no trustworthy basis for a guess. It does not, for the further reason that the primary object of customs duties has for many years past been not the raising of revenue, but the protection of American industries by subjecting foreign products to a very high tariff. This tariff brings in an income far exceeding the current needs of the government. The Ways and Means Committee has, therefore, no motive for adapting taxation to expenditure. The former will always be in excess so long as the protective tariff stands for commercial or political reasons unconnected with national finance.

The business of spending money belongs primarily to two standing committees, the old Committee on Appropriations and the new Committee on Rivers and Harbors, created in 1883. The Committee on Appropriations starts from, but does not adopt, the estimates sent in by the Secretary of the Treasury, for the appropriation bills it prepares usually make large and often reckless reductions in these estimates. The Rivers and Harbors Committee proposes grants of money for what are called "internal improvements," nominally in aid of navigation, but practically in order to turn a stream of public money into the State or States where each "improvement" is to be executed. More money is wasted in this way than what the parsimony of the Appropriations Committee can save. There are several committees on the departments, such as those on the navy, the army, the judiciary. There is the Committee on Pensions, a source of infinite waste. Each of these proposes grants of money, not knowing nor heeding what is being proposed by other committees, and guided by the Executive no further than the members choose. All the expenditures recommended must be met by appropriation bills, but into their propriety the Appropriations Committee cannot inquire.

Every revenue bill must, of course, come before the House; and the House, whatever else it may neglect, never neglects the discussion of taxation and money grants. These are discussed as fully as the pressure of work permits, and are often added to by the insertion of fresh items, which members interested in getting money voted for a particular purpose or locality suggest. These bills then go to the Senate, which forthwith refers them to its committees. The Senate Committee on Finance deals with revenue-raising bills; the Committee on Appropriations with supply bills. Both sets then come before the whole Senate. Although it cannot initiate appropriation bills, the Senate has long ago made good its claim to amend them, and does so without stint, adding new items and often greatly raising the total of the grants. When the bills go back to the House, the House usually rejects the amendments; the Senate adheres to them, and a Conference Committee is appointed, consisting of three Senators and three members of the House, by which a compromise is settled, hastily and in secret, and accepted, generally in the last days of the session, by a hard-pressed but reluctant House. Even as enlarged by this committee, the supply voted is usually found inadequate, so a deficiency bill is introduced in the following session, including a second series of grants to the departments.

What I have said may be summarized as follows:

There is practically no connection between the policy of revenue-raising and the policy of revenue-spending, for these are left to different committees.

There is no relation between the amount proposed to be spent and the amount proposed to be raised. But for the fact that the high tariff produces a large annual surplus, a financial breakdown would speedily ensue.

Little check exists on the tendency of members to deplete the public treasury by securing grants for their friends or constituents, or by putting through financial jobs for which they are to receive some private consideration.

The nation becomes so puzzled by a financial policy varying from year to year, and controlled by no responsible leaders, as to feel diminished interest in congressional discussions and diminished confidence in Congress.

It may be remarked that the enormous income, added to the fact that the tariff is imposed for protection rather than for revenue, is not only the salvation of the United States Government under the present system, but also the cause of that system. The present state of things is evidently exceptional. America is the only country in the world whose difficulty is not to raise money, but to spend it. Still, Congress is contracting lax habits, and ought to change them.

It may be said: Yet the nation has developed rapidly and has been paying off its debt rapidly since 1865. That is due to the following causes: to the prosperity of the country; to the spending habits of the people, who allow themselves luxuries such as the masses enjoy in no other country, and therefore pay more than any other people in the way of indirect taxation; to the absence of the military and naval charges which press so heavily on European states; to the maintenance of an exceedingly high tariff at the instance of numerous interested persons who have obtained the public ear and can influence Congress.

Under the system of congressional finance here described America wastes millions annually. But her wealth is so great, her revenue so elastic, that she is not sensible of the loss. She has the glorious privilege of youth—the privilege of committing errors without suffering from their consequences.

Chapter XI

THE RELATIONS OF THE TWO HOUSES

THE creation by the Constitution of 1789 of two chambers in the United States, in place of the one chamber which existed under the Confederation, has been usually ascribed by Europeans to mere imitation of England. There were, however, better reasons than deference to English precedents to justify the division of Congress into two houses and no more. Not to dwell upon the fact that there were two chambers in all but two of the thirteen original States, the Convention of 1787 had two solid motives for fixing on this number, a motive of principle and theory, a motive of immediate expediency.

The chief advantage of dividing a legislature into two branches is that the one may check the haste and correct the mistakes of the other. To these considerations there was added the practical ground that the division of Congress into two houses supplied a means of settling the dispute which raged between the small and the large States. The country remained a federation in respect of the Senate, it became a nation in respect of the House: there was no occasion for a third chamber.

The respective characters of the two bodies are wholly unlike those of the so-called upper and lower chambers of Europe. Both the Senate and the House equally represent the people, the whole people, and nothing but the people. What is perhaps stranger, the two branches of Congress have not exhibited that contrast of feeling and policy which might be expected from the different methods by which they are chosen. The House has never been the organ of the large States, nor prone to act in their interest; neither has the Senate been the stronghold of the small States, for American politics have never turned upon an antagonism between these two sets of commonwealths. Questions relating to States' rights and the greater or less extension of the powers of the national government have played a leading part in the history of the Union.

The real differences between the two bodies have been indicated in speaking of the Senate. They are due to the smaller size of the latter, to the somewhat superior capacity of its members, to the habits which its executive functions form in individual Senators, and have formed in the whole body.

Although the Senate does draw off from the House many of its ablest men, it is not clear, paradoxical as the observation may appear, that the House would be much the better for retaining those men. The faults of the House are mainly due, not to want of talent among individuals, but to its defective methods, and especially to the absence of leadership. The merits of the Senate are largely due to the fact that it trains to higher efficiency the ability which it has drawn from the House, and gives that ability a sphere in which it can develop with better results.

Collisions between the two Houses are frequent. The fact that one House has passed a bill goes but a little way in inducing the other to pass it. Yet deadlocks are not common, and little bitterness is engendered.

The United States is the only great country in the world in which the two Houses are really equal and co-ordinate. Such a system could hardly work, and therefore could not last, if the Executive were the creature of either or of both, nor unless both were in close touch with the sovereign people.

When each chamber persists in its own view, the regular proceeding is to appoint a Committee of Conference, consisting of three members of the Senate and three of the House. These six meet in secret, and generally settle matters by a compromise, which enables each side to retire with honor. If no compromise can be arranged, the conflict continues till one side yields or it ends by an adjournment, which of course involves the failure of the measure disagreed upon. The House at one time tried to coerce the Senate into submission by adding "riders," as they are called, to appropriation bills, *i. e.,* annexing or "tacking" (to use an English expression) pieces of general legislation to bills granting sums of money. This puts the Senate in the dilemma of either accepting the unwelcome rider, or rejecting the whole bill, and thereby withholding from the executive the funds it needs. This happened in 1855 and 1856. However, the Senate stood firm, and the House gave way. The device had previously been attempted in 1849 by the Senate in tacking a pro-slavery provision to an appropriation bill which it was returning to the House, and it was revived in both Houses against President Andrew Johnson.

Chapter XII

GENERAL OBSERVATIONS ON CONGRESS

THE English reader must bear in mind three points which, in following the details of the last few chapters, he may have forgotten. The first is that Congress is not like the Parliaments of England, France, and Italy, a sovereign assembly, but is subject to the Constitution, which only the people can change. The second is that it neither appoints nor dismisses the executive government, which springs directly from popular election. The third is, that its sphere of legislative action is limited by the existence of forty-five governments in the several States, whose authority is just as well based as its own, and cannot be curtailed by it.

1. The choice of members of Congress is locally limited by law and by custom. Under the Constitution every Representative and every Senator must when elected be an inhabitant of the State whence he is elected. Moreover, State law has in many and custom practically in all States, established that a Representative must be a resident in the congressional district which elects him.

The causes of this are,—Firstly. In the existence of States, originally separate political communities, still for many purposes independent, and accustomed to consider the inhabitant of another State as almost a foreigner. This sentiment has spread by a sort of sympathy, this reasoning has been applied by a sort of analogy, to the counties, the cities, the electoral districts of the State itself.

Secondly. Much of the interest felt in the proceedings

of Congress relates to the raising and spending of money, and each locality thinks that no one but an inhabitant can duly comprehend the needs or zealously advocate the demands of a neighborhood.

Thirdly. A district would think it a slur to be told that it ought to look beyond its own borders for a representative; and as the post is a paid one, the people feel that a good thing ought to be kept for one of themselves rather than thrown away on a stranger.

The practice in America thus differs from England owing to special causes, and the American practices that which is natural to a free country, where local self-government is fully developed and rooted in the habits of the people. It is from their local government that the political ideas of the American people have been formed; and they have applied to their State assemblies and their national assembly the customs which grew up in the smaller area.

Its results are unfortunate. So far as the restriction to residents in a State is concerned it is intelligible. The Senator was—to some extent is still—a sort of ambassador from his State. Even a Representative in the House from one State who lived in another might be perplexed by a divided allegiance. But what reason can there be for preventing a man resident in one part of a State from representing another part? In England it is not found that a member is less active or successful in urging the local interests of his constituency because he does not live there. In case of conflict of interests he always feels his efforts to be owing first to his constituents, and not to the place in which he happens to reside.

The mischief is twofold. Inferior men are returned, because there are many parts of the country which do not grow statesmen. And men of marked ability and zeal are prevented from forcing their way in. Such men are pro-

duced chiefly in the great cities of the older States. There is
not room enough there for nearly all of them, but no other
doors to Congress are open. Careers are moreover interrupted. A promising politician may lose his seat in his own
district through some fluctuation of opinion, or perhaps because he has offended the local wire-pullers by too much
independence. Since he cannot find a seat elsewhere, as
would happen in England, he is stranded. Custom is so
strong in this matter that it would be hard to change.

2. Every Senator and Representative receives a salary,
at present fixed at $5000 per annum, besides an allowance
(called mileage) of 20 cents per mile for traveling expenses
to and from Washington, besides stationery and clerk hire.
The salary is looked upon as a matter of course. It was not
introduced for the sake of enabling workingmen to be returned as members, but on the general theory that all public
work ought to be paid for. The reasons for it are stronger
than in England or France, because the distance to Washington from most parts of the United States is so great, and
the attendance required there so continuous, that a man cannot attend to his profession or business while sitting in Congress. If he loses his livelihood in serving the community,
the community ought to compensate him, not to add that the
class of persons whose private means put them above the
need of a lucrative calling, or of compensation for inter-
rupting it, is comparatively small even now, and hardly existed when the Constitution was framed. Cynics defend the
payment of Congressmen on another ground, viz., that " they
would steal worse if they didn't get it," and would make
politics, as Napoleon made war, support itself. I do not
believe that the practice works ill by preventing good men
from entering politics. It may strengthen the tendency of
members to regard themselves as mere delegates, but that
tendency has other and deeper roots. It contributes to keep

up a class of professional politicians, but the supposed benefit of the introduction of a large number of representative
workingmen, has hitherto been little desired and nowise
secured.

3. 'A Congressman's tenure of his place is usually short.
Senators are sometimes returned for two, three, or even
four successive terms, but a member of the House can seldom feel safe in the saddle. If he is so eminent as to be
necessary to his party, or "stands in" with the politicians
he may in the Eastern, Middle, and Southern States hold his
ground for three or four Congresses, i. e., for six or eight
years. In the West a member is extremely lucky if he does
even this. Out there a seat is regarded as a good thing
which ought to go around. It has a salary. It sends a man,
free of expense, for two winters and springs to Washington. Rotation in office, dear to the Democrats of Jefferson's school a century ago, still charms the less educated, who
see in it a recognition of equality. An ambitious Congressman is therefore forced to think day and night of his renomination, and secure it by procuring Federal grants or
offices for influential constituents. This prevents growth of
experience and training in political problems.

4. The short duration of Congress forbids learning
statesmanship. Short as it seems, the two-years' term was
warmly opposed, when the Constitution was framed, as being too long. In most of the States at the time the legislative term was one year. So essential to republicanism was
this principle deemed, that the maxim "where annual elections end, tyranny begins" had passed into a proverb. At
present the two-years' term is justified on the ground that
it furnishes a proper check on the President, the election for
a new Congress coming as it does in the middle of his term.
Thus the people can, if they please, express disapproval of
the policy which he has so far followed. One is also told

that these frequent elections are necessary to keep up popular interest in current politics, nor do some fail to hint that the temptations to jobbing would overcome the virtue of members who had a longer term before them.

5. The members of the two American Houses seem small to a European when compared on the one hand with the population of the country, on the other with the practice of European States. The Senate has 90 members against the British House of Lords with about 560, and the French Senate with 300. The House has 386 against the British House of Commons with 670, and the French and Italian Chambers with 584 and 508 respectively.

The Americans, however, doubt whether both their Houses have not already become too large. They began with 26 in the Senate, 65 in the House, numbers then censured as too small, but which worked well, and gave less encouragement to idle talk and vain display than the crowded halls of to-day. The proportion of Representatives to inhabitants, originally 1 to 30,000, is now 1 to 194,000, having constantly fallen as the population increased. The inclination of wise men is to stop further increase, for they perceive that the House already suffers from disorganization, and fear that a much larger one would prove unmanageable.

6. American Congressmen are more assiduous in their attendance than the members of most European legislatures. The great majority not only remain steadily at Washington through the session, but are usually to be found at the Capitol, often in the Chamber itself, while a sitting lasts. There is therefore comparatively little trouble in making a quorum, though a quorum consists of one-half of each house. This requirement of a high quorum, which is prescribed in the Constitution, has doubtless helped to secure a good attendance. Other causes are the distance from Washington of

the residences of most members, so that it is not worth while
to take the journey home for a short sojourn, and the fact
that very few attempt to carry on any regular business or
profession while the session lasts.   The more democratic
a country is, so much the more regular is the attendance, so
much closer the attention to the requests of constituents
which a member is expected to render.

7. There are several reasons which make a political
career unattractive to most Americans.   It takes a new
member at least a session to learn the procedure of the
House.   Full dress debates are rare, newspaper reports of
speeches delivered are curt and little read.   The most serious
work is done in committees; it is not known to the world,
and much of it results in nothing, because many bills which
a committee has considered are perhaps never even voted on
by the House.   Ability, tact, and industry make their way
in the long run in Congress, as they do everywhere else.
But in Congress there is, for most men, no long run.   Nowhere, therefore, does the zeal of a young politician sooner
wax cold than in the House of Representatives.   His toil
is usually unfruitful unless it helps him to a renomination
or a senatorship.   Now a seat in the Senate is the highest
ambition ·of the Congressman.   When I first went to
America, I used to ask the ablest and most ambitious of the
friends I made among young men whether they looked forward to entering Congress.   Out of many scarcely one
seemed drawn toward the career to which those who have
won success at the universities of England naturally look
forward.   Presently I came to understand their attitude,
and to feel that the probable disappointments and vexations
of a life in Congress so far outweighed its attractions that
nothing but a strong sense of public duty would induce a
man of fine tastes and high talents to adopt it.   Law, education, literature, the higher walks of commerce, finance, or

railroad work, offer a better prospect of usefulness, enjoyment, or distinction.

Inside Washington, the Representative is dwarfed by the Senator and the Federal judge. Outside Washington he enjoys no great social consideration. Rich men therefore do not seek, as in England, to enter the legislature in order that they may enter society. They will get no *entrée* which they could not have secured otherwise. The country does not go to Congress to look for its Presidential candidates as England looks to Parliament for its Prime Ministers. Congress, in short, is not a focus of political life as are the legislatures of France, Italy, and England.

8. Neither in the Senate nor in the House are there any recognized leaders. In other words, no regular means exist for securing either that members shall be apprised of the approach of an important division, or that they shall vote in that division in a particular way.

There are not, as in the English Parliament, any " whips," one for each party, whose duties are (1) to inform every member belonging to the party when an important division may be expected, and if he sees the member in or about the House, to keep him there until the division is called; (2) to direct the members of his own party how to vote; (3) to obtain pairs for them if they cannot be present to vote; (4) to "tell," *i e.,* count the members in every party division; (5) to " keep touch " of opinion within the party, and convey to the leader a faithful impression of that opinion. A ministerial whip is further bound to " keep a house," *i. e.,* a quorum. The whip is a necessity of government. In America it is different. Whips are not so necessary at Washington as at Westminster. A sort of substitute for them has been devised. Congress does suffer from the want of them, that is, it suffers from the inadequacy of the substituted device.

A division in Congress has not the importance it has in the House of Commons, where it may throw out the ministry. In Congress it merely affirms or negatives some particular bill or resolution. Hence it is not essential to a majority that its full strength should be always at hand, nor has a minority party any great prize set before it as the result of a successful vote.

Questions, however, arise in which some large party interest is involved. In such cases it is important to bring up every vote. Accordingly a meeting of the party is convened, called a senatorial caucus or congressional (*i. e.,* House) caucus, as the case may be. The attitude to be assumed by the party is debated with closed doors, and a vote taken as to the course to be adopted. By this vote every member of the party is deemed bound. The most important caucus of a Congress is that held at the opening to select the party candidate for the speakership, selection by the majority being of course equivalent to election. As the views and tendencies of the Speaker determine the composition of the committees, and thereby the course of legislation, his selection is a matter of supreme importance, and is preceded by weeks of intrigue and canvassing.

This process of " going into caucus " is the regular American substitute for recognized leadership, and has the advantage of seeming more consistent with democratic equality, because every member of the party has in theory equal weight in the party meeting. Anyhow his vote is doubtful, unpredictable; and consequently divisions on minor questions are uncertain. This is a further reason, added to the power of the standing committees, why there is a want of consistent policy in the action of Congress. The freedom thus enjoyed by members on minor questions has the interesting result of preventing dissensions and splits in the parties.

The congressional caucus is more or less called into action according to the number and gravity of the party issues that come before Congress. In troublous times it has to be supplemented by something like obedience to regular leaders. The Senate is rather more jealous of the equality of all its members. But of course a senatorial caucus, since it rarely consists of more than forty persons, is a better working body than a House caucus, which may reach two hundred.

The House of Representatives is for the purpose of serious party issues fully as much a party body as the House of Commons. A member voting against his party on such an issue is more certain to forfeit his party reputation and his seat than is an English member. This is true of both the Senate and the House. But for the purpose of ordinary questions, of issues not involving party fortunes, a Representative is less bound by party ties than an English member, because he has neither leaders to guide him by their speeches nor whips by their private instructions. The apparent gain is that a wider field is left for independent judgment on nonpartisan questions. The real loss is that legislation becomes weak and inconsistent. This conclusion is not encouraging to those who expect us to get rid of party in our legislatures. A deliberative assembly is, after all, only a crowd of men; and the more intelligent a crowd is, so much the more numerous are its volitions; so much greater the difficulty of agreement. Like other crowds, a legislature must be led and ruled. Its merit lies not in the independence of its members, but in the reflex action of its opinion upon the leaders, in its willingness to defer to them in minor matters, reserving disobedience for the issues in which some great principle overrides both the obligation of deference to established authority and the respect due to special knowledge.

Secondly, the spirit of party may seem to be weaker in Congress than in the people at large. But this is only because the questions which the people decide at the polls are always questions of choice between candidates for office. Were the people to vote at the polls on matters not explicitly comprised within a party platform, there would be the same uncertainty as Congress displays. But of course it cannot be employed every day or for every bill. Hence when no party meeting has issued its orders, a member is free to vote as he pleases, or rather as he thinks his constituents desire.

THE HOUSE OF REPRESENTATIVES, CAPITOL BUILDING, WASHINGTON, D. C.

Chapter XIII

THE RELATION OF CONGRESS TO THE PRESIDENT

ALTHOUGH the Constitution forbids any Federal official to be chosen a member of either the House or the Senate, there is nothing in it to prevent officials from speaking there. Now, however, no Federal official appears on the floor. In the early days Washington came down and delivered his opening speech. Occasionally he remained in the Senate during a debate, and even expressed his opinion there. When Hamilton, the first Secretary of the Treasury, prepared his famous report on the national finances, he asked the House whether they would hear him speak it, or would receive it in writing. They chose the latter course, and the precedent then set has been followed by subsequent ministers, while that set in 1801 by President Jefferson when he transmitted his message in writing instead of delivering a speech, has been similarly respected by all his successors. Thus neither House now hears a member of the executive. There is therefore little direct intercourse between Congress and the administration, and no sense of interdependence and community of action such as exists in other parliamentary countries. Cabinet ministers may never have sat in Congress, and the President himself is not necessarily the leader of his party. Hence he does not sway the councils and guide the policy of those members of Congress who belong to his own side. No duty lies on Congress to take up a subject to which he has called attention as needing legislation; and, in fact, the suggestions which he makes, year after year, are

97

usually neglected, even when his party has a majority in both Houses, or when the subject lies outside party lines.

The President and his Cabinet have no recognized spokesman in either House. The only means the President possesses of influencing members of Congress is through patronage. The consequence has been to encourage secret influence, which may of course be used for legitimate purposes, but which, being exerted in darkness, is seldom above suspicion. Thus by its exclusion from Congress the Executive is deprived of the power of leading and guiding the legislature and of justifying in debate its administrative acts.

Next as to the power of Congress over the Executive. Either House of Congress, or both Houses jointly, can pass resolutions calling on the President or his ministers to take certain steps, or censuring steps they have already taken. The President need not obey such resolutions, need not even notice them. They do not shorten his term or limit his discretion. Either House of Congress can direct a committee to summon and examine a minister, who, though he might legally refuse to attend, never does refuse. The committee, when it has got him, can do nothing more than question him.

Congress may refuse to the President the legislation he requests, and thus, by mortifying and embarrassing him, may seek to compel his compliance with its wishes. Congress can pass bills requiring the President or any minister to do or abstain from doing certain acts of a kind hitherto left to his free will and judgment, may, in fact, endeavor to tie down the officials by prescribing certain conduct for them in great detail. The President will presumably veto such bills, as contrary to sound administrative policy. If, however, he signs them, or if Congress passes them by a two-thirds vote in both Houses over his veto, the further question may arise whether they are within the constitutional powers of Congress. If brought before a court, and decided against the President, then if he still refuses to obey, nothing remains but to impeach him. This is too large a proceeding for ordinary use. Since 1789 it has been used only once against a President, and then, although that President (Andrew Johnson) had for two years constantly, and with great intemperance of language, so defied and resisted Congress that the whole machinery of government had been severely strained by the collision of the two authorities, yet the Senate did not convict him, because no single offense had been clearly made out. Thus impeachment does not tend to secure, and indeed was never meant to secure, the co-operation of the Executive with Congress.

It accordingly appears that Congress cannot compel the dismissal of any official. Thus we arrive at the result, surprising to a European, that while Congress may examine the servants of the public to any extent, may censure them, may lay down rules for their guidance, it cannot get rid of them. There remains the power which in free countries has been long regarded as the citadel of parliamentary supremacy, the power of the purse. Congress has the sole right of raising money and appropriating it to the service of the state. But this right means much less power than in European countries. Congress may check any particular scheme which the President favors by refusing supplies for it. But if, keeping within the limits of his constitutional functions, he takes a different course from that they recommend, they would have to look on. To withhold the ordinary supplies, and thereby stop the machine of government, would injure the country and themselves far more than the President. They could not lawfully refuse to vote his salary, for that is guaranteed to him by the Constitution. They could not, except by a successful impeachment, turn him out of the White House or deprive him of his title to the obedience of all Federal officials.

Accordingly, when Congress has endeavored to coerce the President by the use of its money powers, it has proceeded not by refusing appropriations altogether, but by attaching what is called a "rider" to an appropriation bill. Nearly forty years ago the House had formed the habit of inserting in bills appropriating money to the purposes of the public service, provisions relating to quite different matters, which there was not time to push through in the ordinary way. In 1879, the majority in Congress attempted to overcome, by this device, the resistance of President Hayes to certain measures affecting the South which they desired to pass. The President vetoed the bills, and Congress was obliged to pass them without the riders. Next session the struggle recommenced in the same form, and the President, by rejecting the money bills, again compelled Congress to drop the tacked provisions. This victory, which was of course due to the fact that the dominant party in Congress could not command a two-thirds majority, was deemed to have settled the question as between the Executive and the legislature, and may have permanently discouraged the latter from recurring to the same tactics.

The practice of "riders" has certainly caused great abuses, and is now forbidden by the constitutions of many States. A recent President urged upon Congress the desirability of so amending the Federal Constitution as to enable him, as a State governor is by some State constitutions allowed to do, to veto single items in an appropriation bill without rejecting the whole bill. Such an amendment would enable the Executive to do its duty without losing the supplies necessary for the public service which the bills provide. But the process of amending the Constitution is so troublesome that even a change which involves no party issues may remain unadopted long after the best opinion has become unanimous in its favor.

Chapter XIV

THE LEGISLATURE AND THE EXECUTIVE

THE fundamental characteristic of the American national government is its separation of the legislative, executive, and judicial departments. This separation is the merit which the Philadelphia Convention chiefly sought to attain, and which Americans have been wont to regard as most completely secured by the Constitution. In Europe, as well as in America, men are accustomed to talk of legislation and administration as distinct. But a consideration of their nature will show that it is not easy to separate these two departments in theory by analysis, and still less easy to keep them apart in practice.

We find that wherever the will of the people prevails, the legislature, since it either is or represents the people, can make itself omnipotent, unless checked by the action of the people themselves. It can do this in two ways. It may, like the republics of antiquity, issue decrees for particular cases as they arise, giving constant commands to all its agents, who thus become mere servants with no discretion left them. Or it may frame its laws with such particularity as to provide by anticipation for the greatest possible number of imaginable cases, in this way also so binding down its officials as to leave them no volition, no real authority.

We also observe that every legislature tends so to enlarge its powers as to encroach on the executive; and that it has great advantages for so doing, because a succeeding legislature rarely consents to strike off any fetter its predecessor has imposed.

Thus the legitimate issue of the process would be the extinction or absorption of the executive as a power in the State. It would become a mere set of employees, obeying the legislature as the clerks in a bank obey the directors. If this does not happen, the cause is generally to be sought in some one or more of the following circumstances:

The legislature may allow the executive the power of appealing to the nation against itself (England).

The people may from ancient reverence or the habit of military submission be so much disposed to support the Executive as to embolden the latter to defy the legislature (Prussia).

The importance of foreign policy and the difficulty of taking it out of the hands of the Executive may be so great that the Executive will draw therefrom an influence reacting in favor of its general weight and dignity (Prussia, England, and, to some extent, France).

Let us now see how the founders of the American Constitution settled the relations of the departments. They were terribly afraid of a strong Executive, and desired to reserve the final and decisive voice to the legislature, as representing the people. They could not adopt what I have called the Greek method of an assembly both executive and legislative, for Congress was to be a body with limited powers. Neither did they adopt the English method of a legislature governing through an Executive dependent upon it, although that was urged in the Philadelphia Convention of 1787. Yet in this case the majority of the convention were fearful of "democratic haste and instability," fearful that the legislature would, in any event, become too powerful, and therefore anxious to build up some counter authority to check and balance it. By making the President independent, and keeping him and his ministers apart from the legislature, the convention thought they were strength-

ening him, as well as protecting it from attempts on his part
to corrupt it. They were also weakening him. He lost the
initiative in legislation which the English Executive enjoys.
He had not the English king's power of dissolving the legislature and throwing himself upon the country. Thus the
executive magistrate seemed left at the mercy of the legislature. It could weave so close a network of statutes about
him that his discretion, his individual volition, seemed to disappear, and he ceased to be a branch of the government,
being nothing more than a servant working under the eye
and at the nod of his master. This would have been an absorption of the Executive into the legislature.

Although the Convention may not have realized how
helpless such a so-called Executive must be, they felt the
danger of encroachments by an ambitious legislature, and
resolved to strengthen him against it. This was done by
giving the President a veto which it required a two-thirds
vote of Congress to override. In doing this, they went
back on their previous action. They had separated the
President and his ministers from Congress. They now bestowed on him legislative functions, though in a different
form. He became a distinct branch of the legislature, but
for negative purposes only. He could not propose, but he
could refuse. Thus the Executive was strengthened, not as
an Executive, but by being made a part of the legislature;
and the legislature, already weakened by being divided into
two coequal houses, was further weakened by finding itself liable to be arrested in any new departure on which two-
thirds of both houses were not agreed. When the two
Houses are of one mind, and the party hostile to the President has a two-thirds majority in both, the Executive is
almost powerless. It may be right that he should be powerless, because such majorities in both houses presumably indicate a vast preponderance of popular opinion against

him.' The fact to be emphasized is, that in this case all "balance of powers" is gone. The legislature has swallowed up the Executive, in virtue of the principle from which this discussion started, *viz.*, that the Executive is in free states only an agent who may be so limited by express and minute commands as to have no volition left him.

The strength of Congress consists in the right to pass statutes; the strength of the President in his right to veto them. But foreign affairs, as we have seen, cannot be brought within the scope of statutes. How then was the American legislature to deal with them? There were two courses open. One was to leave foreign affairs to the Executive, as in England, giving Congress the same indirect control as the English Parliament enjoys over the crown and ministry. This course could not be taken, because the President is independent of Congress and irremovable during his term. The other course would have been for Congress, like a Greek assembly, to be its own foreign office, or to create a foreign affairs committee of its members to handle these matters. As the objections to this course, which would have excluded the chief magistrate from functions naturally incidental to his position as official representative of the nation, were overwhelmingly strong, a compromise was made. The initiative in foreign policy and the conduct of negotiations were left to him, but the right of declaring war was reserved to Congress, and that of making treaties to one, the smaller and more experienced, branch of the legislature. A measure of authority was thus suffered to fall back to the Executive which would have served to raise materially his position had foreign questions played as large a part in American politics as they have in French or English.

An authority which depends on a veto capable of being overthrown by a two-thirds majority may seem frail. But the experience of a century has shown that, owing to the almost equal strength of the two great parties, the Houses often differ, and there is rarely a two-thirds majority of the same color in both. Hence the Executive has enjoyed some independence. He is strong for defense, if not for attack. Congress can, except within that narrow sphere which the Constitution has absolutely reserved to him, baffle the President, can interrogate, check, and worry his ministers. But it can neither drive him the way it wishes him to go, nor dismiss them for disobedience or incompetence.

An individual man has some great advantages in combating an assembly. His counsels are less distracted. His secrets are better kept. He may sow discord among his antagonists. He can strike a more sudden blow. Hence, when the President happens to be a strong man, resolute, prudent, and popular, he may well hope to prevail against a body whom he may divide by the dexterous use of patronage, may weary out by inflexible patience, may overawe by winning the admiration of the masses, always disposed to rally round a striking personality. But in a struggle extending over a long course of years an assembly has advantages over a succession of officers, especially of elected officers. Men come and go, but an assembly goes on forever; it is immortal, because while the members change, the policy, the passion for extending its authority, the tenacity in clinging to what has once been gained, remain persistent. A weak magistrate comes after a strong magistrate, and yields what his predecessor had fought for; but an assembly holds all it has ever won. Its pressure is steady and continuous; it is always, by a sort of natural process, expanding its own powers and devising new methods for fettering its rival. Thus Congress, though it is no more respected or loved by the people now than it was ninety years ago, though it has developed no higher capacity for promoting the best in-

terests of the State, has succeeded in occupying nearly all
the ground which the Constitution left debatable between
the President and itself; and would, did it possess a better
internal organization, be even more plainly than it now is
the supreme power in the government.

In their effort to establish a balance of power, the
framers of the Constitution so far succeeded that neither
power has subjected the other. But they underrated the inconveniences that arise from the disjunction of the two chief
organs of government. They relieved the administration
from a duty which European ministers find exhausting and
hard to reconcile with the proper performance of administrative work—the duty of giving attendance in the legislature—and taking the lead in its debates. They secured
continuity of executive policy for four years at least, instead
of leaving the government at the mercy of fluctuating majorities in an excitable assembly. But they so narrowed the
sphere of the Executive as to prevent it from leading the
country, or even its own party in the country. They sought
to make members of Congress independent, but in so doing
they deprived them of some of the means which European
legislators enjoy of learning how to administer, of learning
even how to legislate on administrative topics. They condemned them to be architects without science, critics without
experience, censors without responsibility.

Chapter XV

THE FEDERAL COURTS

WHEN in 1788 the loosely confederated States of North America united themselves into a nation, national tribunals were felt to be a necessary part of the national government. Under the Confederation there had existed no means of enforcing treaties or orders of Congress. Now that a Federal legislature had been established, whose laws were to bind directly the individual citizen, a Federal judicature was evidently needed to interpret and apply these laws, and to compel obedience to them. State courts were not fitted to deal with matters of a quasi-international character, such as admiralty jurisdiction and rights arising under treaties, and supplied no means for deciding questions between different States. They could not be trusted to do complete justice between their own citizens and those of another State, and being under the control of their own State governments, they might be forced to disregard any Federal law which the State disapproved. And being authorities coördinate with and independent of one another, with no common court of appeal placed over them to correct their errors or harmonize their views, they would be likely to interpret the Federal Constitution and statutes in different senses, and make the law uncertain by the variety of their decisions. These reasons pointed imperatively to the establishment of a new tribunal or set of tribunals, altogether detached from the States, as part of the machinery of the new government. The Constitution drew the outlines of the system. Congress perfected it by statutes; and as the details rest upon these statutes, Congress retains the power of altering them. Few American institutions are better worth studying than this intricate judicial machinery: few deserve more admiration for the smoothness of their working: few have contributed more to the peace and well-being of the country.

The Federal courts fall into three classes:

The Supreme Court, which sits at Washington.

The circuit courts.

The district courts.

The Supreme Court is directly created by Art. iii. sec. 1 of the Constitution, but with no provision as to the number of its judges. Originally there were six; at present there are nine, a chief justice, with a salary of $13,000, and eight associate justices (salary $12,500 each). The justices are nominated by the President and confirmed by the Senate. They hold office during good behavior, i $e.,$ they are removable only by impeachment. Moreover, the provisions of the American Constitution are held to apply to the inferior as well as to the superior Federal judges. The Fathers of the Constitution were extremely anxious to secure the independence of their judiciary, regarding it as a bulwark both for the people and for the States against aggressions of either Congress or the President. They affirmed the life tenure by an unanimous vote in the Convention of 1787. The result has justified their expectations. The judges have shown themselves independent of Congress and of party, yet the security of their position has rarely tempted them to breaches of judicial duty. Impeachment has been five times resorted to, once only against a justice of the Supreme Court, and then unsuccessfully.

The Supreme Court sits at Washington from October to July in every year. The presence of six judges is required to pronounce a decision, a rule which, by preventing the division of the court into two or more branches, retards the dispatch of business, though it has the advantage of securing a thorough consideration of every case.

The circuit courts have been created by Congress under a power in the Constitution to establish "inferior courts." There are at present nine judicial circuits, in which courts are held annually. For each of these there has been appointed a circuit judge (salary $7000), and to each there is also allotted one of the justices of the Supreme Court. The circuit court may be held either by the circuit judge alone, or by the Supreme Court circuit justice alone, or by both together, or by either sitting along with the district judge (hereafter mentioned) of the district wherein the particular circuit court is held. An appeal lies from the circuit court to the Supreme Court, except in certain cases where the amount in dispute is small.

The district courts are the third and lowest class of Federal tribunals. There are at present ninety-two and the salary of a judge is $6000. For the purpose of dealing with the claims of private persons against the Federal government there has been established in Washington a special tribunal called the Court of Claims, with five justices (salaries, chief justice, $6500, justices, $6000), from which an appeal lies direct to the Supreme Court.

The jurisdiction of the Federal courts extends to the following classes of cases, on each of which I say no more than what seems absolutely necessary to explain their nature. All other cases have been left to the State courts, from which there does not lie (save as hereinafter specified) any appeal to the Federal courts.

1. "Cases in law and equity arising under the Constitution, the laws of the United States and treaties made under their authority."

In order to enforce the supremacy of the national Constitution and laws over all State laws, it was necessary to place the former under the guardianship of the national judiciary. This provision accordingly brings before a Federal court every cause in which either party to a suit relies upon any Federal enactment. The rule has been that where in any legal proceeding a Federal enactment has to be construed or applied by a State court, if the latter supports the Federal enactment, *i. e.,* considers it to govern the case, and applies it accordingly, the supremacy of Federal law is thereby recognized and admitted, and there is therefore no reason for removing the case to a Federal tribunal. But if the decision of the State court has been against the applicability of the Federal law, it is only fair that the party who suffers by the decision should be entitled to Federal determination of the point, and he has accordingly an absolute right to carry it before the Supreme Court.

2. " Cases affecting ambassadors, other public ministers, and consuls."

As these persons have an international character, it would be improper to allow them to be dealt with by a State court which has nothing to do with the national government, and for whose learning and respectability there may exist no such securities as those that surround the Federal courts.

3. " Cases of admiralty and maritime jurisdiction."

These are deemed to include not only prize cases, but all maritime contracts, and all transactions relating to navigation, as well on the navigable lakes and rivers of the United States as on the high seas.

4. " Controversies to which the United States shall be a party."

This provision is obviously needed to protect the United States from being obliged to sue or be sued in a State court, to whose decision the national government could not be expected to submit. When a pecuniary claim is sought to be established against the Federal government, the proper tribunal is the Court of Claims.

5. " Controversies between two or more States, between a State and citizens of another State, between citizens of different States, between citizens of the same State claiming lands under grants of different States, and between a State, or the citizens thereof, and foreign states, citizens, or subjects."

In all these cases a State court is likely to be, or at any rate to seem, a partial tribunal, and it is therefore desirable to vest the jurisdiction in judges equally unconnected with the plaintiff and the defendant.

One important part of the jurisdiction here conveyed has been subsequently withdrawn from the Federal judicature. When the Constitution was submitted to the people, a principal objection urged against it was that it exposed a State, although a sovereign commonwealth, to be sued by the individual citizens of some other State. The question was in doubt until in 1793 the Supreme Court, in the famous case of Chisholm v. The State of Georgia (2 Dall. 419), construed the Constitution to hold that an action did lie against the State of Georgia. The latter's cries of rage filled the Union, and brought other States to her help. An amendment (the eleventh) to the Constitution was passed through Congress and duly accepted by the requisite majority of the States, which declares that " the judicial power of the United States shall not be construed to extend to any suit commenced or prosecuted against one of the United States by citizens of another State or by citizens or subjects of any foreign state." Under the protection of this amendment, not a few States have with impunity repudiated their debts.

The jurisdiction of the Supreme Court is original in

cases affecting ambassadors, and wherever a State is a party; in other cases it is appellate; that is, cases may be brought to it from the inferior Federal courts and (under the circumstances before mentioned) from State courts. But the State courts cannot be invested by Congress with any jurisdiction, for Congress has no authority over them, and is not permitted by the Constitution to delegate any judicial powers to them.

The criminal jurisdiction of the Federal courts, which extends to all offenses against Federal law, is purely statutory, for the United States as such can have no common law. The procedure of the Federal courts is prescribed by Congress, subject to some few rules contained in the Constitution, such as those which preserve the right of trial by jury in criminal cases and suits at common law. The law applied in the Federal courts is of course first and foremost that enacted by the Federal legislature, which, when it is applicable, prevails against any State law. But very often, as for instance in suits between citizens of different States, Federal law does not, or does only in a secondary way, come in question. In such instances the first thing is to determine what law it is that ought to govern the case, each State having a law of its own; and when this has been ascertained, it is applied to the facts, following the decisions of the State courts as of highest authority. Needless to say, the State courts follow the decisions of the Federal courts upon questions of Federal law.

For the execution of its powers each Federal court has attached to it an officer called the United States marshal, corresponding to the sheriff in the State governments, whose duty it is to carry out its writs, judgments, and orders by arresting prisoners, levying execution, putting persons in possession, and so forth. He is entitled, if resisted, to call on all good citizens for help; if they will not or cannot render it, he must refer to Washington and obtain the aid of Federal troops. There exists also in every judiciary district a Federal public prosecutor, called the United States district attorney, who institutes proceedings against persons transgressing Federal laws or evading the discharge of obligations to the Federal treasury. Both sets of officials are under the direction of the Attorney General, as head of the department of justice. They constitute a network of Federal authorities covering the whole territory of the Union, and independent of the officers of the State courts and of the public prosecutors who represent the State governments. Where a State maintains a jail for the reception of Federal prisoners, the United States marshal delivers his prisoners to the State jailer; where this provision is wanting, he must himself arrange for their custody.

This complex system of two jurisdictions (Federal and State) over the whole country, after a hundred and twenty years of experience, despite the wonder of foreigners, works smoothly. It leads to few conflicts or heartburnings, because the key to all difficulties is found in the principle that wherever Federal law is applicable Federal law must prevail, and that every suitor who contends that Federal law is applicable is entitled to have the point decided by a Federal court. The acumen of the lawyers and judges, the wealth of accumulated precedents, make the solution of these questions of applicability and jurisdiction easier than a European practitioner can realize: while the law-abiding habits of the people and their sense that the supremacy of Federal law and jurisdiction works to the common benefit of the whole people, secure general obedience to Federal judgments.

A word in conclusion as to the separation of the judicial from the other two departments, a point on which the framers of the Constitution laid great stress. The legislature makes the law, the judiciary applies it to particular cases by investigating the facts and, when these have been ascertained, by declaring what rule of law governs them. Nevertheless, there are certain points in which the functions of the two departments touch, certain ground which is debatable between the judiciary on the one hand and the legislature on the other.

In most points America has followed the principles and practices of England. She creates no administrative tribunals, she has given the judges (*i. c.,* the Federal judges) a position secured against the caprice of the legislature or Executive, she recognizes judicial decisions as law until some statute has set them aside. She has improved on England in forbidding the legislature to exercise the powers of a criminal court by passing acts of attainder or of pains and penalties, measures still legal, though virtually obsolete, in England. In other points she stands behind England. She still, occasionally, throws upon one House of Congress the trial of impeachments; she still reserves the trial of contested congressional elections for committees of Congress. Special and local bills which vest in private hands certain rights of the State, such as public franchises, or the power of taking private property against the owner's will, are, though in form exercises of legislative power, really fitter to be examined and settled by judicial methods than by the loose opinion, the private motives, the lobbying, which determine legislative decisions where the control of public opinion is insufficiently provided for. England accordingly, though she refers such bills to committees of Parliament, directs these committees to apply a quasi-judicial procedure, and to decide according to the evidence tendered. America takes no such securities, but handles these bills like any others. Here, therefore, we see three pieces of ground debatable between the legislature and the judiciary. All of them originally belonged to the legislature All in America still belong to it. England, however, has abandoned the first, has delivered over the second to the judges, and treats the third as matter to be dealt with by judicial, rather than legislative, methods. Such points of difference are worth noting, because the impression has prevailed in Europe that America is the country in which the province of the judiciary has been most widely extended.

Chapter XVI

THE COURTS AND THE CONSTITUTION

NO feature in the government of the United States has awakened so much curiosity in the European mind, caused so much discussion, received so much admiration, and been more frequently misunderstood, than the duties assigned to the Supreme Court and the functions which it discharges in guarding the ark of the Constitution. Yet there is really no mystery about the matter. It is not a novel device. It is not a complicated device. It is the simplest thing in the world if approached from the right side. In America the name Constitution designates a particular instrument adopted in 1788, amended in some points since, which is the foundation of the national government. This Constitution was ratified and made binding, not by Congress, but by the people acting through conventions assembled in the thirteen States which then composed the Confederation. It created a legislature of two houses; but that legislature, which we call Congress, has no power to alter it in the smallest particular. That which the people have enacted, the people only can alter or repeal.

Suppose, however, that Congress does so transgress, or does overpass the specified purposes. The question remains: How and by whom, in case of dispute, is the validity or invalidity of a statute to be determined?

Such determination is to be effected by setting the statute side by side with the Constitution, and considering whether there is any discrepancy between them. Is the purpose of the statute one of the purposes mentioned or implied in the Constitution? Does it in pursuing that purpose contain anything which violates any clause of the Constitution? It is a question of interpretation, that is, of determining the true meaning both of the superior law and of the inferior law, so as to discover whether they are inconsistent. Congress cannot interpret the law, because Congress is a party interested. The President cannot, because he is not a lawyer, and he also may be personally interested. There remain only the courts, and these must be the national or Federal courts, because no other courts can be relied on in such cases. As the nation takes precedence of the States, the Federal Constitution, which is the supreme law of the land everywhere, and the statutes duly made by Congress under it, are preferred to all State constitutions and statutes; and if any conflict arise between them, the latter must give way.

It will be observed that in all this there is no conflict between the law courts and any legislative body. The conflict is between different kinds of laws. The four kinds of American laws are: 1. The Federal Constitution; 2. Federal statutes; 3. State constitutions; 4. State statutes. The American law court therefore does not itself enter on any conflict with the legislature. It merely secures to each kind of law its due authority.

This is the abstract statement of the matter; but there is also an historical one. In the American colonies, the validity of statutes passed by assemblies under charter from England was often determined by colonial or English courts or by the Privy Council in England. After independence was declared and State constitutions were formed the same question was liable to recur with regard to a statute passed by one of the State assemblies. When the Constitution of the United States came into operation in 1789, and was declared to be paramount to all State constitutions and State statutes, no new principle was introduced; there was merely a new application, as between the nation and the States, of the old doctrine that a subordinate and limited legislature cannot pass beyond the limits fixed for it. For the determination of such questions it became necessary to call in courts created by the central Federal authority and coextensive with it—that is to say, those Federal courts which have been already described.

It is, therefore, no mere technicality to point out that the American judges do not, as Europeans are apt to say, " control the legislature," but simply interpret the law. All that the judges have to do is to discover from the enactments before them what the will of the people is, and apply that will to the facts of a given case. The more general or ambiguous the language which the people have used, so much the more difficult is the task of interpretation, so much greater the need for ability and integrity in the judges. But the task is always the same in its nature. The judges have no concern with the motives or the results of an enactment. To construe the law, that is, to elucidate the will of the people as supreme lawgiver, is the beginning and end of their duty.

The importance of those functions can hardly be exaggerated. It arises from two facts. One is that as the Constitution cannot easily be changed, a bad decision on its meaning, *i. e.*, a decision which the general opinion of the profession condemns, may go uncorrected.

The other fact which makes the function of an American judge so momentous is the brevity, the laudable brevity, of the Constitution. The words of that instrument are general, laying down a few large principles. The cases which will arise as to the construction of these general words cannot be foreseen till they arise. It is therefore hardly an exaggeration to say that the American Constitution as it now stands, with the mass of fringing decisions which explain it, is a far more complete and finished instrument than it was when it came fire-new from the hands of the Convention. It is not merely their work, but the work of the judges, and most of all of one man, the great Chief Justice Marshall.

It is, nevertheless, true that there is no part of the American system which reflects more credit on its authors or has worked better in practice. It has had the advantage of relegating questions not only intricate and delicate, but peculiarly liable to excite political passions, to the cool, dry atmosphere of judicial determination. The relations of the central Federal power to the States, and the amount of authority which Congress and the President are respectively entitled to exercise, have been the most permanently grave questions in American history, with which nearly every other political problem has become entangled.

By leaving constitutional questions to be settled by the courts of law another advantage was incidentally secured. The court does not go to meet the question; it waits for the question to come to it. In America the Constitution is at all times very hard to change: much more, then, must political issues turn on its interpretation. And if this be so, must not the interpreting court be led to assume a control over the executive and legislative branches of the government, since it has the power of declaring their acts illegal?

The causes which have enabled the Federal courts to avoid it, and to maintain their dignity and influence almost unshaken, are the following:

The Supreme Court—I speak of the Supreme Court because its conduct has governed that of inferior Federal courts—has steadily refused to interfere in purely political questions. Occasionally, however, the court has come into collision with the Executive. Occasionally it has been required to give decisions which have worked with tremendous force on politics, as in the Dred Scott decision, which did much to precipitate the Civil War.

Some questions, and among them many which involve political issues, can never come before the Federal courts, because they are not such as are raisable in an action between parties. Looking upon itself as a pure organ of the law, commissioned to do justice between man and man, but to do nothing more, the Supreme Court has steadily refused to decide abstract questions, or to give opinions in advance by way of advice to the Executive. Other causes have sustained the authority of the court by saving it from immersion in the turbid pool of politics. These are the strength of professional feeling among American lawyers, the relation of the bench to the bar, the power of the legal profession in the country. As the respect of the bench for the bar tends to keep the judges in the straight path, so the respect and regard of the bar for the bench, a regard grounded on the sense of professional brotherhood, ensure the moral influence of the court in the country.

The maintenance of judicial influence has been largely due to the personal eminence of the judges. One must not call that a result of fortune which was the result of the wisdom of successive Presidents in choosing capable men to sit on the supreme Federal bench. Yet one man was so singularly fitted for the office of Chief Justice, and rendered such incomparable services in it, that the Americans have been wont to regard him as a special gift of a favoring Providence. This was John Marshall, who presided over the Supreme Court from 1801, till his death in 1835 at the age of seventy-seven, and whose fame overtops that of all other American judges more than Papinian overtops the jurists of Rome or Lord Mansfield the jurists of England.

No other man did half so much either to develop the Constitution by expounding it, or to secure for the judiciary its rightful place in the government as the living voice of the Constitution. The admiration and respect which he and his colleagues won for the Court remain its bulwark: the traditions which were formed under him and them have continued in general to guide the action and elevate the sentiments of their successors.

Nevertheless, the Court has not always had smooth seas to navigate. It has more than once been shaken by blasts of unpopularity. It has not infrequently found itself in conflict with other authorities.

The first attacks arose out of its decision that it had jurisdiction to entertain suits by private persons against a State. This point was set at rest by the eleventh amendment; but the States then first learned to fear the Supreme Court as an antagonist. In 1801, in an application requiring the Secretary of State to deliver a commission, it declared itself to have the power to compel an executive officer to fulfill a ministerial duty affecting the rights of individuals. President Jefferson protested angrily against this claim, but it has been repeatedly reasserted, and is now undoubted law. It was in this same case that the court first explicitly asserted its duty to treat as invalid an act of Congress inconsistent with the Constitution. In 1806 it for the first time pronounced a State statute void; in 1816 and 1821 it rendered decisions establishing its authority as a Supreme Court of Appeal from State courts on " Federal questions," and unfolding the full meaning of the doctrine that the Constitution and acts of Congress duly made in pursuance of the Constitution are the fundamental and supreme law of the land. This was a doctrine which had not been adequately apprehended even by lawyers, and its development, legitimate as we now deem it, roused opposition. The Democratic party, which came into power under President Jackson in 1829, was specially hostile to a construction of the Constitution which seemed to trench upon State rights. A new period in the history of the Court came about now, during which, in the hands of judges mostly appointed by the Democratic party, it made no further advance in power.

.In 1857 the Dred Scott judgment, pronounced by a majority of the judges, excited the strongest outbreak of displeasure yet witnessed. During the Civil War the court did not, as was feared, attempt to throw legal difficulties in the prosecution of the measures needed for reestablishing the authority of the Union. In 1868, having then become Republican in its sympathies by the appointment of new members as the older judges disappeared, it sustained the congressional plan of reconstruction which President Johnson was endeavoring to defeat, and in subsequent cases it has given effect to most, though not to all, of the statutes passed by Congress under the three amendments which abolished slavery and secured the rights of the negroes.

Two of its later acts are thought by some to have affected public confidence. One of these was the reversal, first in 1871, and again, upon broader but not inconsistent grounds, in 1884, of the decision, given in 1869, which declared invalid the act of Congress making government paper a legal tender for debts. The reversal came after a change in the composition of the court. The other misfortune was the interposition of the court in the Presidential electoral count dispute of 1877, in which the Supreme Court members of the Electoral Commission voted strictly on party lines.

Notwithstanding this occurrence, which after all was quite exceptional, the credit and dignity of the Supreme Court stand very high. No one of its members has ever been suspected of corruption, and comparatively few have allowed their political sympathies to disturb their official judgment. Though for many years back every President has appointed only men of his own party, and frequently leading politicians of his own party, the new-made judge has left partisanship behind him.

Federal judgeships of the second and third rank (circuit and district) are invariably given to the members of the President's party, and by an equally well-established usage, to persons resident in the State or States where the circuit or district court is held. But cases of corruption, or even of pronounced partisanship, are practically unknown.

One question remains to be put and answered. The Supreme Court is the living voice of the Constitution—that is, of the will of the people expressed in the fundamental law they have enacted, " the conscience of the people," the guarantee of the minority. To discharge these momentous functions, the court must be stable even as the Constitution is stable.

Does it possess, has it displayed, this strength and stability?

It has not always followed its own former decisions. This is natural in a court whose errors cannot be cured by the intervention of the legislature.

The Supreme Court feels the touch of public opinion. Opinion is stronger in America than anywhere else in the world, and judges are only men. To yield a little may be prudent, for the tree that cannot bend to the blast may be broken. When the terms of the Constitution admit of more than one construction, and when previous decisions have left the true construction so far open that the point in question may be deemed new, is a court to be blamed if it prefers the construction which the bulk of the people deem suited to the needs of the time?

The Supreme Court has changed its color, *i. e.*, its temper and tendencies, from time to time, according to the political proclivities of the men who composed it. It changes very slowly, because the vacancies in a small body happen rarely, and its composition therefore often represents the predominance of a past, and not of the present ruling party. But in none of its three periods can the judges be charged with any prostitution of their functions to party purposes. Their action flowed naturally from the habits of thought they had formed before their accession to the bench, and from the sympathy they could not but feel with the doctrines on whose behalf they had contended.

The Fathers of the Constitution studied nothing more than to secure the complete independence of the judiciary. The President was not permitted to remove the judges, nor Congress to diminish their salaries. One thing only was either forgotten or deemed undesirable, because highly inconvenient, to determine—the number of judges in the Supreme Court. Here was a weak point, a joint in the court's armor through which a weapon might some day penetrate. As the Constitution does not prescribe the number of justices, a statute may increase or diminish the number as Congress thinks fit, and it is possible the court might be "packed" for a purpose. What prevents assaults on the fundamental law—assaults which, however immoral in substance, would be perfectly legal in form? Not the mechanism of government, for all its checks have been evaded; not the conscience of the legislature and the President, for heated combatants seldom shrink from justifying the means by the end. Nothing but the fear of the people, whose broad good sense and attachment to the great principles of the Constitution may generally be relied on to condemn such a perversion of its forms. Yet if excitement has risen high over the country, a majority of the people may acquiesce;

and then it matters little whether what is really a revolution be accomplished by openly violating or by merely distorting the forms of law. To the people we come sooner or later: it is upon their wisdom and self-restraint that the stability of the most cunningly devised scheme of government will in the last resort depend.

Chapter XVII

SUMMARY OF THE FRAME OF NATIONAL GOVERNMENT

THE American Constitution was not a copy of the English parliamentary system. This was so for several reasons.

Very few of the members of the convention had been in England so as to know her constitution, such as it then was, at first hand. Yet there were three sources whence light fell upon it, and for that light they were grateful. One was their experience in dealing with the mother country since the quarrel began. They saw in Britain an executive largely influenced by the personal volitions of the king.

The second source was the legal presentation of the English constitution in scientific text-books, and particularly in Blackstone, whose famous " Commentaries " was first published in 1765.

The third source was the view of the English constitution given by the political philosophers of the eighteenth century, among whom, since he was by far the most important, we need look at Montesquieu alone, with his famous treatise on " The Spirit of Laws," dwelling upon the separation of the executive, legislative, and judicial powers in the British constitution as the most remarkable feature of that system. Now Montesquieu's treatise was taken by the thinkers of the next generation as a sort of Bible of political philosophy.

The views of the British constitution tallied with and were strengthened by their experience of representative gov-

ernment in the colonies—ideas and habits which were after
all the dominant factor in the construction of their political
system. There was a loyally appointed governor or a pro-
prietor, separate from the elected assemblies. Thus the
Americans found and admired in their colonial (or State)
systems, a separation of the legislative from the executive
branch, more complete than in England, because in the colonies no ministers sat in the legislature. And being already
proud of their freedom, they attributed its amplitude chiefly
to this cause.

From their colonial experience, coupled with these no-
tions of the British constitution, the men of 1787 drew three
conclusions: Firstly, that the vesting of the executive and
the legislative powers in different hands was the normal and
natural feature of a free government. Secondly, that the
power of the Executive was dangerous to liberty, and must
be kept within well-defined boundaries. Thirdly, that in
order to check the head of the state it was necessary not only
to define his powers, and appoint him for a limited period,
but also to destroy his opportunities of influencing the legislature. Ministers were forbidden in the Congress, but to
keep Congress from being omnipotent the suggestion that
it elect the President was voted down, and the election made
indirect, and the President was given a veto. Thus it was believed in 1787 that a due balance had been arrived at, the
independence of Congress being secured on the one side and
the independence of the President on the other. There was
of course the risk that controversies as to their respective
rights and powers would arise between these two departments. But the creation of a court entitled to place an au-
thoritative interpretation upon the Constitution in which the
supreme will of the people was expressed, provided a remedy
available in many, if not all, of such cases, and a security
for the faithful observance of the Constitution which Eng-

land did not, and under her system of an omnipotent Parliament could not, possess.

"They builded better than they knew." They divided the legislature from the Executive so completely as to make each, not only independent, but weak even in its own proper sphere.

These observations may suffice to show why the Fathers of the Constitution did not adopt the English parliamentary or cabinet system.

The American system results as follows: A dispute between the President and Congress may arise over an executive act or over a bill. If over an executive act, the Senate can check the President. If over a bill which the President has returned to Congress unsigned, the two Houses can, by a two-thirds majority, pass it over his veto, and so end the quarrel. Should there not be a two-thirds majority, the bill drops; and nothing can be done till the current term of Congress expires. The matter is then remitted to the people. If the President has still two more years in office, the people may signify their approval of his policy by electing a House in political agreement with him, or disapprove it by reëlecting a hostile House. If the election of a new President coincides with that of the new House, the people have a second means provided of expressing their judgment. They may choose not only a House of the same or an opposite complexion to the last, but a President of the same or an opposite complexion. Anyhow they can now establish accord between one house of Congress and the Executive. The Senate, however, may still remain opposed to the President, and may not be brought into harmony with him until a sufficient time has elapsed for the majority in it to be changed by the choice of new Senators by the State legislatures. This method may fail in a crisis needing immediate action; but it escapes the danger of a hurried and perhaps irrevocable decision.

UNITED STATES TREASURY BUILDING, WASHINGTON, D. C.

Thus, in the United States, however, not only in the national government, but in every one of the States, the theory is that the Executive should be wholly independent of the legislative branch. Americans understand that this scheme involves a loss of power and efficiency, but they believe that it makes greatly for safety in a popular government. They expect the Executive and the legislature to work together as well as they can, and public opinion does usually compel a degree of cooperation and efficiency, which perhaps could not be expected theoretically. It is an interesting commentary on the tendencies of democratic government, that in America reliance is coming to be placed more and more, in the nation, in the State, and in the city, upon the veto of the Executive as a protection to the community against the legislative branch.

It is another and a remarkable consequence of the absence of cabinet government in America, that there is also no party government in the European sense. Men do, no doubt, talk of one party as being "in power," meaning thereby the party to which the President belongs. But they do so because that party enjoys the spoils of office in which to so many politicians the value of power consists. The House or Senate or both may be of a different party. Though party feeling has generally been stronger in America than in England, and even now covers a larger proportion of the voters, and enforces a stricter discipline, party government is distinctly weaker.

We are now in a position to sum up the practical results of the system which purports to separate Congress from the Executive, instead of uniting them as they are united under a cabinet government. I say " purports to separate," because it is plain that the separation, significant as it is, is less complete than current language imports, or than the Fathers of the Constitution would seem to have intended.

The necessary coherence of the two powers baffled them. These results are five:

The President and his ministers have no initiative in Congress, little influence over Congress, except what they can exert upon individual members, through the bestowal of patronage.

Congress has, together with unlimited powers of inquiry, imperfect powers of control over the administrative departments.

The nation does not always know how or where to fix responsibility for misfeasance or neglect. The person and bodies concerned in making and executing the laws are so related to one another that each can generally shift the burden of blame on someone else, and no one acts under the full sense of direct accountability.

There is a loss of force by friction, *i. e.,* part of the energy, force, and time of the men and bodies that make up the government is dissipated in struggles with one another. This belongs to all free governments, because all free governments rely upon checks. But the more checks, the more friction.

There is a risk that executive vigor and promptitude may be found wanting at critical moments.

We may include these defects in one general expression. There is in the American government, considered as a whole, a want of unity. A President can do little, for he does not lead either Congress or the nation. Congress cannot guide or stimulate the President, nor replace him by a man fitter for the emergency. The Cabinet neither receives a policy from Congress nor gives one to it. Each power in the state goes its own way.

This want of unity is painfully felt in a crisis. When a sudden crisis comes upon a free state, the Executive needs two things, a large command of money and powers in excess of those allowed at ordinary times. When dangers thicken the only device may be the Roman one of a temporary dictatorship. Something like this happened in the War of Secession, for the powers then conferred upon President Lincoln, or exercised without congressional censure by him, were almost as much in excess of those enjoyed under the ordinary law as the authority of a Roman dictator exceeded that of a Roman consul. When the emergency had passed away the torrent which had overspread the plain fell back at once into its safe and well-worn channel. The reign of legality returned; and only four years after the power of the Executive had reached its highest point in the hands of President Lincoln, it was reduced to its lowest point in those of President Johnson. Such a people can work any Constitution. The danger for them is that this reliance on their skill and their star may make them heedless of the faults of their political machinery, slow to devise improvements which are best applied in quiet times.

Before leaving this subject a few remarks may be added on the general features of the national government.

1. No part of the Constitution cost its framers so much time and trouble as the method of choosing the President. The result has, however, so completely falsified their expectations that it is hard to comprehend how they came to be entertained.

2. The choice of the President, by what is now practically a simultaneous popular vote, not only involves once in every four years a tremendous expenditure of energy, time, and money, but induces of necessity a crisis which, if it happens to coincide with any passion powerfully agitating the people, may be dangerous to the commonwealth.

3. There is always a risk that the result of a Presidential election may be doubtful or disputed on the ground of error, fraud, or violence.

4. The change of the higher executive officers, and of many of the lower executive officers also, which usually takes place once in four years, gives a jerk to the machinery, and causes a discontinuity of policy, unless, of course, the President has served only one term and is reëlected. Moreover, there is generally a loss either of responsibility or of efficiency in the executive chief magistrate during the last part of his term.

5. The Vice-President's office is ill conceived. His only function is to act as chairman of the Senate with very little power, yet he may succeed to the highest office in the land.

6. The defects in the structure and working of Congress, and in its relations to the Executive, have been so fully dwelt on already that it is enough to refer summarily to them. They are—

The discontinuity of congressional policy.

The want of adequate control over officials.

The want of opportunities for the Executive to influence the legislature.

The want of any authority charged to secure the passing of such legislation as the country needs.

The frequency of disputes between three coördinate powers, the President, the Senate, and the House.

The maintenance of a continuous policy is a difficulty in all popular governments. In the United States it is specially so, because—

The executive head and his ministers are necessarily (unless when a President is reëlected) changed once every four years.

One House of Congress is changed every two years.

Neither House recognizes permanent leaders.

No accord need exist between Congress and the Executive.

There is no true leadership in political action, because the most prominent man has no recognized party authority.

There is often no general and continuous cabinet policy, because the Cabinet has no authority over Congress and may, perhaps have no influence with it.

There is no general or continuous legislative policy, because the legislature, having no recognized leaders, and no one guiding committee, acts through a large number of committees, independent of one another, and seldom able to bring their measures to maturity.

These defects are all reducible to two. There is an excessive friction in the American system, a waste of force in the strife of various bodies and persons created to check and balance one another. There is a want of executive unity, and therefore a possible want of executive vigor.

7. The relations of the people to the legislature are far from perfect. Legislators are not responsible to their constituents because of the committee system and the want of recognized leadership in Congress.

One may say in general that the reciprocal action and reaction between the electors and Congress, what is commonly called the " touch " of the people with their agents, is not sufficiently close, quick, and delicate. Conversely, Congress does not guide and illuminate its constituents.

8. The independence of the judiciary, due to its holding for life, has been a conspicuous merit of the Federal system, as compared with the popular election and short terms of judges in most of the States. Yet even the Federal judiciary is not secure from the attacks of the two other powers, if combined.

It is worth remarking that the points in which the American frame of national government has proved least successful are those which are most distinctly artificial, i. e., those which are not the natural outgrowth of old institutions and well-formed habits, but devices consciously introduced to attain specific ends. The election of the President and Vice President by electors appointed *ad hoc* is such a device.

All the main features of American government may be deduced from two principles. One is the sovereignty of the people. The second principle, itself a consequence of this first one, is the distrust of the various organs and agents of government.

In general what keeps a free government going is the good sense and patriotism of the people, or of the guiding class, embodied in usages and traditions which it is hard to describe, but which find, in moments of difficulty, remedies for the inevitable faults of the system. Now, this good sense and that power of subordinating sectional to national interests which we call patriotism, exist in higher measure in America than in any of the great states of Europe. And the United States, more than any other country, is governed by public opinion, that is to say, by the general sentiment of the mass of the nation, which all the organs of the national government and of the State governments look to and obey.

Every constitution, like every man, has "the defects of its good qualities." If a nation desires perfect stability it must put up with a certain slowness and cumbrousness; it must face the possibility of a want of action, where action is called for. If, on the other hand, it seeks to obtain executive speed and vigor by a complete concentration of power, it must run the risk that power will be abused and irrevocable steps too hastily taken. Those faults on which I have laid stress, the waste of power by friction, the want of unity and vigor in the conduct of affairs by Executive and legislature, are the price which the Americans pay for the autonomy of their States, and for the permanence of the equilibrium among the various branches of their government. They pay this price willingly, because these defects are far less dangerous to the body politic than they would be in a European country. Since the War of Secession ended, no serious danger has arisen either from within or from without to alarm American statesmen. Social convulsions from within, warlike assaults from without, seem now as unlikely to try the fabric of the American Constitution, as an earthquake to rend the walls of the Capitol. This is why the Americans submit, not merely patiently, but hopefully, to the defects of their government. The vessel may not be any better built, or found, or rigged than are those which carry the fortunes of the great nations of Europe. She is certainly not better navigated. But for the present at least—it may not always be so—she sails upon a summer sea.

It must never be forgotten that the main object which the framers of the Constitution set before themselves has been achieved. The Constitution as a whole has stood and stands unshaken. The scales of power have continued to hang fairly even. The President has not corrupted and enslaved Congress; Congress has not paralyzed and cowed the President. The legislative may have gained somewhat on the executive department; but neither the legislature nor the Executive has for a moment threatened the liberties of the people. The States have not broken up the Union, and the Union has not absorbed the States. No wonder that Americans are proud of an instrument under which this great result has been attained, which has passed unscathed through the furnace of civil war, which has been found capable of embracing a body of commonwealths three times as numerous and with twenty-fold the population of the original States, which has cultivated the political intelligence of the masses to a point reached in no other country, which has fostered and been found compatible with a larger measure of local self-government than has existed elsewhere. Nor is it the least of its merits to have made itself beloved. Exceptions may be taken to particular features, and these objections point, as most American thinkers are agreed, to practical improvements which would preserve the excellences and remove some of the inconveniences. But reverence for the Constitution has become so potent a conservative influence, that no proposal of fundamental change seems likely to be entertained. And this reverence is itself one of the most wholesome and hopeful elements in the character of the American people.

Chapter XVIII

THE FEDERAL SYSTEM

THE contests in the Convention of 1787 over the framing of the Constitution, and in the country over its adoption, turned upon two points: the extent to which the several States should be recognized as independent and separate factors in the construction of the national government, and the quantity and nature of the powers which should be withdrawn from the States to be vested in that government. We may say that in the America of to-day there exists a general agreement—

That every State on entering the Union finally renounced its sovereignty, and is now forever subject to the Federal authority as defined by the Constitution.

That the functions of the States as factors of the national government are satisfactory, *i.e.* sufficiently secure its strength and the dignity of these communities.

That the delimitation of powers between the national government and the States, contained in the Constitution, is convenient, and needs no fundamental alteration.

As to the Federal system—

1. The distribution of powers between the national and State governments is effected in two ways—Positively, by conferring certain powers on the national government; negatively, by imposing certain restrictions on the States. Thus we may distinguish the following classes of governmental powers—

Powers vested in the national government alone.

Powers vested in the States alone.

Powers exercisable by either the national government or the States.

Powers forbidden to the national government.

Powers forbidden to the State governments.

2. The powers vested in the national government alone are such as relate to the conduct of the foreign relations of the country and to such common national purposes as the army and navy, internal commerce, currency, weights and measures, and the post office, with provisions for the management of the machinery, legislative, executive, and judicial, charged with these purposes.

The powers which remain vested in the States alone are all the other ordinary powers of internal government, such as legislation on private law, civil and criminal, the maintenance of law and order, the creation of local institutions, the provision for education, and the relief of the poor, together with taxation for the above purposes.

3. The powers which are exercisable concurrently by the national government and by the States are—

Powers of legislation on some specified subjects, such as bankruptcy and certain commercial matters (*e. g.,* pilot laws and harbor regulations), but so that State legislation shall take effect only in the absence of Federal legislation.

Powers of taxation, direct or indirect, but so that neither Congress nor a State shall tax exports from any State, and so that neither any State shall, except with the consent of Congress, tax any corporation or other agency created for Federal purposes or any act done under Federal authority, nor the national government tax any State or its agencies or property.

Powers of determining matters relating to the election of Representatives and Senators (but if Congress determines, the State law gives way).

4. The prohibitions imposed on the national govern-

ment are set forth in Art. i. sec. 9, and in the first ten amendments. The most important are—

Writ of *habeas corpus* may not be suspended, nor bill of attainder or *ex post facto* law passed.

No commercial preference shall be given to one State over another.

No title of nobility shall be granted.

No law shall be passed establishing or prohibiting any religion, or abridging the freedom of speech or of the press, or of public meeting, or of bearing arms.

No religious test shall be required as a qualification for any office under the United States.

No person shall be tried for a capital crime unless on the presentment of a grand jury, or be subjected to a second capital trial for the same offense, or be compelled to be a witness against himself, or be tried otherwise than by a jury of his State and district.

No common law action shall be decided except by a jury where the value in dispute exceeds $20, and no fact determined by a jury shall be reëxamined otherwise than by the rules of the common law.

5. The prohibitions imposed on the States are contained in Art. i. sec. 10, and in the three last amendments. They are intended to secure the national government against attempts by the States to trespass on its domain, and to protect individuals against oppressive legislation.

No State shall make any treaty or alliance; coin money: make anything but gold and silver coin a legal tender: pass any bill of attainder, *ex post facto* law, or law impairing the obligation of contracts: grant any titles of nobility.

No State shall without the consent of Congress lay duties on exports or imports (the produce of such, if laid going to the national treasury) : keep troops or ships of war in peace time: enter into an agreement with another State or with any foreign power: engage in war, unless actually invaded or in imminent danger.

Every State must give credit to the records and judicial proceedings of every other State: extend the privileges and immunities of citizens to the citizens of other States: deliver up fugitives from justice to the State entitled to claim them.

No State shall have any but a republican form of government.

No State shall maintain slavery: abridge the privileges of any citizen of the United States, or deny to him the right of voting, in respect of race, color, or previous servitude: deprive any person of life, liberty, or property without due process of law: deny to any person the equal protection of the laws.

Note that this list contains no prohibition to a State to do such things as the following: Establish a particular form of religion: endow a particular form of religion, or educational or charitable establishments connected therewith: abolish trial by jury in criminal or civil cases: which shows that the framers of the Constitution had no wish to produce uniformity among the States in government or institutions, and little care to protect the citizens against abuses of State power.

6. The powers vested in each State are all of them original and inherent powers, which belonged to the State before it entered the Union. Hence they are *prima facie* unlimited. The powers granted to the national government are delegated powers, enumerated in and defined by the instrument which has created the Union. Hence the rule that when a question arises whether the national government possesses a particular power, proof must be given that the power was positively granted.

7. The authority of the national government over

the citizens of every State is direct and immediate, not exerted through the State organization, and not requiring the coöperation of the State government.

On the other hand, the State in no wise depends on the national government for its organization or its effective working. It is the creation of its own inhabitants.

8. It is a further consequence of this principle that the national government has but little to do with the States as States. Its relations are with their citizens, who are also its citizens, rather than with them as ruling commonwealths. In the following points, however, the Constitution does require certain services of the States—

It requires each State government to direct the choice of, and accredit to the seat of the national government, two Senators and so many Representatives as the State is entitled to send.

It requires similarly that Presidential electors be chosen, meet, and vote in the States, and that their votes be transmitted to the national capital.

It requires each State to organize and arm its militia, which, when duly summoned for active service, are placed under the command of the President.

It requires each State to maintain a republican form of government.

Note in particular that the national government does not, as in some other federations—

Call upon the States, as commonwealths, to contribute funds to its support.

Issue (save in so far as may be needed in order to secure a republican form of government) administrative orders to the States, directing their authorities to carry out its laws or commands.

Require the States to submit their laws to it, and veto such as it disapproves.

Neither does the national government allow its structure to be dependent on the action of the States.

9. A State is, within its proper sphere, just as legally supreme, just as well entitled to give effect to its own will, as is the national government within its sphere; and for the same reason.

10. There are several remarkable omissions in the Constitution of the American federation.

One is that there is no grant of power to the national government to coerce a recalcitrant or rebellious state. Another is that nothing is said as to the right of secession. Anyone can understand why this right should not have been granted. But neither is it mentioned to be negatived, and there is no abstract or theoretic declaration regarding the nature of the federation and its government, nothing as to the ultimate supremacy of the central authority outside the particular sphere allotted to it, nothing as to the so-called sovereign rights of the States.

Chapter XIX

WORKING OF THE FEDERAL SYSTEM

THE working relations of the national government to the States may be considered under two heads, *viz.,* its relations to the States as corporate bodies, and its relations to the citizens of the States as individuals, they being also citizens of the Union.

The national government touches the States as corporate commonwealths in three points. One is their function in helping to form the national government; another is the control exercised over them by the Federal Constitution through the Federal courts; the third is the control exercised over them by the Federal legislature and Executive in the discharge of the governing functions which these latter authorities possess.

1. The States serve to form the national government by choosing Presidential electors, by choosing Senators, and by fixing the franchise which qualifies citizens to vote for members of the House of Representatives. The only restriction imposed on State discretion in this respect is that of the fifteenth amendment, which forbids any person to be deprived of suffrage, on "account of race, color, or previous condition of servitude."

2. The Federal Constitution deprives the States of certain powers they would otherwise enjoy. They are liable to be sued in the Federal courts by another State or by a foreign power. They cannot, without the consent of Congress,

tax exports or imports, or in any case pass a law impairing the obligation of a contract. They must surrender fugitives from the justice of any other State.

The President as national Executive, and Congress as national legislature, have also received from the Constitution the right of interfering in certain specified matters with the governments of the States. Congress of course does this by way of legislation, and an act of Congress overrides any State act.

Where the President interferes with a State, he does so either under his duty to give effect to the legislation of Congress, or under the discretionary executive functions which the Constitution has entrusted to him, *e. g.*, to carry out the guarantee of a republican form of government, or to suppress insurrection.

Offenses against Federal statutes are justiciable in Federal courts, and punishable under Federal authority. There is no Federal common law of crimes.

Resistance offered to the enforcement of a Federal statute may be suppressed by Federal authority.

Attacks on the property of the Federal government may be repelled, and disturbances thence arising may be quelled by Federal authority.

The judgments pronounced in civil causes by Federal courts are executed by the officers of these courts.

All other offenses and disorders whatsoever are left to be dealt with by the duly constituted authorities of the State, who are, however, entitled to summon the power of the Union to their aid in case of the breaking out in a State of serious disturbances.

So far we have been considering the relations of the national government to the States as political communities. Let us now see what are its relations to the individual citizens of these States. They are citizens of the Union as well as

CONGRESSIONAL LIBRARY, WASHINGTON, D. C.

of the States, and owe allegiance to both powers. In general the right of the State to obedience is wider in the area of matters which it covers. But within the limits of its power, the authority of the national government is higher than that of the State.

The limits of judicial power are more difficult of definition. Every citizen can sue and be sued or indicted both in the courts of his State and in the Federal courts, but in some classes of cases the former, in others the latter, is the proper tribunal, while in many it is left to the choice of the parties before which tribunal they will proceed.

The Federal authority acts upon the citizens of a State directly by means of its own officers, who are quite distinct from and independent of the State officials. Federal indirect taxes, for instance, are levied all along the coast and over the country by Federal custom-house collectors and excisemen, acting under the orders of the Treasury Department at Washington. The judgments of Federal courts are carried out by United States marshals, likewise dispersed over the country and supplied with a staff of assistants. The same is, of course, true of the army: but the army is rarely seen by the majority of the people.

If the duly constituted authorities of a State resist the laws and orders of the national government, a difficult question arises. This has several times happened. The question was finally settled by the Civil War of 1861-1865, since which time the following doctrines may be deemed established—

No State has a right to declare an act of the Federal government invalid.

No State has a right to secede from the Union.

The only authority competent to decide finally on the constitutionality of an act of Congress or of the national Executive is the Federal judiciary.

Any act of a State legislature or State executive conflicting with the Constitution, or with an act of the national government done under the Constitution, is really an act not of the State government, which cannot legally act against the Constitution, but of persons falsely assuming to act as such government, and is therefore *ipso jure* void.

But in general unless the legislation or administration of such a State transgresses some provision of the Federal Constitution (such as that forbidding *ex post facto* laws, or laws impairing the obligation of a contract), the national government not only ought not to interfere, but cannot interfere. The State must go its own way, with whatever injury to private rights and common interests its folly or perversity may cause. So far from lamenting as a fault, though an unavoidable fault, of their Federal system, the State independence I have described, the Americans are inclined to praise it as a merit. They argue not merely that the best way on the whole is to leave a State to itself, but that this is the only way in which a permanent cure of its diseases will be effected.

A European may say that there is a dangerous side to this application of democratic faith in local majorities and in *laissez-aller*. Doubtless there is: yet those who have learned to know the Americans will answer that no nation so well understands its own business.

Chapter XX

FAULTS AND MERITS OF THE FEDERAL SYSTEM

THE faults generally charged on federations as compared with unified governments (and the experience of America in these points) are the following—

1. Weakness in the conduct of foreign affairs.

In its early years the Union was not successful in the management of its foreign relations. But for many years the principle of abstention from Old World complications was so heartily and consistently adhered to that the capacities of the Federal system were little tried, while the unanimity of opinion in the conduct of later affairs did not strain the system.

2. Weakness in home government, that is to say, deficient authority over the component States and the individual citizens.

For the purposes of domestic government the Federal authority is now, in ordinary times, sufficiently strong. However, there have been occasions when the resistance of even a single State disclosed its weakness, *e. g.*, South Carolina in 1832 with her "nullification." The only general conclusion on this point which can be drawn from history is that while the central government is likely to find less and less difficulty in enforcing its will against a State or disobedient subjects, because the prestige of its success in the Civil War has strengthened it, because the Union sentiment is still growing, and because the facilities of communication make the raising and moving of troops more easy, nevertheless recalcitrant States, or groups of States, still enjoy certain advantages for resistance, advantages due partly to their legal position, partly to their local sentiment, which rebels might not have in unified countries like England, France, or Italy.

3. Liability to dissolution by the secession or rebellion of States.

This was tried and failed in 1861-1865.

4. Liability to division into groups and factions by the formation of separate combinations of the component States.

This was a favorite feature before the war. At present, though there are several sets of States whose common interests lead their representatives in Congress to act together, it is no longer the fashion for States to combine in an official way through their State organizations, and their so doing would excite reprehension. It is easier, safer, and more effective to act through the great national parties.

5. Want of uniformity among the States in legislation and administration.

The want of uniformity in private law and methods of administration is an evil which different minds will judge by different standards. Some may think it a positive benefit to secure a variety which is interesting in itself and makes possible the trying of experiments from which the whole country may profit. On the whole, far less inconvenience than could have been expected seems to be caused by the varying laws of different States, partly because commercial law is the department in which the diversity is smallest, partly because American practitioners and judges have become expert in applying the rules for determining which law, where those of different States are in question, ought to be deemed to govern a given case.

6. Trouble, expense, and delay due to the complexity

of a double system of legislation and administration. Americans do not seem to feel this. They tell you that smoothness of working is secured by elaboration of device, that complex as the mechanism of their government may appear, the citizens have grown so familiar with it that its play is smooth and easy, attended with less trouble, and certainly with less suspicion on the part of the people, than would belong to a scheme which vested all powers in one administration and one legislature. The expense is admitted, but is considered no grave defect when compared with the waste which arises from untrustworthy officials and legislators whose depredations would, it is thought, be greater were their sphere of action wider, and the checks upon them fewer.

There is a blemish characteristic of the American federation which Americans seldom notice because it seems to them unavoidable. This is the practice in selecting candidates for Federal office of regarding not so much the merits of the candidate as the effect which his nomination will have upon the vote of the State to which he belongs.

I have left to the last the gravest reproach which Europeans have been wont to bring against Federalism in America. They attributed to it the origin, or at least the virulence, of the great struggle over slavery which tried the Constitution so severely. That struggle created parties which tended more and more to become identified with States. It gave tremendous importance to legal questions arising out of the differences between the law of the Slave States and of the Free States. It shook the credit of the Supreme Court. It disposed the extreme men on both sides to hate the Federal Union which bound them in the same body with their antagonists. Thus at last it brought about secession and the great Civil War. Even when the war was over, the dregs of the poison continued to haunt and vex the system, and bred fresh disorders in it. All these mischiefs, it has often been argued, are the results of the Federal structure.

It may be answered not merely that the national government has survived this struggle and emerged from it stronger than before, but also that Federalism did not produce the struggle, but only gave to it the particular form of a series of legal controversies over the Federal pact followed by a war of States against the Union.

On the merit side, there are two distinct lines of argument by which their Federal system was recommended to the framers of the Constitution, and upon which it is still held forth for imitation to other countries.

The first set of arguments point to Federalism proper, and are the following—

1. That Federalism furnishes the means of uniting commonwealths into one nation under one national government without extinguishing their separate administrations, legislatures, and local patriotisms. As the Americans of 1787 would probably have preferred complete State independence to the fusion of their States into a unified government, Federalism was the only resource.

2. That Federalism supplies the best means of developing a new and vast country.

3. That it prevents the rise of a despotic central government, absorbing other powers, and menacing the private liberties of the citizen.

The second set of arguments relate to and recommend not so much Federalism as local self-government. I state them briefly because they are familiar.

4. Self-government stimulates the interest of people in the affairs of their neighborhood, sustains local political life, educates the citizen in his daily round of civic duty, teaches him that perpetual vigilance and the sacrifice of his own time

and labor are the price that must be paid for individual liberty and collective prosperity.

5. Self-government secures the good administration of local affairs by giving the inhabitants of each locality due means of overseeing the conduct of their business.

Three further benefits to be expected from a Federal system may be mentioned, benefits which seem to have been unnoticed or little regarded by those who established it in America.

6. Federalism enables a people to try experiments in legislation and administration which could not be safely tried in a large centralized country.

7. Federalism, if it diminishes the collective force of a nation, diminishes also the risks to which its size and the diversities of its parts expose it.

8. Federalism, by creating many local legislatures with wide powers, relieves the national legislature of a part of that large mass of functions which might otherwise prove too heavy for it. Thus business is more promptly dispatched, and the great central council of the nation has time to deliberate on those questions which most nearly touch the whole country.

All of these arguments recommending Federalism have proved valid in American experience. Although many blunders have been committed in the process of development, greater evils might have resulted had the creation of local institutions and the control of new communities been left to the central government.

The arguments which set forth the advantages of local self-government were far more applicable to the States of 1787 than now. Those were communities to which the expression " local self-government " might be applied, for, although the population was scattered, the numbers were small enough for the citizens to have a personal knowledge of their leading men, and a personal interest (especially as a large proportion were landowners) in the economy and prudence with which common affairs were managed. Now, however, with the larger States, the stake of each citizen is relatively smaller, and generally too small to sustain his activity in politics, and the party chiefs of the State are known to him only by the newspapers or by their occasional visits on a stumping tour.

All that can be claimed for the Federal system under this head is that it handles taxation better—for the educative effect (which is claimed) of frequent elections is neutralized by overtaxing the citizen's attention and interest.

The utility of the State system in localizing disorders or discontents, and the opportunities it affords for trying easily and safely experiments which ought to be tried in legislation and administration, constitute benefits to be set off against a risk, referred to in the last preceding chapters, of injustice to the minority and imitation of bad legislation.

A more unqualified approval may be given to the division of legislative powers, for the existence of the State legislatures relieves Congress of a burden too heavy for its shoulders, and different economic and social conditions in different parts of the country are treated with the varying legislation they require.

The characteristic merit of the American Constitution lies in that it has given the national government a direct authority over all citizens, irrespective of the State governments, and has therefore been able safely to leave wide powers in the hands of those governments. And by placing the Constitution above both the national and the State governments, it has referred the arbitrament of disputes between them to an independent body, charged with the interpretation of the Constitution, a body which is to be deemed the living voice of the Constitution.

Yet even these devices would not have succeeded but for the presence of a mass of moral and material influences stronger than any political devices, which have maintained the equilibrium of centrifugal and centripetal forces. On the one hand there has been the love of local independence and self-government; on the other, the sense of community in blood, in language, in habits and ideas, a common pride in the national history and the national flag.

Chapter XXI

GROWTH AND DEVELOPMENT OF THE CONSTITUTION

THERE is another point of view from which we have still to consider the Constitution. It is not only a fundamental law, but an unchangeable law, unchangeable, that is to say, by the national legislature, and changeable even by the people only through a slow and difficult process. How can a country whose very name suggests movement and progress be governed by a system and under an instrument which remains the same from year to year and from century to century?

The Americans have what may be called a rigid Constitution, *i. e.*, one which cannot be bent or twisted by the action of the legislature, but stands stiff and solid, opposing a stubborn resistance to the attacks of any majority who may desire to transgress or evade its provisions. As the English constitution is the best modern instance of the flexible type, so is the American of the rigid type.

Historical inquiry verifies this expectation. Yet the Constitution of the United States, rigid though it be, has changed, has developed. It has developed in three ways to which I devote the following paragraphs.

It has been changed by Amendment. Certain provisions have been struck out of the original document of 1787-1788; certain other, and more numerous, provisions have been added. This method needs little explanation, because it is open and direct. It resembles the method in which laws are changed in England, the difference being that whereas in England statutes are changed by the legislature, here in the United States the fundamental law is changed in a more roundabout fashion by the joint action of Congress and the States.

It has been developed by Interpretation, that is, by the unfolding of the meaning implicitly contained in its necessarily brief terms; or by the extension of its provisions to cases which they do not directly contemplate, but which their general spirit must be deemed to cover.

It has been developed by Usage, that is, by the establishment of rules not inconsistent with its express provisions, but giving them a character, effect, and direction which they would not have if they stood alone, and by which their working is materially modified. These rules are sometimes embodied in statutes passed by Congress and repealable by Congress. Sometimes they remain in the stage of mere convention or understanding which has no legal authority, but which everybody knows and accepts. Whatever their form, they must not conflict with the letter of the Constitution, for if they do conflict with it, they will be deemed invalid whenever a question involving them comes before a court of law.

1. The men who sat in the Convention of 1787 were not sanguine enough, like some of the legislating sages of antiquity, or like such imperial codifiers as the Emperor Justinian, to suppose that their work could stand unaltered for all time to come. They provided (Art. v.) that "Congress, whenever two-thirds of both houses shall deem it necessary, shall propose amendments to this Constitution, or on the application of the legislatures of two-thirds of the several States, shall call a convention for proposing amendments, which, in either case, shall be valid to all intents and purposes as part of this Constitution when ratified by the legislatures of three-fourths of the several States, or by con-

ventions in three-fourths thereof, as the one or the other mode may be prescribed by Congress."

All the amendments so far adopted have been proposed in the first manner (by Congress) and ratified in the first manner (by State legislatures).

There is only one provision in the Constitution which cannot be so amended. It is that which secures to each and every State equal representation in one branch of the legislature. "No State without its consent shall be deprived of its equal suffrage in the Senate" (Art. v.).

Following President Lincoln, Americans speak of the Union as indestructible; and the expression. "An indestructible Union of indestructible States," has been used by the Supreme Court in a famous case. But looking at the Constitution simply as a legal document, one finds nothing in it to prevent the adoption of an amendment providing a method for dissolving the existing Federal tie, whereupon such method would be applied so as to form new unions, or permit each State to become an absolutely sovereign and independent commonwealth.

The amendments made to the Constitution have been in all fifteen in number. These have been made on four occasions, and fall into four groups, two of which consist of one amendment each. The first group, including ten amendments made immediately after the adoption of the Constitution, ought to be regarded as a supplement or postscript to it, rather than as changing it. They constitute what Americans, following the English precedent, call a Bill of Rights, securing the individual citizen and the States against the encroachments of Federal power. The second and third groups, if a single amendment can be properly called a group (viz., amendments xi. and xii.) are corrections of minor defects which had disclosed themselves in the working of the Constitution. The fourth group is the only one which marked a political crisis and registered a political victory. It comprises three amendments (xiii , xiv., xv.) which forbid slavery, define citizenship, secure the suffrage of citizens against attempts by States to disciiminate to the injury of particular classes, and extend Federal protection to those citizens who may suffer from the operation of certain kinds of unjust State laws. These three amendments are the outcome of the War of Secession, and were needed in order to confirm and secure for the future its results.

Many amendments to the Constitution have been at various times suggested to Congress by Presidents, or brought forward in Congress by members, but very few of these have ever obtained the requisite two-thirds vote of both Houses.

Why then has the regular procedure for amendment proved in practice so hard to apply?

Partly, of course, owing to the inherent disputatiousness and perversity (what Americans call " cussedness ") of bodies of men. It is difficult to get two-thirds of two assemblies (the Houses of Congress) and three-fourths of forty-five commonwealths, each of which acts by two assemblies, for the State legislatures are all double-chambered, to agree to the same practical proposition.

Ought the process of change to be made easier? American statesmen think not. A swift and easy method would not only weaken the sense of security which the rigid Constitution now gives, but would increase the troubles of current politics by stimulating a majority in Congress to frequently submit amendments to the States. The habit of mending would turn into the habit of tinkering.

From this there has followed another interesting result. Since modifications or developments are often needed, and since they can rarely be made by amendment, some other way of making them must be found. The ingenuity of lawyers has discovered one method in interpretation, while the dexterity of politicians has invented a variety of devices whereby legislation may extend, or usage may modify, the express provisions of the apparently immovable and inflexible instrument.

2. The second method of change is by interpretation.

It is plain that the shorter a law is, the more general must its language be, and the greater therefore the need for interpretation. So too the greater the range of a law, and the more numerous and serious the cases which it governs, the more frequently will its meaning be canvassed. The Constitution of the United States is so concise and so general in its terms, that even had America been as slow moving a country as China, many questions must have arisen on the interpretation of the fundamental law which would have modified its aspect. But America has been the most swiftly expanding of all countries. Hence the questions that have presented themselves have often related to matters which the framers of the Constitution could not have contemplated.

Three points chiefly need discussion.

(1) To whom does it belong to interpret the Constitution? Any question arising in a legal proceeding as to the meaning and application of this fundamental law will evidently be settled by the courts of law. But there are always questions of construction which have not been settled by the courts. Here every authority and every citizen must be guided by the best view he can form. In points of "a purely political nature," which a court will not decide, the Executive and legislature must follow their own views.

'(2) The Constitution has been expanded by construction in two ways. Powers have been exercised, sometimes by the President, more often by the legislature in passing statutes, and the question has arisen whether the powers so exercised were rightfully exercised, *i. e.*, were really contained in

the Constitution. When the question was resolved in the
affirmative by the court, the power has been henceforth
recognized as a part of the Constitution. The other way is
where some piece of State legislation alleged to contravene
the Constitution has been judicially decided to contravene it,
and to be therefore invalid.

Questions of the above kinds sometimes arise as questions of interpretation in the strict sense of the term, i. e.,
as questions of the meaning of a term or phrase which is so
far ambiguous that it might be taken either to cover or not
to cover a case apparently contemplated by the people when
they enacted the Constitution. Sometimes they are rather
questions to which we may apply the name of construction,
i. e., the case that has arisen is one apparently not contemplated by the enacters of the Constitution, or one which,
though possibly contemplated, has for brevity's sake been
omitted; but the Constitution has nevertheless to be applied
to its solution.

Now the doctrines laid down by Chief Justice Marshall,
and on which the courts have constantly since proceeded, may
be summed up in two propositions.

(1) Every power alleged to be vested in the national
government, or any organ thereof, must be affirmatively
shown to have been granted.

(2) When once the grant of a power by the people to
the national government has been established that power
will be construed broadly. The people—so Marshall and
his successors have argued—when they confer a power, must
be deemed to confer a wide discretion as to the means whereby
it is to be used in their service.

But other instances of development besides those
worked out by the courts of law are due to the action of the
Executive, or of the Executive and Congress conjointly, as
thus, in 1803, when President Jefferson negotiated and com-

pleted the purchase of Louisiana, and in 1807 and 1808, when Congress laid, by two statutes, an embargo on all shipping in United States ports, thereby practically destroying the lucrative carrying trade of the New England States. More startling, and more far-reaching in their consequences, were the assumptions of Federal authority made during the War of Secession by the Executive and confirmed, some expressly, some tacitly, by Congress and the people.

The process of changing the Constitution by interpretation shows no signs of stopping, nor can it, for the new conditions of economics and politics bring up new problems for solution. But the most important work was that done during the first half-century, and especially by Chief Justice Marshall during his long tenure of the presidency of the Supreme Court (1801-1835). It is scarcely an exaggeration to call him, as an eminent American jurist has done, a second maker of the Constitution. His work of building up and working out the Constitution was accomplished not so much by the decisions he gave as by the judgments in which he expounded the principles of these decisions, judgments which for their philosophical breadth, the luminous exactness of their reasoning, and the fine political sense which pervades them, have never been surpassed and rarely equaled by the most famous jurists of modern Europe or of ancient Rome. That admirable flexibility and capacity for growth which characterize the Constitution beyond all other rigid or supreme constitutions, is largely due to him, yet not more to his courage than to his caution.

We now come to a third question: How is the interpreting authority restrained? If the American Constitution is capable of being so developed by this expansive interpretation, what security do its written terms offer to the people and to the States?

The answer is twofold. In the first place the interpreting authority is, in questions not distinctly political, different from the legislature and the Executive. There is, therefore, a probability that it will disagree with either of them when they attempt to transgress the Constitution, and will decline to stretch the law so as to sanction encroachments those authorities may have attempted.

In the second place, there stands above and behind the legislature, the Executive, and the judiciary, another power, that of public opinion. The President, Congress, and the courts are all, the two former directly, the latter practically, amenable to the people, and anxious to be in harmony with the general current of its sentiment.

A singular result of the importance of constitutional interpretation in the American government may be here referred to. It is this, that the United States legislature has been very largely occupied in purely legal discussions, i. e., when it is proposed to legislate on a subject which has been heretofore little dealt with, the opponents of a measure have two lines of defense, that of expediency, and also that of constitutionality.

The interpretation of the Constitution has become at times so momentous as to form a basis for the formation of political parties. Soon after the establishment of the national government in 1789 two parties grew up, one advocating a strong central authority, the other championing the rights of the States. There has always been a party professing itself disposed to favor the central government, and therefore a party of broad construction. There has always been a party claiming that it aimed at protecting the rights of the States, and therefore a party of strict construction. But the two great parties have several times changed sides on the very question of interpretation. Constitutional interpretation has been a pretext rather than a cause, a matter of form rather than of substance.

The results have been both good and evil. They were good in so far as they made both parties profess themselves defenders of the Constitution, zealous only that it should be interpreted aright; as they familiarized the people with its provisions, and made them vigilant critics of every legislative or executive act which could affect its working. They were evil in distracting public attention from real problems to the legal aspect of those problems, and in cultivating a habit of casuistry which threatened the integrity of the Constitution itself.

Since the Civil War there has been much less of this casuistry because there have been fewer occasions for it, the broad construction view of the Constitution having practically prevailed.

(3) There is yet another way in which the Constitution has been developed. This is by laying down rules on matters which are within its general scope, but have not been dealt with by its words.

Although the Constitution is curiously minute upon some comparatively small points, such as the qualifications of members of Congress and the official record of their votes, it passes over in silence many branches of political action, many details essential to every government. The government when formed had to make many laws on points not provided for at all in the Constitution, and the earlier Congresses passed statutes some of which still are in force.

Besides legislation, usage has developed the Constitution. Custom, which is a law-producing agency in every department, is specially busy in matters which pertain to the practical conduct of government. Here are some instances.

The Presidential electors have by usage and by usage only lost the right the Constitution gave them of exercising their discretion in the choice of a chief magistrate.

The President is not reelected more than once, though

the Constitution places no restriction whatever on re-eligibility.

Both the House and the Senate conduct their legislation by means of standing committees.

The custom of going into caucus, by which the parties in each of the two Houses of Congress determine their action, and the obligation on individual members to obey the decision of the caucus meeting, are mere habits or understandings, without legal sanction.

As to the so-called spoils system, which has been applied also to State and municipal offices, and has been made the corner-stone of " practical politics " in America, the Constitution is nowise answerable for it, and legislation only partially.

The most extraordinary instance of all is the choice of Presidential candidates by the great parties assembled in their national conventions.

One of the changes which the last seventy years have brought about is so remarkable as to deserve special mention. This is the electoral franchise.

In the first days of the Constitution the suffrage was in nearly all States limited by various conditions (e. g., property qualification, length of residence, etc.). At present the suffrage is in every State practically universal. Here is an advance toward pure democracy effected without the action of the national legislature, but solely by the legislation of the several States, a legislation which, as it may be changed at any moment, is, so far as the national government is concerned, mere custom.

So it is seen that the American Constitution has stood, although developing, because it has submitted to a process of constant, sometimes scarcely perceptible, change which has adapted it to the conditions of a new age.

Chapter XXII

THE RESULTS OF CONSTITUTIONAL DEVELOPMENT

W E have seen that the American Constitution has changed, is changing, and by the laws of its existence must continue to change, in its substance and practical working even when its words remain the same. "Time and habit," said Washington, "are at least as necessary to fix the true character of governments as of other human institutions"; and while habit fixes some things, time remolds others.

The Constitution was avowedly created as an instrument of checks and balances. Each branch of the national government was to restrain the others, and maintain the equipoise of the whole. The legislature was to balance the Executive, and the judiciary both. The two houses of the legislature were to balance one another. The national government, taking all its branches together, was balanced against the State governments. Each branch of the American government has striven to extend its range and its powers; each has advanced in certain directions, but in others has been restrained by the equal or stronger pressure of other branches.

In the other struggle that has gone on in America, that between the national government and the States, the results have been still more considerable, though the process of change has sometimes been interrupted. During the first few decades after 1789 the States, in spite of a steady and often angry resistance, sometimes backed by threats of secession, found themselves more and more entangled in the network of Federal powers which sometimes Congress. sometimes the President, sometimes the judiciary, as the expounder of the Constitution, flung over them. Provisions of the Constitution whose bearing had been inadequately realized in the first instance were put in force against a State, and when once put in force became precedents for the future.

The dominance of the centralizing tendencies is due partly to the amendments, but also:

To the extensive interpretation by the judiciary of the powers which the Constitution vests in the national government.

To the passing by Congress of statutes on topics not exclusively reserved to the States, statutes which have sensibly narrowed the field of State action.

To exertions of executive power which, having been approved by the people, and not condemned by the courts, have passed into precedents.

The underlying causes belong to history. They are partly economical, partly moral. Steam and electricity have knit the various parts of the country closely together, have made each State and group of States more dependent on its neighbors, have added to the matters in which the whole country benefits by joint action and uniform legislation. The power of the national government to stimulate or depress commerce and industries by tariff legislation has given it a wide control over the material prosperity of part of the Union. There has grown up a pride in the national flag, and in the national government as representing national unity. All over the country there is a great army of Federal officeholders who look to Washington as the center of their hopes and fears.

All this inquiry bears on the discussion of the worth of a rigid Constitution. But because the United States rigid Constitution has been changed, as we have seen, it is not to be concluded that rigid constitutions are a delusion and a snare.

To expect any form of words, however weightily conceived, with whatever sanctions enacted, permanently to restrain the passions and interests of men is to expect the impossible. Beyond a certain point, you cannot protect the people against themselves. To cling to the letter of a constitution when the welfare of the country for whose sake the constitution exists is at stake, would be to seek to preserve life at the cost of all that makes life worth having—*propter vitam vivendi perdere causas.*

Nevertheless the rigid Constitution of the United States has rendered, and renders now, inestimable services. It opposes obstacles to rash and hasty change. It secures time for deliberation. It forces the people to think seriously before they alter it or pardon a transgression of it. It makes legislatures and statesmen slow to overpass their legal powers, slow even to propose measures which the Constitution seems to disapprove. It tends to render the inevitable process of modification gradual and tentative, the result of admitted and growing necessities rather than of restless impatience. It altogether prevents some changes which a temporary majority may clamor for, but which will have ceased to be demanded before the barriers interposed by the Constitution have been overcome.

It does still more than this. It forms the mind and temper of the people. It trains them to habits of legality. It strengthens their conservative instincts, their sense of the value of stability and permanence in political arrangements. It makes them feel that to comprehend their supreme instrument of government is a personal duty, incumbent on each one of them. It familiarizes them with, it attaches them by ties of pride and reverence to, those fundamental truths on which the Constitution is based.

Chapter XXIII

NATURE OF THE AMERICAN STATES

FROM the study of the national government, we may go on to examine that of the several States which make up the Union. This is the part of the American political system which has received least attention both from foreign and from native writers. Yet the States are full of interest; and he who would understand the changes that have passed over American democracy will find far more instruction in a study of the State governments than of the Federal Constitution.

The American State is a peculiar organism, unlike anything in modern Europe, or in the ancient world (except, possibly, the cantons of Switzerland).

There are forty-five States in the American Union, varying in size from Texas, with an area of 265,780 square miles, to Rhode Island, with an area of 1250 square miles; and in population from New York, with 7,268,894 inhabitants, to Nevada, with 42,335. Considering not only these differences of size, but the differences in the density of population (which in Nevada is .4, and in Wyoming .9, to the square mile, while in Rhode Island it is 407, and in Massachusetts 348 9, to the square mile) ; in its character (in South Carolina the blacks are 782,321 against 557,807 whites, in Mississippi 907,630 against 641,200 whites) ; in its birthplace (in North Carolina the foreign-born persons are less than $\frac{1}{420}$ of the population, in Minnesota more than $\frac{1}{3}$) ; in the occupations of the people, in the amount of accumulated wealth, in the proportion of educated persons to the rest of

the community—it is plain that immense differences might
be looked for between the aspects of politics and conduct
of government in one State and in another.

Be it also remembered that the older colonies had different historical origins. Virginia and North Carolina were
unlike Massachusetts and Connecticut; New York, Pennsylvania, and Maryland different from both; while in recent times the stream of European immigration has filled
some States with Irishmen, others with Germans, others with
Scandinavians, and has left most of the Southern States
wholly untouched.

Nevertheless, the form of government is in its main
outlines, and to a large extent even in its actual working, the
same in all these forty-five republics, and the differences,
instructive as they are, relate to points of secondary consequence.

The States fall naturally into five groups: The New
England States—Massachusetts, Connecticut, Rhode Island,
New Hampshire, Vermont, Maine. The Middle States—
New York, New Jersey, Pennsylvania, Delaware, Maryland,
Ohio, Indiana. The Southern, or old Slave States—Virginia, West Virginia (separated from Virginia during the
war), North Carolina, South Carolina, Georgia, Alabama,
Florida, Kentucky, Tennessee, Mississippi, Louisiana, Arkansas, Missouri, Texas. The Northwestern States—Michigan, Illinois, Wisconsin, Minnesota, Iowa, Nebraska, Kansas, Colorado, Utah, Montana, North Dakota, South Dakota, Idaho, Wyoming. The Pacific States—California,
Nevada, Oregon, Washington.

Each of these groups has something distinctive in the
character of its inhabitants, which is reflected, though more
faintly now than formerly, in the character of its government and politics.

New England is the old home of Puritanism, the traces

whereof, though waning under the influence of Irish and French-Canadian immigration, are by no means yet extinct. The Southern States will long retain the imprint of slavery, not merely in the presence of a host of negroes, but in the degradation of the poor white population, and in certain attributes, laudable as well as regrettable, of the ruling class. The Northwest is the land of hopefulness, and consequently of bold experiment in legislation: its rural inhabitants have the honesty and narrow-mindedness of agriculturists. The Pacific west, or rather California and Nevada, for Washington and Oregon belong in political character to the Upper Mississippi or Northwestern group, tinges the energy and sanguine good nature of the Westerners with a speculative recklessness natural to mining communities, where great fortunes have grown and vanished, and into which elements have been suddenly swept together from every part of the world.

As the dissimilarity of population and external conditions seems to make for a diversity of constitutional and political arrangements between the States, so also does the large measure of legal independence which each of them enjoys under the Federal Constitution. No State can, as a commonwealth, politically deal with or act upon any other State. No diplomatic relations can exist nor treaties be made between States, no coercion can be exercised by one upon another. And although the government of the Union can act on a State, it rarely does act, and then only in certain limited directions, which do not touch the inner political life of the commonwealth.

Let us pass on to consider the circumstances which work for uniformity among the States, and work more powerfully as time goes on. For one thing the States are not natural growths. The State boundaries are artificial. This absence of physical lines of demarcation has tended and must tend to prevent the growth of local distinctions. Each State makes its own Constitution; that is, the people agree on their form of government for themselves, with no interference from the other States or from the Union. This form is subject to one condition only: it must be republican. But the influence of the older States makes their constitutions examples for newer ones. Nowhere is population in such constant movement as in America. In such a constant flux of population local peculiarities are not readily developed. Each State takes from its neighbors and gives to its neighbors, so that the process of assimilation is always going on over the whole wide area.

Still more important is the influence of railroad communication, of newspapers, of the telegraph. The inhabitants of each State know every morning the events of yesterday over the whole Union.

Finally the political parties are the same in all the States. Hence, State politics are largely swayed by forces and motives external to the particular State, and common to the whole country, or to great sections of it; and the growth of local parties, the emergence of local issues and development of local political schemes, are correspondingly restrained.

These considerations explain why the States, notwithstanding the original diversities between some of them, and the wide scope for political divergence which they all enjoy under the Federal Constitution, are so much less dissimilar and less peculiar than might have been expected.

I return to indicate the points in which the legal independence and right of self-government of the several States appears. Each of the forty-five has its own:

Constitution (whereof more anon). Executive, consisting of a governor, and various other officials. Legislature of two Houses. System of local government in counties, cities, townships, and school districts. System of State and local taxation. Debts, which it may (and sometimes does) repudiate at its own pleasure. Body of private law, including the whole law of real and personal property, of contracts, of torts, and of family relations. Courts, from which no appeal lies (except in cases touching Federal legislation or the Federal Constitution) to any Federal court. System of procedure, civil and criminal. Citizenship, which may admit persons (e. g., recent immigrants) to be citizens at times, or on conditions, wholly different from those prescribed by other States.

Three points deserve to be noted as illustrating what these attributes include.

1. A man gains active citizenship in the United States (i. e., a share in the government of the Union) only by becoming a citizen of some particular State. The only restriction on the States in this matter is that of the fourteenth and fifteenth constitutional amendments, intended to secure equal treatment to the negroes.

2. The power of a State over all communities within its limits is absolute. It may grant or refuse local government as it pleases.

3. A State commands the allegiance of its citizens and may punish them for treason against it.

These are illustrations of the doctrine which Europeans often fail to grasp, that the American States were originally in a certain sense, and still for certain purposes remain, sovereign States. Each of the original thirteen became sovereign when it revolted from the mother country in 1776. By entering the Confederation of 1781-1788 it parted with one or two of the attributes of sovereignty; by accepting the Federal Constitution in 1788 it subjected itself for certain specified purposes to a central government, but claimed to retain its sovereignty for all other purposes. That is to say, the authority of a State is an inherent, not a delegated authority.

What State sovereignty means and includes is a question which incessantly engaged the most active legal and political minds of the nation, from 1789 down to 1870. It ranged from considering it paramount to the rights of the Union, to the renouncing of State authority in accepting that of the Union. Since the defeat of the Secessionists, the last of these views may be deemed to have been established, and the term " State sovereignty " is now but seldom heard.

What, then, do the rights of a State now include? Every right or power of a government, except:

The right of secession (not abrogated in terms, but admitted since the war to be no longer claimable. It is expressly negatived in the recent constitutions of several Southern States). Powers which the Constitution withholds from the States (including that of intercourse with foreign governments). Powers which the Constitution expressly confers on the Federal government.

As respects some powers of the last class, however, the States may act concurrently with, or in default of action by, the Federal government.

A reference to the preceding list of what each State may create in the way of distinct institutions will show that these rights practically cover nearly all the ordinary relations of citizens to one another and to their government. An American may, through a long life, never be reminded of the Federal government, except when he votes at Presidential and congressional elections, lodges a complaint against the post office, and opens his trunks for a custom-house officer on the pier at New York when he returns from a tour in Europe. His direct taxes are paid to officials acting under State laws. The State, or a local authority constituted by State statutes, registers his birth, appoints his guardian, pays for his schooling, gives him a share in the estate of his father deceased, licenses him when he enters a trade (if it be one needing a license), marries him, divorces him, entertains civil actions against him, declares him a bankrupt, hangs him for murder. The police that guard his house, the local boards which look after the poor, control highways, impose water rates, manage schools—all these derive their legal powers from his State alone.

But although the national government touches the direct interest of the citizen less than does the State government, it touches his sentiment more. Hence the strength of his attachment to the former and his interest in it must not be measured by the frequency of his dealings with it. In the partitionment of governmental functions between nation and State, the State gets the most, but the nation the highest, so the balance between the two is preserved.

Chapter XXIV

STATE CONSTITUTIONS

THE government of each of the forty-five States is determined by and set forth in its constitution, a comprehensive fundamental law, or rather group of laws included in one instrument, which has been directly enacted by the people of the State, and is capable of being repealed or altered, not by their representatives, but by themselves alone. As the Constitution of the United States stands above Congress and out of its reach, so the constitution of each State stands above the legislature of that State, cannot be varied in any particular by acts of the State legislature, and involves the invalidity of any statute passed by the legislature which a court of law may find to be inconsistent with it.

The State constitutions are the oldest things in the political history of America, for they are the continuations and representatives of the royal colonial charters, whereby the earliest English settlements in America were created, and under which their several local governments were established, subject to the authority of the English Crown and ultimately of the British Parliament.

When in 1776 the thirteen colonies threw off their allegiance to King George III. and declared themselves independent States, the colonial charter naturally became the State constitution. In most cases it was remodeled, with large alterations, by the revolting colony. But in three States it was maintained unchanged, except, of course, so far as crown authority was concerned, *viz.*, in Massachusetts till 1780, in Connecticut till 1818, and in Rhode Island till 1842. The other thirty-two States admitted to the Union in addition to the original thirteen, have all entered it as organized self-governing communities, with their constitutions already made by their respective peoples. Each act of Congress which admits a new State admits it as a subsisting commonwealth, recognizing rather than affecting to sanction its constitution. Congress may impose conditions which the State constitution must fulfill. But the authority of the State constitutions does not flow from Congress, but from acceptance by the citizens of the States for which they are made. Of these instruments, therefore, no less than of the constitutions of the thirteen original States, we may say that although subsequent in date to the Federal Constitution, they are, so far as each State is concerned, *de jure* prior to it. Their authority over their own citizens is nowise derived from it.

The original constitutions of the States, whether of the old thirteen or of the newer thirty-two, have been in nearly every case subsequently recast, in some instances five, six, or even seven times, as well as amended in particular points. Thus constitutions of all dates are now in force in different States.

Every existing constitution is the work of the people, not of the legislature of the State. The constitutions of the revolutionary period were in a few instances enacted by the State legislature, acting as a body with plenary powers, but more usually by the people acting through a convention, *i. e.*, a body especially chosen by the voters at large for the purpose, and invested with full powers, not only of drafting, but of adopting the instrument of government. But since 1792, when Kentucky framed her constitution, the usual practice has been for the convention, elected by the voters, to submit, in accordance with the precedent set by Massachusetts in 1780, the draft constitution framed by it to the citizens of the

State at large, who vote upon it yes or no. They usually vote on it as a whole, and adopt or reject it *en bloc,* but sometimes provision is made for voting separately on some particular point or points.

The people of a State retain forever in their hands, altogether independent of the national government, the power of altering their constitution. When a new constitution is to be prepared, or the existing one amended, the initiative usually comes from the legislature, which (either by a simple majority, or by a two-thirds majority, or by a majority in two successive legislatures, as the constitution may in each instance provide) submits the matter to the voters in one of two ways. It may either propose to the people certain specific amendments, or it may ask the people to decide by a direct popular vote on the propriety of calling a constitutional convention to revise the whole existing constitution. In the former case the amendments suggested by the legislature are directly voted on by the citizens; in the latter the legislature, so soon as the citizens have voted for the holding of a convention, provides for the election by the people of this convention. When elected, the convention meets, sets to work, goes through the old constitution, and prepares a new one, which is then presented to the people for ratification or rejection at the polls. Some States provide for the submission to the people at fixed intervals, of seven, ten, sixteen, or twenty years, of the propriety of calling a convention to revise the constitution, so as to secure that the attention of the people shall be drawn to the question whether their scheme of government ought or ought not to be changed. Be it observed, however, that whereas the Federal Constitution can be amended only by a vote of three-fourths of the States, a constitution can in nearly every State be changed by a bare majority of the citizens voting at the polls. Hence we may expect, and shall find that these instruments are altered more

State, Army, and Navy Building, Washington, D. C.

frequently and materially than the Federal Constitution has been.

A State constitution is not only independent of the central national government (save in certain points already specified), but it is also the fundamental law of the State itself. The State exists as a commonwealth by virtue of its constitution, and all State authorities, legislative, executive, and judicial, are the creatures of, and subject to, the State constitution. All State statutes must be consistent with the State constitution, and the State courts will determine the question when brought before them, the same as in the interpretation of the United States Constitution by the Federal courts.

A State constitution is really nothing but a law made directly by the people voting at the polls upon a draft submitted to them.

The importance of this character of a State constitution as a properly-enacted law, overriding every minor State law, becomes all the greater when the contents of these constitutions are examined. It not only creates a frame of government, but deals with a variety of topics which in Europe would be left to the ordinary action of the legislature, or of administrative authorities; and it pursues these topics into a minute detail hardly to be looked for in a fundamental instrument.

A normal constitution consists of five parts:

1. The definition of the boundaries of the State. (This does not occur in the case of the older States.)

2. The so-called Bill of Rights—an enumeration (whereof more anon) of the citizens' primordial rights to liberty of person and security of property. This usually stands at the beginning of the constitution, but occasionally at the end.

3. The frame of government—*i. e.*, the names, func-

tions, and powers, of the executive officers, the legislative bodies, and the courts of justice. This occupies several articles.

4. Miscellaneous provisions relating to administration and law, including articles treating of schools, of the militia, of taxation and revenue, of the public debts, of local government, of State prisons and hospitals, of agriculture, of labor, of impeachment, and of the method of amending the constitution, besides other matters, still less political in their character. The order in which these occur differs in different instruments, and there are some in which some of the above topics are not mentioned at all. The more recent constitutions and those of the newer States are much fuller on these points.

5. The schedule, which contains provisions relating to the method of submitting the constitution to the vote of the people, and arrangements for the transition from the previous constitution to the new one which is to be enacted by that vote. Being of a temporary nature, the schedule is not strictly a part of the constitution.

The Bill of Rights is historically the most interesting part of these constitutions, for it is the legitimate child and representative of declarations from Magna Charta down, which secure the liberty of the people. A few points which occur in them may be mentioned.

All provide for full freedom of religious opinion and worship, and for the equality before the law of all religious denominations and their members; and many forbid the establishment of any particular church or sect, and declare that no public money ought to be applied in aid of any religious body or sectarian institution.

Twenty-six States declare that "all men have a natural, inherent, and inalienable right to enjoy and defend life and liberty."

Eighteen declare that all men have " a natural right to acquire, possess, and protect property."

All in one form or another secure the freedom of writing and speaking opinions, and some add that the truth of a libel may be given in evidence.

Nearly all secure the freedom of public meeting and petition.

Many provide that no *ex post facto* law, nor law impairing the obligation of a contract, shall be passed by the State legislature; and that private property shall not be taken by the State without just compensation.

Many forbid the creation of any title of nobility.

Some forbid imprisonment for debt, except in case of fraud, and secure the acceptance of reasonable bail, except for the gravest charges.

Several declare that " perpetuities and monopolies are contrary to the genius of a free State, and ought not to be allowed."

These instances, a few out of many, may suffice to show how remote from the common idea of a Bill of Rights, are some of the enactments which find a place under that heading. The Constitution-makers seem to have inserted here such doctrines or legal reforms as seemed to them matters of high import or of wide application, especially when they could find no suitable place for them elsewhere in the instrument.

The frame of government will be discussed later. I pass on, therefore, to what have been classed as the miscellaneous provisions. These are of great interest as revealing the spirit and tendencies of popular government in America, the economic and social condition of the country, the mischiefs that have arisen, the remedies applied to these mischiefs, the ideas and beliefs of the people in matters of legislation.

Among such provisions we find a great deal of matter

which is in no distinctive sense constitutional law, but general law, *e. g.,* administrative law, the law of judicial procedure, the ordinary private law of family, inheritance, contract, and so forth; matter therefore which seems out of place in a constitution because fit to be dealt with in ordinary statutes. We find minute provisions regarding the management and liabilities of banking companies, of railways, or of corporations generally; regulations as to the salaries of officials, the quorum of courts sitting *in banco,* the length of time for appealing, the method of changing the venue, the publication of judicial reports; detailed arrangements for school boards and school taxation; we find a prohibition of lotteries, of bribery, of the granting of liquor licenses, of usurious interest on money, an abolition of the distinction between sealed and unsealed instruments, a declaration of the extent of a mechanic's lien for work done. The framers of these more recent constitutions have in fact neither wished nor cared to draw a line of distinction between what is proper for a constitution and what ought to be left to be dealt with by the State legislature. And, in the case of three-fourths at least of the States, no such distinction now, in fact, exists.

Four reasons may be suggested for this confusion.

1. Americans, like the English, have no love for scientific arrangement.

2. The people found the enactment of a new constitution a convenient opportunity for enunciating doctrines they valued and carrying through reforms they desired.

3. The peoples of the States have come to distrust their respective legislatures. There is an unmistakable wish in the minds of the people to act directly rather than through their representatives in the legislature.

4. The State constitutions in comparison with the United States Constitution, have less capacity for development, whether by interpretation or by usage: firstly, because they

are more easily, and therefore more frequently, amended or
recast; secondly, because they are longer, and go into much
more minute detail.

The rules of interpretation are in the main the same as
those applied to the Federal Constitution. There is this ex-
ception—that a State legislature is presumably able to pass
any law unless it is positively shown that the Federal Constitution, or its own constitution, forbids it.

The ultimate expounder of the meaning of the constitution is, of course, the judiciary, and it is a well-established rule that the judges will always lean in favor of the
validity of a legislative act.

Chapter XXV

THE DEVELOPMENT OF STATE CON-
STITUTIONS

THE State constitutions furnish invaluable materials for history. Their interest is all the greater, because the succession of constitutions and amendments to constitutions from 1776 till to-day enables the annals of legislation and political sentiment to be read in these documents more easily and succinctly than in any similar series of laws in any other country. They are a mine of instruction for the natural history of democratic communities.

Three periods may be distinguished in the development of State governments, as set forth in the constitution, each period marked by an increase in the length and minuteness of those instruments.

The first period covers about thirty years from 1776 downwards, and includes the earlier constitutions of the original thirteen States, as well as of Kentucky, Vermont, Tennessee, and Ohio.

Most of these constitutions were framed under the impressions of the Revolutionary War. They manifest a dread of executive power and of military power, together with a disposition to leave everything to the legislature, as being the authority directly springing from the people. The election of a State governor is in most States vested in the legislature. He has not (except in Massachusetts) a veto on the acts of the legislature. He has not, like the royal governors of colonial days, the right of adjourning or dis-

solving it. The idea of giving power to the people directly
has scarcely appeared, because the legislature is conceived
as the natural and necessary organ of popular government,
much as the House of Commons is in England. And hence
many of these early constitutions consist of little beyond
an elaborate Bill of Rights and a comparatively simple out-
line of a frame of government, establishing a representative
legislature, with a few executive officers and courts of justice carefully separated therefrom.

The second period covers the first half of the nineteenth
century down to the time when the intensity of party struggles over slavery (1850-1860) interrupted to some extent
the natural processes of State development. It is a period
of the democratization of all institutions, a democratization
due not only to causes native to American soil, but to the influence upon the generation which had then come to manhood of French republican ideas, an influence which declined
after 1815 and ended with 1851, since which time French
examples and ideas have counted for very little. Such provisions for the maintenance of religious institutions by the
State as had continued to exist are now swept away. The
principle becomes established that constitutions must be
directly enacted by popular vote. The choice of a governor
is taken from the legislature to be given to the people.
Property qualifications are abolished, and a suffrage practically universal, except that it often excludes free persons
of color, is introduced. Even the judges are not spared.
Many constitutions shorten their term of office, and direct
them to be chosen by popular vote. The State has emerged
from the English conception of a community acting through
a ruling legislature, for the legislature begins to be regarded
as being only a body of agents exercising delegated and restricted powers, and obliged to recur to the sovereign people
(by asking for a constitutional amendment) when it seeks

to extend these powers in any particular direction. The increasing length of the constitutions during this half century shows how the range of the popular vote has extended, for these documents now contain a mass of ordinary law on matters which in the early days would have been left to the legislatures.

In the third period, which begins from about the time of the Civil War, a slight reaction may be discerned, not against popular sovereignty, which is stronger than ever, but in the tendency to strengthen the executive and judicial departments. The governor had begun to receive in the second period a veto on the acts of the legislature. His tenure of office has been generally lengthened; the restrictions on his reëligibility generally removed. In many States the judges have been granted larger salaries, and their terms of office lengthened. Some constitutions have even transferred judicial appointments from the vote of the people to the executive. But the most notable change of all has been the narrowing of the competence of the legislature, and the tying up of its action by a variety of complicated restrictions. Such provisions are conservative in their results and are really checks imposed by the citizens upon themselves. This process of development, which has first exalted and then depressed the legislature, which has extended the direct interference of the people, which has changed the constitution itself from a short into a long, from a simple into a highly complex document, has of course not yet ended.

Of the new constitutions there are some tendencies to be seen everywhere. One is for the constitutions to grow longer. This is an absolutely universal rule. The new constitutions are longer, not only because new topics are taken up and dealt with, but because the old topics are handled in far greater detail.

I have already referred to the progress which the newer

constitutions show toward more democratic arrangements. The suffrage is now in almost every State enjoyed by all adult males. Citizenship is quickly and easily accorded to immigrants. And, most significant of all, the superior judges, who were formerly named by the governor, or chosen by the legislature, and who held office during good behavior, are now in most States elected by the people for fixed terms of years.

On the whole, therefore, there can be no doubt that the democratic spirit is now more energetic and pervasive than it was in the first generation. Yet there has been a certain anti-democratic reaction since the Jacksonian age noticeable as showing that the people do learn by experience, and are not indisposed to reverse their action and get clear of the results of past mistakes. Nor does the history of State constitutions confirm the notion that democracies are uncertain and fond of change. In the older and more conservative States there have been but few revisions. In the newer States the more rapidly moving population, and swifter economic and social changes tend more to induce changes in the fundamental law. It must be remarked, however, that both whole constitutions and particular amendments are frequently rejected by the people when submitted to them at the polls.

A few more observations on what the constitutions disclose are needed before I conclude this necessarily brief sketch of the most instructive sources for the history of popular government which our century has produced.

The constitutions witness to a singular distrust by the people of its own agents and officers, not only of the legislatures, but also of local authorities.

They witness also to a jealousy of the Federal government. They show a wholesome anxiety to protect and safeguard private property in every way. The only exceptions to this rule are to be found in the case of anything approaching a monopoly, and in the case of wealthy corporations.

The extension of the sphere of State interference, with the corresponding departure from the doctrine of *laissez-faire,* is not carried so far in American States as in some European countries. For instance, the States neither own nor manage railroads, or telegraphs, or mines, or forest, and they sell their public lands instead of working them. There is, nevertheless, visible in recent constitutions a tendency to extend the scope of public administrative activity.

A spirit of humanity and tenderness for suffering, very characteristic of the American people, appears in the directions which many constitutions contain for the establishment of charitable and reformatory institutions.

In the older Northern constitutions, and in nearly all the more recent constitutions of all the States, ample provision is made for the creation and maintenance of schools. Even universities are the object of popular zeal, though a zeal not always according to knowledge.

Although a Constitution is the fundamental and supreme law of the State, one must not conclude that its provisions are any better observed and enforced than those of an ordinary statute. There is sometimes reason to suspect that when an offense is thought worthy of being specially mentioned in a constitution, this happens because it is specially frequent, and because it is feared that the legislature may shrink from applying due severity to repress it.

Chapter XXVI

DIRECT LEGISLATION BY THE PEOPLE

THE difficulties and defects inherent in the method of legislating by a constitution are obvious enough. Inasmuch as the people cannot be expected to distinguish carefully between what is and what is not proper for a fundamental instrument, there arises an inconvenient as well as unscientific mixture and confusion of private law and administrative regulation with the frame of government and the general doctrines of public law. There follows in due course an abundant crop of questions as to the constitutionality of statutes. The habit of putting into the constitution matters proper for an ordinary statute has the further disadvantage that it heightens the difficulty of correcting a mistake or supplying an omission. It is also sometimes difficult to induce the people to take a proper interest in the amendment of the constitution.

These defects are so obvious that we ask, Why do the Americans tend more and more to remove legislation from the legislature and entrust it to the people? We could quite well imagine the several State governments working without fundamental instruments to control them. Each American State might now, if it so pleased, conduct its own business, and govern its citizens as a commonwealth " at common law," with a sovereign legislature, whose statutes formed the highest expression of popular will. This, however, no American State does, or has ever done, or is likely to do.

In the United States, the conception that the people (*i. e.,* the citizens at large) are and ought of right to be the

187

supreme legislators, has taken the form of legislation by enacting or amending a constitution. The Americans take subjects which belong to ordinary legislation out of the category of statutes, place them in the constitution, and then handle them as parts of this fundamental instrument.

I have already explained the historical origin of this system. As the republic went on working out both in theory and in practice those conceptions of democracy and popular sovereignty which had been only vaguely apprehended when enunciated at the Revolution, the faith of the average man in himself became stronger, his love of equality greater, his desire, not only to rule, but to rule directly in his own proper person, more constant. These sentiments would have told still further upon State governments had they not found large scope in local government. However, even in State affairs they made it an article of faith that no constitution could be enacted save by the direct vote of the citizens. Concurrently with the growth of these tendencies there had been a decline in the quality of the State legislatures, and of the legislation which they turned out. Hence the people had the further excuse for superseding the legislature, that they might reasonably fear it would neglect or spoil the work they desired to see done. Instead of being stimulated by this distrust to mend their ways and recover their former powers, the State legislatures fell in with the tendency, and promoted their own supersession. They welcomed the direct intervention of the people as relieving them of embarrassing problems. They began to refer to the decision of a popular vote matters clearly within their own proper competence, such as the question of liquor traffic, or the creation of a system of gratuitous schools.

It is chiefly, however, in the form of amendment to the constitution that we find the American voters exercising direct legislative power. And this method comes very near to the Swiss referendum, because the amendment is first discussed and approved by the legislature, a majority greater than a simple majority being required in some States, and then goes before the citizens voting at the polls. It is not uncommon for proposals submitted by the legislature in the form of constitutional amendments to be rejected by the people.

The demerits of this plan of direct legislation by the people are obvious. It tends to lower the authority and sense of responsibility in the legislature; and it refeis matters needing much elucidation by debate to the determination of those who cannot, on account of their numbers, meet together for discussion, and many of whom may have never thought about the matter.

But the Americans, in despair of improving the legislature, fall back on the referendum as the best course available under the circumstances of the case, and in such a world as the present. But they remark with truth that the mass of the people are equal in intelligence and character to the average State legislator, and are exposed to 'fewer temptations. Nor should it be forgotten that in a country where law depends for its force on the consent of the governed, it is eminently desirable that law should not outrun popular sentiment, but have the whole weight of the people's deliverance behind it.

If the practice of recasting or amending State constitutions were to grow common, one of the advantages of direct legislation by the people would disappear, for the sense of permanence would be gone, and the same mutability which is now possible in ordinary statutes would become possible in the provisions of the fundamental law. But this fault of small democracies, especially when ruled by primary assemblies, is unlikely to recur in large democracies, such as most States have now become, nor does it seem to be on the increase among them. Reference to the people, therefore, acts as a conservative force; that is to say, it is a conservative method as compared with action by the legislature.

This method of legislating by means of a constitution or amendments thereto was a historical accident, so to speak, and its invention has been used for other purposes far more extensively than its creators foresaw. It is now, moreover, serviceable in a way which those who first used it did not contemplate, though they are well pleased with the result. It acts as a restraint not only on the vices and follies of legislators, but on the people themselves. Having solemnly bound themselves by their constitution to certain rules and principles, the people come to respect those principles.

State constitutions, considered as laws drafted by a convention and enacted by the people at large, are better both in form and substance than laws made by the legis-lature, because they are the work of abler men, acting under a special commission which imposes special responsibilities on them. The appointment of a constitutional convention is an important event, which excites general interest in a State. Its functions are weighty and difficult, far transcend-ing those of the regular legislature. Hence the best men in the State desire a seat in it, and, in particular, eminent law-yers become candidates, knowing how much it will affect the law they practice. It is therefore a body superior in com-position to either the Senate or the House of a State. Or if the work of altering the constitution is carried out by a series of amendments, these are likely to be more fully considered by the legislature than ordinary statutes would be, and to be framed with more regard to clearness and precision.

In the interval between the settlement by the convention of its draft constitution, or by the legislature of its draft amendments, and the putting of the matter to the vote of the people, there is copious discussion in the press and at public meetings, so that the citizens always go well prepared to the polls. An all-pervading press does the work which speeches did in the ancient republics, and the fact that constitutions and amendments so submitted are frequently rejected, shows that the people, whether they act wisely or not, do not at any rate surrender themselves blindly to the judgment of a convention, or obediently adopt the proposals of a legislature.

Chapter XXVII

STATE LEGISLATURES

THE similarity of the frame of government in the forty-five republics which make up the United States, a similarity which appears the more remarkable when we remember that each of the republics is independent and self-determined as respects its frame of government, is due to the common source whence the governments flow. They are all copies, some immediate, some mediate, of ancient English institutions which existed in the charters of the colonies.

We may sketch out a sort of genealogy of governments as follows—

First. The English incorporated company, a self-governing body, with its governor, deputy governor, and assistants chosen by the freemen of the company, and meeting in what is called the general court or assembly.

Next. The colonial government, which out of this company evolves a governor or executive head and a legislature, consisting of representatives chosen by the citizens and meeting in one or two chambers.

Thirdly. The State government, which is nothing but the colonial government developed and somewhat democratized, with a governor chosen originally by the legislature, now always by the people at large, and now in all cases with a legislature of two chambers. From the original thirteen States this form has spread over the Union and prevails in every State.

Lastly. The Federal government, modeled after the

State governments, with its President chosen, through electors, by the people, its two-chambered legislature, and its judges named by the President.

Out of such small beginnings have great things grown.

It would be endless to describe the minor differences in the systems of the forty-five States. I will sketch the outlines only, which, as already observed, are in the main the same everywhere.

Every State has—

An executive elective head, the governor.

A number of other administrative officers.\

A legislature of two houses.

A system of courts of justice.

Various subordinate local self-governing communities—counties, cities, townships, villages, school districts.

The governor and the other chief officials are not now chosen by the legislature, as was the case under most of the older State constitutions, but by the people. They are as far as possible disjoined from the legislature. Neither the governor nor any other State official can sit in a State legislature. He cannot lead it. It cannot, except of course by passing statutes, restrain him. There can therefore be no question of any government by ministers who link the executive to the legislature according to the system of the free countries of modern Europe and of the British colonies.

Of these several powers it is best to begin by describing the legislature, because it is by far the strongest and most prominent.

An American State legislature always consists of two houses, the smaller called the Senate, the larger, usually called the House of Representatives, though in six States it is entitled "The Assembly," and in three "The House of Delegates." The origin of this very interesting feature is to be sought in history. Now, however, the need for two chambers has become an axiom of political science, being based on the belief that the innate tendency of an assembly to become hasty, tyrannical, and corrupt, needs to be checked by the coëxistence of another house of equal authority.

Both houses are chosen by popular vote, generally in equal electoral districts, and by the same voters, although in a few States there are minor variations as to modes of choice.

The following differences between the rules governing the two Houses are general—

1. The senatorial electoral districts are always larger.

2. A Senator is usually chosen for a longer term than a Representative.

3. In most cases the Senate instead of being elected all at once like the House, is only partially renewed. This gives it a sense of continuity which the House lacks.

4. In some States the age at which a man is eligible for the Senate is fixed higher than that for the House of Representatives.

Local feeling applies not less in State elections than in national, and the effects of keeping out good men are not less serious.

The unfortunate results of this local sentiment have been aggravated by the tendency to narrow the election areas, allotting one Senator or Representative to each district.

Universal manhood suffrage, subject to certain disqualifications in respect of crime (including bribery) and of the receipt of poor law relief, which prevail in many States, is the rule in nearly all the States. The payment of a tax is still required in a few States, but if he does not pay it, his party usually pays it for him, so the restriction is of little practical importance. In Massachusetts, Connecticut, and some of the Southern States (by recent constitutions) there is an educational requirement. Of course certain terms of residence within the United States, in the particular States, and in the voting districts, are also prescribed: these vary greatly from State to State, but are usually short.

The suffrage is generally the same for other purposes as for that of elections to the legislature, and is in every State but four confined to male inhabitants. In other States, women are permitted to vote at school district and in one at municipal elections. It is important to remember that, by the Constitution of the United States, the right of suffrage in Federal or national elections (*i. e.,* for Presidential electors and members of Congress) is in each State that which the State confers on those who vote at the election of its more numerous House. Thus there might exist great differences between one State and another in the free bestowal of the Federal franchise. That such differences are at present insignificant is due, partly to the prevalence of democratic theories of equality over the whole Union, partly to the provision of the fourteenth amendment to the Federal Constitution, which reduces the representation of a State in the Federal House of Representatives, and therewith also its weight in a Presidential election, in proportion to the number of adult male citizens disqualified in that State.

The number of members in the legislature varies greatly from State to State, the Senate ranging from 9 to 51, and the House of Representatives from 21 to 321, the most being in New England and the States which follow New England precedents, where local feeling is strong and local units must be represented.

In all States the members of both Houses receive salaries, which in some cases are fixed at an annual sum, or more frequently, are calculated at so much for every day during which the session lasts, besides a small allowance, called mileage, for traveling expenses. The length of the legislative sessions, has in some cases been restricted to a fixed number of days. The States which pay by the day are also those which limit the session.

It was formerly usual for the legislature to meet annually, but the experience of bad legislation and over legislation has led to fewer as well as shorter sittings; and sessions are now quadrennial in one State and biennial in all others except six in which they are annual. There is, however, in nearly all States a power reserved to the governor to summon the Houses in extraordinary session should a pressing occasion arise, but the provisions for daily pay do not usually apply to these extra sessions.

Bills may originate in either House, save that in nineteen States money bills must originate in the House of Representatives, a rule which, in the present condition of things, is merely a historical perpetuation.

In one point a State Senate enjoys a special power, obviously modeled on that of the English House of Lords and the Senate,—the trial of impeachments. Like the Federal Senate, it has in many States the power of confirming or rejecting appointments to office made by the governor. The power is an important one in those States which allow the governor to nominate the higher judges. In other respects the powers and procedure of the two Houses of a State legislature are identical;   except that, whereas the lieutenant governor of a State is generally *ex officio* president of the Senate, with a casting vote therein, the House always chooses its own Speaker. The legal quorum is usually fixed, by the constitution, at a majority of the whole number of members elected, though a smaller number may adjourn and compel the attendance of absent members. Both Houses do most of their work by committees, much after the fashion of Congress, and the committees are in both usually chosen by the presiding officer.

The State governor has of course no right to dissolve

the legislature, nor even to adjourn it unless the Houses, while agreeing to adjourn, disagree as to the date. Such control as the legislature can exercise over the State officers by way of inquiry into their conduct is generally exercised by committees. The proceedings are rarely reported. Sometimes when a committee takes evidence on an important question reporters are present, and the proceedings more resemble a public meeting than a legislative session. It need scarcely be added that neither House separately, nor both Houses acting together, can control an executive officer otherwise than either by passing a statute prescribing a certain course of action for him, which if it be in excess of their powers will be held unconstitutional and void, or by withholding the appropriations necessary to enable him to carry out the course of action he proposes to adopt. One State vests legislative authority in the legislature alone. All the rest require a bill to be submitted to the governor, and permit him to return it to the legislature with his objections. If he so returns it, it can only be again passed—" over the veto "—by something more than a bare majority. To so pass a bill over the veto there is required—a majority of three-fifths in each House, or two-thirds, or a simple majority of all the members elected to that House.

Here, therefore, as in the Federal Constitution, we find a useful safeguard against the unwisdom or misconduct of a legislature, and a method provided for escaping, in extreme cases, from those deadlocks which the system of checks and balances tends to occasion.

I have adverted in a preceding chapter to the restrictions imposed on the legislatures of the various States by their respective constitutions. These restrictions, which are numerous, elaborate, and instructive, take two forms—

1. Exclusions of a subject from legislative competence, *i. e.,* prohibitions to the legislature to pass any law on certain

enumerated subjects. The most important classes of prohibited statutes are—

Statutes inconsistent with democratic principles, as for example, granting titles of nobility.

Statutes against public policy, *c. g.*, tolerating lotteries or impairing the obligation of contracts.

Statutes special or local in their application.

Statutes increasing the State or local debts beyond a certain limited amount.

2. Restrictions on the procedure of the legislature, *i. e.*, directions as to the particular forms to be observed and times to be allowed in passing bills, sometimes all bills, sometimes bills of a certain specified nature.

Where statutes have been passed by a legislature upon a prohibited subject, or where the prescribed forms have been transgressed or omitted, the statute will be held void so far as inconsistent with the constitution.

Debates in these bodies are seldom well reported, and sometimes not reported at all. One result is that the conduct of members escapes the scrutiny of their constituents; a better one that speeches are generally short and practical, the motive for rhetorical displays being absent. If a man does not make a reputation for oratory, he may for quick good sense and business habits. However, so much of the real work is done in committees that talent for intrigue or " management " usually counts for more than debating power.

Chapter XXVIII

THE STATE EXECUTIVE

THE executive department in a State consists of a governor (in all the States), a lieutenant governor (in most), and of various minor officials. The governor, who, under the earlier constitutions of most of the original thirteen States, was chosen by the legislature, is now always elected by the people, and by the same suffrage, practically universal, as the legislature. He is elected directly, not as the President under the Federal Constitution, by a college of electors. His term of office is in twenty-one States, four years: in one State, three years: in twenty-one States, two years: and in two States (Massachusetts and Rhode Island), one year. His salary varies from $10,000 (New York, New Jersey, Pennsylvania) to $1500 (Oregon and Vermont). Some States limit his reeligibility; but in those which do not there seems to exist no tradition forbidding a third term of office similar to that which has prevailed in the Federal government since the days of Washington.

The earlier constitutions of the original States (except South Carolina) associated with the governor an executive council, but these councils have long since disappeared, except in Massachusetts, Maine, and North Carolina, and the governor remains in solitary glory the official head and representative of the majesty of the State. His powers are, however, in ordinary times more specious than solid, and only one of them is of great practical value. He is charged with the duty of seeing that the laws of the State are faithfully administered by all officials and the judgments of the courts carried out. He has, in nearly all States, the power of reprieving and pardoning offenders, with occasional restrictions. He is commander-in-chief of the armed forces of the State, can embody the militia, repel invasion, suppress insurrection. He appoints some few officials, but seldom to high posts, and in many States his nominations require the approval of the State Senate. Patronage, in which the President of the United States finds one of his most desired and most disagreeable functions, is in the case of a State governor of slight value, because the State offices are not numerous, and the more important and lucrative ones are filled by the direct election of the people. However, in a few States the governor still retains the nomination of the judges. He has in many the power of suspending or removing certain officials, usually local officials, from office, upon proof of their misconduct. He has the right of requiring information from the executive officials, and is usually bound to communicate to the legislature his views regarding the condition of the commonwealth. He may also recommend measures to them, but does not frame and present bills. In a few States he is directed to present estimates. He has in all the States but one a veto upon bills passed by the legislature. This veto may be overridden by the legislatures in the manner before indicated, but generally kills the measure, because if the bill is a bad one, it calls the attention of the people to the fact and frightens the legislature, whereas if the bill be an unobjectionable one, the governor's motive for vetoing it is probably a party motive, and the requisite overriding majority can seldom be secured in favor of a bill which either party dislikes. The use of his veto is, in ordinary times, a governor's most serious duty, and chiefly by his discharge of it is he judged.

Although much less sought after and prized than in "the days of the Fathers," when a State governor sometimes refused to yield precedence to the President of the United States, the governorship is still, particularly in New England, and such great States as New York or Ohio, a post of some dignity, and affords an opportunity for the display of character and talents. Cleveland and Hayes were put forward for President, having commended themselves by their governorships of New York and Ohio. The Civil War governors had great responsibilities and some of them became quite "heroes" to the North. In most States there is an elective lieutenant governor who steps into the governor's place if it becomes vacant, and who is usually also *ex officio* president of the Senate, as the Vice President of the United States is of the Federal Senate. Otherwise he is an insignificant personage, though sometimes a member of some of the executive boards.

The names and duties of the other officers vary from State to State. The most frequent are a secretary of state (in all States), a treasurer (in all), an attorney-general, a comptroller, an auditor, a superintendent of public instruction. Now and then we find a State engineer, a surveyor, a superintendent of prisons. Some States have also various boards of commissioners, *e. g.*, for railroads, for canals, for prisons, for the land office, for agriculture, for immigration. Most of these officials are in nearly all States elected by the people at the general State election. Sometimes, however, they, or some of them, are either chosen by the legislature, or, more rarely, appointed by the governor, whose nomination usually requires the confirmation of the Senate. Their salaries vary with the importance of the office and the parsimony of the State. So too does the length of the term of office.

It has already been observed that the State officials are in no sense a ministry or cabinet to the governor. Holding independently of him, and responsible neither to him nor to the legislature, but to the people, they do not take generally his orders, and need not regard his advice. Each has his own department to administer, and as there is little or nothing political in the work, a general agreement in policy, such as must exist between the Federal President and his ministers, is not required. Policy rests with the legislature, whose statutes, prescribing minutely the action to be taken by the officials, leave little room for executive discretion.

Of the subordinate civil service of a State there is little to be said. It is not large, for the sphere of administrative action which remains to the State between the Federal government on the one side, and the county, city, and township governments on the other, is not wide. It is ill-paid, for the State legislatures, especially in the West, are parsimonious. It is seldom well manned, for able men have no inducement to enter it; and the so-called " Spoils System," which has been hitherto applied to State no less than to Federal offices, makes places the reward for political work, *i. e.*, electioneering and wirepulling. Efforts to secure civil service reform in State administration as in national have been successful in part, to the benefit of securing permanency of competent officials.

Every State except Oregon, which is content to rely on the ordinary law, provides for the impeachment of executive officers for grave offenses. Impeachments are rare in practice. There is also in many States a further power of removing officials, sometimes by the vote of the legislature, sometimes by the governor on the address of both houses, or by the governor alone, or with the concurrence of the Senate.

Chapter XXIX

THE STATE JUDICIARY

THE judiciary in every State includes three sets of courts: A supreme court or court of appeal; superior courts of record; local courts; but the particular names and relations of these several tribunals and the arrangements for criminal business vary greatly from State to State. We hear of courts of common pleas, probate courts, surrogate courts, prerogative courts, courts of oyer and terminer, orphans' courts, court of general sessions of the peace and good delivery, quarter sessions, hustings courts, county courts, etc. All sorts of old English institutions have been transferred bodily, and sometimes look odd in the midst of their new surroundings. As respects the distinction which Englishmen used to deem fundamental, that of courts of common law and courts of equity, there has been great diversity of practice. Most of the original States continued their colonial separate courts of chancery, and were imitated by a few of the earlier among the new States. In some of the old States, however, the hostility to equity jurisdiction was so great as to prevent the establishment of such courts. These States held out for some time, but now administer equity, as indeed every civilized State must do in substance, dispensing it, however, through the same judges as those who apply the common law, and having more or less worked into it the texture of the older system. Special chancery courts now exist only in a few of the States, chiefly older Eastern or Southern States, which, in judicial matters, have shown themselves more conservative than their sisters in the West. In three States only has there been a complete fusion of law and equity. Five States provide for the establishment of tribunals of arbitration and conciliation.

The jurisdiction of the State courts, both civil and criminal, is absolutely unlimited, in other words, there is no appeal from them to the Federal courts, except in certain cases specified by the Federal Constitution. Certain classes of cases are, of course, reserved for the Federal courts and in some the State courts enjoy a concurrent jurisdiction. All crimes, except such as are punishable under some Federal statute, are justiciable by a State court; and it is worth remembering that in most States there exist much wider facilities for setting aside the verdict of a jury finding a prisoner guilty, by raising all sorts of points of law, than are permitted by the law and practice of England. Such facilities have been and are abused, to the great detriment of the community.

One or two other points relating to law and justice in the States require notice. Each State recognizes the judgments of the courts of a sister State, gives credit to its public acts and records, and delivers up to its justice any fugitive from its jurisdiction charged with a crime. Of course the courts of one State are not bound either by law or usage to follow the reported decisions of those of another State. Most of the States have within the last half century made sweeping changes, not only in their judicial system, but in the form of their law. They have revised and codified their statutes, a carefully corrected edition whereof is issued every few years. They have in many instances adopted codes of procedure, and in some cases have even enacted codes embodying the substance of the common law, and fusing it with the statutes. Such codes, however, have been condemned by the judgment of the abler and more learned part of the profession, as tending to confuse the law and make it more uncertain and less scientific. But with the masses of the people the proposal is popular, for it holds out a prospect of a system whose simplicity will enable the layman to understand the law, and render justice cheaper and more speedy. Codification, however, increases the variations of the law between different States.

Important as are the functions of the American judiciary, the powers of a judge are limited by the State constitutions in a manner surprising to Europeans. He is not allowed to charge the jury on questions of fact, but only to state the law. His power of committing for contempt of court is often restricted. Express rules forbid him to sit in causes wherein he can have any family or pecuniary interest.

I come now to three points, which are not only important in themselves, but instructive as illustrating the currents of opinion which have influenced the people of the States. These are—

The method of appointing the judges.

Their tenure of office.

Their salaries.

In colonial days the superior judges were appointed by the governors, except in Rhode Island and Connecticut, where the legislature elected them. In and after 1776, the tendency was toward legislative election.

In the period between 1812 and 1860, when the tide of democracy was running strong, the function was in several of the older States taken from the governor or the legislature to be given to the people voting at the polls; and the same became the practice among the new States as they were successively admitted to the Union.

At present we find that in a majority of the States the judges are elected by the people, in a few by the legislature, and in a few more are appointed by the governor, subject, however, to confirmation either by the council, or by the legislature, or by one House thereof. It is the older commonwealths that have clung to the less democratic methods of choosing judicial officers.

Originally the superior judges were, in most States, like those of England since the Revolution of 1688, appointed for life, and held office during good behavior. A judge may now be removed upon an address from the legislature in thirty States, a majority of two-thirds in each house being usually required. But the wave of democracy has in nearly all States swept away the old system of life-tenure. Only four now retain it. In the rest a judge is elected or appointed for a term, varying from two years to twenty-one years.

Any one of the three phenomena I have described—popular elections, short terms, and small salaries—would be sufficient to lower the character of the judiciary. Putting the three sources of mischief together, no one will be surprised to hear that in many of the United States the State judges are men of moderate abilities and scanty learning, inferior, and sometimes, vastly inferior, to the best of the advocates who practice before them.

Pecuniary corruption seems to be rare, but there are other influences which can be used. And apart from that it is an evil that the bench should not be, intellectually and socially at least, on a level with the bar.

The mischief is serious. But I must own that it is smaller than a European observer is prepared to expect. Justice in civil causes between man and man is fairly administered over the whole Union, because:

1. Of the coexistence in every State of the Federal tribunals.

2. Of the influence of a public opinion which not only recognizes the interest the community has in an honest admin-

istration of the law, but recoils from turpitude in a highly placed official.

3. There is the influence of the bar, a potent influence even in the present day, when its *rôle* is less brilliant than in former generations. It has a professional liking for a good judge, and also a personal interest in getting fairly competent men before whom to plead, often forcing good judicial nominations on party conventions.

These causes, and especially the last, go far to nullify the malign effects of popular election and short terms. But they cannot equally nullify the effect of small salaries. Accordingly, while corruption and partiality are uncommon among State judges, inferiority to the practicing counsel is a conspicuous and frequent fault.

During the last few years there has been a distinct change for the better, some States vesting appointments in governors, and raising salaries or lengthening terms. In this point at least, the tide of democracy which went on rising for so many years, seems to have begun to recede from the high-water mark of 1840-1860. The American people, if sometimes bold in their experiments, have a fund of good sense which makes them watchful of results, and not unwilling to reconsider their former decisions.

Chapter XXX

STATE FINANCE

THE financial systems in force in the several States furnish one of the widest and most instructive fields of study that the whole range of American institutions presents to a practical statesman, as well as to a student of comparative politics. What I have to say falls under the heads of—

Purposes for which State revenue is required.

Forms of taxation.

Exemptions from taxation.

Methods of collecting taxes.

Limitations imposed on the power of taxing.

State indebtedness.

Restriction imposed on the borrowing power.

1. The budget of a State is seldom large, in proportion to the wealth of its inhabitants, because the chief burden of administration is borne not by the State, but by its subdivisions, the counties, and still more the cities and townships. The chief expenses which a State undertakes in its corporate capacity are—(1) The salaries of its officials, executive and judicial, and the incidental expenses of judicial proceedings, such as payments to jurors and witnesses; (2) the State volunteer militia; (3) charitable and other public institutions, such as State lunatic asylums, State universities, agricultural colleges, etc.; (4) grants to schools; (5) State prisons, comparatively few, since the prison is usually supported by the county; (6) State buildings and public works, including, in a few cases, canals; (7) payment of interest

Patent Office, Washington, D. C.

on State debts. Of the whole revenue collected in each State under State taxing laws, a comparatively small part is taken by the State itself and applied to State purposes.

2. The Federal government raises its revenue by indirect taxation, and by duties of customs and excise, though it has the power of imposing direct taxes, and used that power freely during the War of Secession. State revenue, on the other hand, arises almost wholly from direct taxation.

The chief tax is in every State a property tax, based on a valuation of all property, real and personal, within the taxing jurisdiction. The valuation is made by officials called appraisers or assessors, appointed by the local communities, though under general State laws. The local assessors have, equally with the property owners, an obvious motive for valuing on a low scale, for by doing so they relieve their community of part of its burden. The State is accordingly obliged to check and correct them by creating what is called a Board of Equalization, which compares and revises the valuations made by the various local officers, so as to secure that taxable property in each locality is equally and fairly valued, and made thereby to bear its due share of public burdens. Similarly a county has often an equalization board. However, the existence of such boards by no means overcomes the difficulty of securing a really equal valuation, and the honest town which puts its property at a fair value suffers by paying more than its share.

A still more serious evil is the fact that so large a part of taxable property escapes taxation. Lands and houses cannot be concealed; cattle and furniture can be discovered by a zealous tax officer. But a great part, often far the largest part of a rich man's wealth, consists in what Americans call "intangible property," notes, bonds, book debts, and Western mortgages. At this it is practically impossible to get, except through the declaration of the owner; and though the owner is required to present his declaration of taxable property upon oath, he is apt to omit this kind of property. Indeed in several States it has been advocated that such taxes be abolished owing to the tendency toward perjury and lack of success in collection.

These difficulties help to explain the occasional bitterness of feeling among American farmers as well as the masses against capitalists, much of whose accumulated wealth escapes taxation, while the farmer who owns his land, as well as the workingman who puts his savings into the house he lives in, is assessed and taxed upon this visible property. We may, in fact, say of most States, that under the present system of taxation the larger the city is the smaller is the proportion of personalty reached by taxation (since concealment is easier in large communities), and the richer a man is the smaller in proportion to his property is the contribution he pays to the State.

Besides the property tax, which is the main source of revenue, the States often levy taxes on particular trades or occupations, sometimes in the form of a license tax, taxes on franchises enjoyed by corporations, taxes on railroad stock, or (in a few States) taxes on collateral inheritances. Comparatively little resort is had to the so-called "death-duties," *i. e.*, probate, legacy, and succession duties, nor is much use made of an income tax. As regards poll taxes there is much variety of practice. The amount of a poll tax is always small, $1 or $2: sometimes the payment of it is made a prerequisite to the exercise of the electoral franchise.

In some States, "foreign" corporations, *i. e.*, those chartered by or domiciled in another State, are taxed more heavily than domestic corporations, and there is always a desire to hit companies, especially banks and railroads.

3. In most States, certain descriptions of property

are exempted from taxation, as for instance, the buildings or other property of the State, or of any local community, burying grounds, schools and universities, educational, charitable, scientific, literary, or agricultural institutions or societies, public libraries, churches and other buildings or property used for religious purposes, cemeteries, household furniture, farming implements, deposits in savings banks. No State can tax any bonds, debt certificates, or other securities issued by, or under the authority of, the Federal government, including the circulating notes commonly called " greenbacks."

4. Some of the State taxes, such, for instance, as license taxes, or a tax on corporations, are directly levied by and paid to the State officials. But others, and particularly the property tax, which forms so large a source of revenue, are collected by the local authorities, being apportioned among the counties and then among the cities and townships, each adding its own tax. Thus, when the township or city authorities assess and collect taxes from the individual citizen, they collect at one and the same time three distinct sets of taxes, the State tax, the county tax, and the city or township tax. Thus trouble and expense are saved in the process of collecting and the citizen sees in one tax-paper all he has to pay.

5. Some States, taught by their sad experience of reckless legislatures, limit by their constitutions the amount of taxation which may be raised for State purposes in any one year.

It may be thought that the self-interest of the people is sufficient to secure economy and limit taxation. But, apart from the danger of a corrupt legislature, it is often remarked that as in many States a large proportion of the voters do not pay State taxes, the power of imposing burdens lies largely in the hands of persons who have no direct interest, and suppose themselves to have no interest at all, in keeping down taxes which they do not pay.

Another illustration of the tendency to restrict the improvidence of representatives is furnished by the prohibitions in many constitutions to pass bills appropriating moneys to any private individual or corporation, or to authorize the payment of claims against the State arising under any contract not strictly and legally binding, or to release the claims which the State may have against railroads or other corporations.

6. Nothing in the financial system of the States better deserves attention than the history of the State debts, their portentous growth, and the efforts made, when the people had taken fright, to reduce their amount, and to set limits to them in the future. Eighty years ago the craze for internal improvements among the newer Western States in the hopes of faster development induced the States to borrow money. The State debts increased rapidly and later were added to by Civil War expenses. There was a good deal in the way of executed works to show for the money borrowed and expended, nevertheless the huge and increasing total startled the people, and, as everybody knows, some States repudiated their debts. State indebtedness has since decreased, but municipal indebtedness has advanced, especially in the larger cities, at a dangerously swift rate. Much of this must be set down to extremely lax and wasteful administration, and much more to mere stealing, facilitated by the habit of subsidizing, or taking share in, corporate enterprises which had excited the hopes of the citizens.

7. The disease spread till it terrified the patient, and a remedy was found in the insertion in the constitutions of the States of provisions limiting the borrowing powers of the State legislatures. For the last fifty years, whenever a State has enacted a constitution, it has inserted sections re-

stricting the borrowing powers of States and local bodies, and often also providing for the discharge of existing liabilities. Many constitutions forbid the assumption by the State of the debts of any individual or municipal corporation.

The care of the people for their financial freedom and safety extends even to local bodies. Many of the recent constitutions limit, or direct the legislature to limit, the borrowing powers of counties, cities, or towns, sometimes even of incorporated school districts, to a sum not exceeding a certain percentage on the assessed value of the taxable property within the area in question. Local authorities are also forbidden to aid any private undertaking.

Cases, of course, occur in which a restriction on the taxing power or borrowing power of a municipality is found inconvenient, because a costly public improvement is rendered more costly if it has to be done piecemeal, but the evils and the abuses incident to an unlimited power of undertaking improvements, have been so great as to make people willing to bear with the occasional inconveniences which are inseparable from restriction. The provisions above described have had the effect of steadily reducing the amount of State and county debts, although the wealth of the country makes rapid strides. In cities, however, there has been, not only no reduction, but an increase. This striking difference between the cities and the States may be explained in several ways. One is that cities cannot repudiate, while sovereign States can and do. Another may be found in the later introduction into State constitutions of restrictions on the borrowing powers of municipalities. But the chief cause is to be found in the conditions of the government of great cities, where the wealth of the community is largest, and is also most at the disposal of a multitude of ignorant voters.

Chapter XXXI

THE WORKING OF STATE GOVERNMENTS

OWING to the lack of power of the State Executive, as already noted, the office has ceased to be of great importance in general, although in the older States and in crises, it still has great influence.

Thus we are led back to the legislature, which is so much the strongest force in the several States that we may almost call it the government and ignore all other authorities.

As the frame of a State government generally resembles the national government, so a State legislature resembles Congress. But, in most States, it exaggerates the characteristic defects of Congress. It has fewer able and high-minded men among its members. It has less of recognized leadership. It is surrounded by temptations relatively greater. It is guarded by a less watchful and less interested public opinion.

The matter of State legislation may be classified under three heads:

1. Ordinary private law, *i. e.,* contracts, torts, inheritance, family relations, offenses, civil and criminal procedure.

2. Administrative law, including the regulation of municipal and rural local government, public works, education, the liquor traffic, vaccination, adulteration, charitable and penal establishments, the inspection of mines or manufactories, together with the general law of corporations, of railroads, and of labor, together also with taxation, both State and local, and the management of the public debt.

3. Measures of a local and special nature, such as

are called in England " private bills," *i. e.*, bills for char-
tering and incorporating gas, water, canal, tramway, or railroad companies, or for conferring franchises in the nature
of monopolies or privileges upon such bodies, or for altering
their constitutions, for incorporating cities and minor communities and regulating their affairs.

Bills of the second class are more numerous than those
of the first, bills of the third more numerous than those of
the other two put together. Ordinary or private law, the
law which guides or secures us in the everyday relations of
life, and upon which nine-tenths of the suits between man
and man are founded, is not greatly changed from year to
year in the United States.

In the second class every session sees experiments, generally with the result of enlarging the province of government, both by interfering with the individual citizen and by
attempting to do things for him which apparently he either
does not do or does not do well for himself. But the general
or " public " legislation, as Englishmen would call it, is
dwarfed by the " private bill " legislation which forms the
third of our classes. One form of this special legislation is
peculiarly attractive and pernicious. It is the power of
dealing by statute with the municipal constitution and actual
management of cities. City revenues are so large as to offer
rich plunder to those who can seize the control of them.
The vote which a city casts is so heavy as to throw great
power into the hands of those who control it, and enable
them to drive a good bargain with the wirepullers of a legislative chamber.

We are now in a position, having seen what the main
business of a State legislature is, to inquire what is likely
to be the quality of the persons who compose it. The conditions that determine their quality may be said to be the
following:

1. The system of selection by party conventions.

2. The habit of choosing none but a resident in any electoral district to represent that district, a habit which narrows the field of choice and excludes competent men.

3. The fact that the capital of a State—*i. e.*, the meeting-place of the legislature and residence of the chief officials, is usually a small town, at a distance from the most populous city or cities of the State, and therefore a place neither attractive socially nor convenient for business men or lawyers, and which, it may be remarked in passing, is more shielded from a vigilant public opinion than is a great city with its keen and curious press.

4. The nature of the business that comes before a State legislature. As already explained, by far the largest part of this business excites little popular interest and involves no large political issues.

After this, it need scarcely be said that the State legislatures are not high-toned bodies. The best seem to be those of some of the New England States, particularly Massachusetts, where the venerable traditions surrounding an ancient commonwealth do something to sustain the dignity of the body and induce good men to enter it. Next come some of the Northwestern States, where the population, consisting almost entirely of farmers, who own as well as work their land, sends up members who fairly represent its average intelligence, and are little below the level of its average virtue. It is hard to present a general view of the Southern States, both because there are great differences among them, and because they are still in a state of transition, generally, it would seem. transition toward a better state of things. Roughly speaking, their legislatures seem to stand below those of the Northwest, though in most a few men of exceptional ability and standing may be found. The lowest place belongs to the States which, possessing the largest cities, have received the largest influx of European immigrants, and have fallen most completely under the control of unscrupulous party managers. New York, Philadelphia, Baltimore, Chicago, San Francisco have done their best to poison the legislatures of the States in which they respectively lie by filling these bodies with members of a low type, as well as by being themselves the centers of enormous accumulations of capital.

The corrupt member has several methods of making gains. One, the most obvious, is to exact money or money's worth for his vote. A second is to secure by it the support of a group of his colleagues in some other measure in which he is personally interested, as for instance a measure which will add to the value of land near a particular city. This is "log-rolling," and is the most difficult method to deal with, because its milder forms are scarcely distinguishable from that legitimate give and take which must go on in all legislative bodies. A third is blackmailing. A member brings in a bill either specially directed against some particular great corporation, probably a railroad or proposing so to alter the general law as in fact to injure such a corporation, or a group of corporations. He intimates privately that he is willing to "see" the directors or the law-agents of the corporation, and is in many cases bought off by them, keeping his bill on the paper till the last moment so as to prevent some other member from repeating the trick.

In these demoralized States the State Senate is apt to be a worse body than the House, whereas in the better States the Senate is usually the superior body. The reason is twofold. As the Senate is smaller the vote of each member is of more consequence, and fetches, when venal, a higher price. And the second reason is that the most adroit and practiced intriguers work their way up into the Senate.

The spirit of localism, surprisingly strong everywhere

in America, completely rules legislatures. When such is
the accepted doctrine as well as invariable practice, log-
rolling becomes natural and almost legitimate. Each member being the judge of the measure which touches his own
constituency, every other member supports that member in
passing the measure, expecting in return the like support in a
like cause. There is in State legislators, particularly in the
West, a restlessness which, coupled with their limited range
of knowledge and undue appreciation of material interests,
makes them rather dangerous. Both this restlessness and the
general character of State legislation are illustrated by the
enormous numbers of bills introduced in each session, comparatively few of which pass, because the time is too short,
or opposing influences can be brought to bear on the
committees.

Nothing is more remarkable about these State legislators than their timidity. No one seems to think of having
an opinion of his own. In matters which touch the interests
of his constituents, a member is, of course, their humble
servant. In burning party questions—they are few, and
mostly personal—he goes with his party. This want of independence has some good results. It has enabled a small
minority of zealous men, backed by a few newspapers, to
carry schemes of reform which the majority regard with
indifference or hostility.

In the recent legislation of many States, especially,
Western States, there is a singular mixture of philanthropy
and humanitarianism with the folly and jobbery which have
been described already, like threads of gold and silver woven
across a warp of dirty sacking. Every year sees bills passed
to restrict the sale of liquor, to prevent the sale of indecent
or otherwise demoralizing literature, to protect women and
children, to stamp out lotteries and gambling houses, to improve the care of the blind, the insane, and the poor, which

testify to a warm and increasing interest in all good works.

The real blemishes in the system of State government are all found in the composition or conduct of the legislatures. The practical result of these blemishes has been to create a large mass of State and local indebtedness which ought never to have been incurred, to allow foolish experiments in law-making to be tried, and to sanction a vast mass of private enterprises, in which public rights and public interests become the sport of speculators, or a source of gain to monopolists, with the incidental consequences of demoralizing the legislators themselves and creating an often unjust prejudice against all corporate undertakings.

All remedies are directed against the legislative power, and may be arranged under four heads.

First, there is the division of the legislature into two houses.

Secondly, there is the veto of the governor.

Thirdly, there are limitations imposed on the competence of the legislature.

The fourth and last of the checks which the prudence of the States imposes is a very simple, not to say naive, one. It consists in limiting the time during which the legislature may sit.

Many recent constitutions have tried another and probably a better expedient than that of limiting the length of sessions. They have made sessions less frequent. At one time every legislature met once a year. Now in only six States (all of these six belonging to the original thirteen) does it meet annually, while the rest are biennial, except one, which is quadrennial.

The chief lesson which a study of the more vicious among the State legislatures teaches, is that power does not necessarily bring responsibility in its train. We know that power does not purify men in despotic governments, but we talk as if it did so in free governments. There must be added to power, in the case of the voter, a direct interest in the choice of good men; in the case of the legislator, responsibility to the voters; in the case of both, a measure of enlightenment and honor. What the legislatures of the worst States show is not merely the need for the existence of a sound public opinion, for such a public opinion exists, but the need for methods by which it can be brought into efficient action upon representatives. The greatness of the scale on which they act, and of the material interests they control, will do little to inspire them. The two largest States in the Union have had legislatures which were confessedly the worst.

The States evidently present some singular conditions for the development of a party system. They are self-governing communities with large legislative and administrative powers, existing inside a much greater community of which they are for many purposes independent. They must have parties, and this community, the Federal Union, has also parties. What is the relation of the one set of parties to the other?

There are three kinds of relations possible, *viz.*:

Each State might have a party of its own, entirely unconnected with the national parties, but created by State issues.

Each State might have parties which, while based upon State issues, were influenced by the national parties, and in some sort of affiliation with the latter.

The parties in each State might be merely local subdivisions of the national parties, the national issues and organizations swallowing up, or rather pushing aside, the State issues and the organizations formed to deal with them.

The nature of the State governments would lead us to

expect to find the first of these relations existing. The contrary has happened. The national parties have engulfed the State parties. The latter have disappeared absolutely as independent bodies, and survive merely as branches of the national parties, working each in its own State for the tenets and purposes which a national party professes and seeks to attain. Historically the strife of the two great national parties became intense within four years from their origin, over the whole Union. From 1793 till 1815 grave issues of foreign policy, complicated with issues of domestic policy, stirred men to fierce passion and strenuous effort. State business was pushed aside, the dividing lines between parties in every State were those drawn by national questions. And from 1827 down to 1877 the renewed keenness of party warfare kept these parties constantly on the stretch, and forced them to use all the support they could win in a State for the purposes of the national struggle.

The States naturally divided on national questions in the elections of Senators. Moreover, there are the offices. The Federal offices in each State are very numerous. They are in the gift of whichever national party happens to be in power. Accordingly the national parties have complete possession of the field.

This system has affected the working of the State governments in preventing the growth within a State of State parties addressing themselves to the questions which belong to its legislature, and really affect its welfare. This may seem to possess the advantage of permitting questions to be considered on their merits, apart from a spirit of faction. However, it is not the practice, for the strength of the national parties prevents it. Every member is elected as a party man.

It is, however, obviously impossible to treat as party matters many of the questions that come before the legislatures. Still, party affiliations often help measures, or parties espouse non-partisan measures to gain votes. Sometimes a real State party does arise on local questions of importance, but more often State divisions are due to personal rivalries.

It will be seen from this fact, as well as from others given in the preceding chapter, that the dignity and magnitude of State politics have declined. This change does not necessarily indicate a feebler sense of political duty. It is due to the shriveling up of the State. In saying this I do not mean to withdraw or modify what was said, in an earlier chapter, of the greatness of a State, and the attachment of its inhabitants to it, but of the practical interest taken in its government.

We may accordingly say that the average American voter, belonging to the laboring or farming or shopkeeping class, troubles himself little about the conduct of State business. The more educated and thoughtful citizen, especially in great States, like New York and Pennsylvania, is apt to be disgusted by the sordidness of many State politicians and the pettiness of most, and prefers to carry his energies into the field of national politics.

Chapter XXXII

THE TERRITORIES

OF the 3,767,053 square miles which constitute the area of the United States, 2,712,760 are included within the bounds of the forty-five States whose government has been described in the last preceding chapters. The 1,054,293 square miles which remain fall into the following divisions:

Four organized Territories, *viz.*, Arizona, New Mexico, Oklahoma, and Hawaii, 281,370 square miles. Two unorganized Territories, viz., Alaska, 590,884 square miles, Indian Territory west of Arkansas, 31,400 square miles. The Federal District of Columbia, 70 square miles. Porto Rico, 3600 square miles. Philippines, 140,000 square miles. Guam, 150 square miles. Tutuila and islets, 79 square miles. Of these three may be dismissed in a word or two. The District of Columbia is a piece of land set apart to contain the city of Washington, which is the seat of the Federal government. It is governed by three commissioners appointed by the President, and has no local legislature nor municipal government, the only legislative authority being Congress.

Alaska (population in 1900, 63,592, of whom 30,507 were whites) and the Indian Territory are also under the direct authority of officers appointed by the President and of laws passed by Congress. Both have been chiefly inhabited by Indian tribes, some of which, however, in the Indian Territory, and particularly the Cherokees, have made considerable progress in civilization.

The organized Territories require a somewhat fuller description, because they present an interesting form of autonomy or local self-government, differing from that which exists in the several States, and in some points more akin to that of the self-governing colonies of Great Britain. This form has in each Territory been created by Federal statutes, beginning with the great Ordinance for the Government of the Territory of the United States northwest of the River Ohio, passed by the Congress of the Confederation in 1787. Since that year many Territories have been organized under different statutes and on different plans out of the Western dominions of the United States, under the general power conferred upon Congress by the Federal Constitution (Art. iv. sec. 3). Most of these Territories have now become States, but there remain the four already mentioned. At first local legislative power was vested in the governor and the judges; it is now exercised by an elective legislature. The present organization of these four is in most respects identical; and in describing it I shall for the sake of brevity ignore minor differences.

The fundamental law of every Territory, as of every State, is the Federal constitution; but whereas every State has also its own popularly enacted State constitution, the Territories are not regulated by any similar instruments, which for them are replaced by the Federal statutes passed by Congress establishing their government and prescribing its form. However, some Territories have created a sort of rudimentary constitution for themselves by enacting a Bill of Rights.

In every Territory, as in every State, the executive, legislative, and judicial departments are kept distinct. The executive consists of a governor, appointed for four years by the President of the United States, with the consent of the Senate, and removable by the President, together with a secretary, treasurer, auditor, and usually also a superintendent of public instruction, and a librarian. The governor

commands the militia, and has a veto upon the acts of the
legislature, which, however, may be overridden by a two-
thirds majority in each House. He is responsible to the Federal government, and reports yearly to the President on the
conditions of the territory, often making his report a sort of
prospectus in which the advantages which his dominions offer
to intending immigrants are fondly set forth. He also sends
a message to the legislature at the beginning of each session.
Important as the post of governor is, it is often bestowed as
a mere piece of party patronage, with no great regard to the
fitness of the appointee.

The legislature is composed of two Houses, a Council
and a House of Representatives elected by districts. Each is
elected by the voters of the Territory for two years, and sits
only once in that period. The session is limited (by Federal
statutes) to sixty days, and the salary of a member is four
dollars a day. The Houses work much like those in the
States, doing the bulk of their business by standing committees, and frequently suspending their rules to run measures through with little or no debate. The sphere of
legislation is wide, but subject to certain Federal restrictions, and also to the still more important right of Congress
to annul or modify by its own statutes any Territorial Act.

The judiciary consists of three or more judges of a
supreme court, appointed for four years by the President,
with the consent of the Senate (salary $3000), together
with a United States district attorney and a United States
marshal. The law they administer is partly Federal,—all
Federal statutes being construed to take effect, where properly applicable, in the Territories,—partly local, created in
each Territory by its own statutes; and appeals, where the
sum in dispute is above a certain value, go to the Federal
Supreme Court. The expenses of Territorial governments
are borne by the Federal treasury.

The Territories send neither Senators nor Representatives to Congress, nor do they take part in Presidential elections. The House of Representatives, under a statute, admits a delegate from each of them to sit and speak, but of course not to vote, because the right of voting in Congress depends on the Federal Constitution. The position of a citizen in a Territory is therefore a peculiar one. What may be called his private or passive citizenship is complete: he has all the immunities and benefits which any other American citizen enjoys. But the public or active side is wanting, so far as the national government is concerned, although complete for local purposes. It must, moreover, be remembered that a Territory, which may be called an inchoate or rudimentary State, looks forward to becoming a complete State. When its population becomes equal to that of an average congressional district, its claim to be admitted as a State is strong, and in the absence of specific objections will be granted. Congress, however, has absolute discretion in the matter, and often uses its discretion under party motives.

When Congress resolves to turn a Territory into a State, it usually passes an enabling act, under which the inhabitants elect a constitutional convention, which frames a draft constitution; and when this has been submitted to and accepted by the voters of the Territory, the act of Congress takes effect: the Territory is transformed into a State, and proceeds to send its Senators and Representatives to Congress in the usual way. The enabling act may prescribe conditions to be fulfilled by the State constitution, but cannot legally narrow the right which the citizens of the newly-formed State will enjoy of subsequently modifying that instrument in any way not inconsistent with the provisions of the Federal Constitution.

The arrangements above described seem to work well. Self-government is practically enjoyed by the Territories,

despite the supreme authority of Congress. The want of
a voice in Congress and Presidential elections, and the fact
that the governor is set over them by an external power, are
not felt to be practical grievances, partly of course because
these young communities are too small and too much absorbed
in the work of developing the country to be keenly interested
in national politics.

Since 1888 most of the Territories have been made into
States—the large Northwestern States of North Dakota,
South Dakota, Montana, Idaho, Wyoming, and Washington, States which are growing in population and are full
of resources, either agricultural or mineral. Utah, which
had been so long kept out on account of its Mormons and
their practices, although it had a large population, was admitted in 1896.

Of the remaining Territories, New Mexico (population
in 1900, 195,310) is still largely peopled by Indo-Spanish
Mexicans, who speak Spanish, and are obviously ill-fitted for
the self-government which organization as a State implies.
Water is too scarce and the soil too hilly to make agriculture
generally available. The same remark applies to Arizona,
the sides of whose splendid mountain groups are barren,
and most of whose plains support only a scanty vegetation.
Both Territories are rich in minerals, but a mining population is not only apt to be disorderly, but is fluctuating, moving from camp to camp as richer deposits are discovered or
old veins worked out. Irrigation, however, will make these
Territories more fruitful and the population is growing
so that they may soon be admitted. In 1890 Oklahoma was
carved out of Indian Territory and opened for settlement.
The population has grown wonderfully and is very stable,
so that the Territory is ready for admission. The Indians
in Indian Territory are being allotted their lands in severalty
so that there will soon be no reason for keeping up their

reservations, and Indian Territory will be joined to Oklahoma to form a single State. In 1898 the islands of the former independent kingdom of Hawaii were annexed to the United States, and in 1900 a regular Territorial form of government was established. In this case, the non-contiguous condition of the islands offers to many persons a bar to their future admission as a State, but the probabilities are that the American mind will be accommodated to that step as soon as the demand is strong enough.

On a review of the whole matter it may safely be said that the American scheme of Territorial government, though it suffers from the occasional incompetence of the governor and is inconsistent with democratic theory, has worked well, and gives little ground for discontent even to the inhabitants of the Territories themselves.

Since the Spanish-American War of 1898 the United States have become possessors of islands in both the Atlantic and Pacific. Porto Rico is absolutely theirs, and is under a modified Territorial form of government, the people electing the House of Delegates (Lower House) and thereby being trained to self-government; the United States controlling the Executive Council (Upper House) and appointing the governor and higher officials, and so holding close control. The Philippine Islands presented a problem never before put to the United States, and the issue to many minds is uncertain. The large number of savages included among the eight million inhabitants, together with the lack of political training of most of the rest, forbids any large measure of self-government as yet. The military government ended in 1902 and complete civil government was established.

Besides these greater possessions the United States secured Tutuila in the Samoan group, with its valuable harbor Pago-Pago, in 1899, and has appropriated numerous small islands as naval bases without any expectation of future self-government.

Chapter XXXIII

LOCAL GOVERNMENT

EACH State has its own system of local areas and authorities, created and worked under its own laws; and though these systems agree in many points, they differ in many others. All I can here attempt is to distinguish the leading types of local government.

Three types of rural local government are discernible in America. The first is characterized by its unit, the town or township, and exists in the six New England States. The second is characterized by a much larger unit, the county, and prevails in the Southern States. The third combines some features of the first with some of the second, and may be called the mixed system. It is found, under a considerable variety of forms, in the Middle and Northwestern States. The differences of these three types are interesting, not only because of the practical instruction they afford, but also because they spring from original differences in the character of the colonists who settled along the American coast, and in the conditions under which the communities there founded were developed.

The first New England settlers were Puritans in religion, and sometimes inclined to republicanism in politics. They were largely townsfolk, accustomed to municipal life and to vestry meetings. They planted their tiny communities along the seashore and the banks of rivers, enclosing them with stockades for protection against the warlike Indians. Each was obliged to be self-sufficing, because divided by rocks and woods from the others. Each such

settlement was called a town, or township, and was in fact
a miniature commonwealth.   Much of that robust, if somewhat narrow, localism which characterizes the representative
system of America is due to this originally distinct and self-
sufficing corporate life of the seventeenth-century towns.

.Very different were the circumstances of the Southern
colonies.   The men who went to Virginia and the Carolinas
settled in scattered communities because the Indians were
peaceable and the climate and soil suitable for large plantations, and there was no attachment to local institutions.   Thus
a semi-feudal society grew up, in which authority naturally
fell to the landowners, each of whom was the center of a
group of free dependents as well as the master of an increasing crowd of slaves.   The county was the practically important unit of local administration controlled by the State
government alone.   The affairs of the county were usually
managed by a board of elective commissioners, and not, like
those of the New England towns, by a primary assembly;
and in an aristocratic society the leading planters had of
course a predominating influence.   Hence this form of local
government was not only less democratic, but less stimulating and educative than that which prevailed in the New
England States.

In the Middle States of the Union the town and town
meeting did not as a rule exist, and the county was the original basis of organization.   There grew up no planting aristocracy like that of Virginia or the Carolinas, and as trade
and manufactures grew, population became denser than in
the South.   New England influenced them, and influenced
still more the newer commonwealths which arose in the Northwest, such as Ohio and Michigan, into which the surplus
population of the East poured.   And the result of this influence is seen in the growth through the Middle and Western States of a mixed system.   The county is perhaps to

be regarded, at least in New York, Pennsylvania, and Ohio, as the true unit, and the townships (for so they are usually called) as its subdivisions. But the townships are vigorous organisms, which largely restrict the functions of the county authority, and give to local government, especially in the Northwest, a character generally similar to that which it wears in New England.

Let us now look at the actual constitution and working of the organs of local government in the three several regions mentioned, beginning with New England and the town system.

The town is in rural districts the smallest local circumscription. It is a rural, not an urban community, with perhaps only a small village, in it. Its area seldom exceeds five square miles; its population is usually small, averaging less than 3000. It is governed by an assembly of all qualified voters resident within its limits, which meets at least once a year, in the spring (a reminiscence of the Easter vestry of England) and from time to time as summoned. There are usually three or four meetings each year. Notice is required to be given at least ten days previously, not only of the hour and place of meeting, but of the business to be brought forward. This assembly has the power both of electing officials and of legislating. It chooses the selectmen, school committee, and executive officers for the coming year; it enacts by-laws and ordinances for the regulation of all local affairs; it receives the reports of the selectmen and the several committees, passes their accounts, hears what sums they propose to raise for the expenses of next year, and votes the necessary taxation accordingly, appropriating to the various local purposes—schools, aid to the poor, the repair of highways, and so forth—the sums directed to be levied. Its powers cover the management of the town lands and other property, and all local matters whatsoever, including police and sanitation. Every resident has the right to make, and to support by speech, any proposal. The meeting, which is presided over by a chairman called the Moderator, is held in the town hall, if the Town possesses one, or in the principal church or schoolhouse, but sometimes in the open air. The attendance is usually good; the debates sensible and practical. Much of course depends on the character and size of the population. When the town meeting has grown to exceed seven or eight hundred persons, and still more when any considerable section are strangers, such as the Irish or French Canadians who have latterly poured into New England, the institution works less perfectly, because the multitude is too large for debate, factions are likely to spring up, and the new immigrants, untrained in self-government, become the prey of wirepullers or petty demagogues.

The executive of a town consists of the selectmen, from three to nine in number. They are elected annually, and manage all the ordinary business, of course under the directions given them by the last preceding meeting. There is also a town clerk, who keeps the records, and minutes the proceedings of the meeting, and is generally also registrar of births and deaths; a treasurer; assessors, who make a valuation of property within the town for the purposes of taxation; the collector, who gathers the taxes, and divers minor officers. There is always a school committee, with sometimes subcommittees for minor school districts if the town be a large one. Town elections are not professedly political, i. e., they are not usually fought on party lines, though occasionally party spirit affects them, and a man prominent in his party is more likely to obtain support.

Next above the town stands the county. Its area and population vary a good deal. The county was originally an aggregation of towns for judicial purposes, and is still in the main a judicial district in and for which civil and criminal courts are held, some by county judges, some by State judges, and in and for which certain judicial officers are elected by the people at the polls, who also choose a sheriff and a clerk. Police belong to the towns and cities, not to the county within which they lie. The chief administrative officers are the county commissioners, of whom there are three in Massachusetts (elected for three years, one in each year), and county treasurer with care of the county buildings, highways, licenses, and apportioning of the tax among the towns and cities. The commissioners are controlled by legislative statutes and have no legislative functions of their own. The functions of the county are in fact of small consequence: it is a judicial district and a highway district and little more.

The system which has prevailed in the Southern States need not long detain us, for it is less instructive and has proved less successful. Here the unit is the county, except in Louisiana, where the equivalent division is called a parish. The county was originally a judicial division, established for the purposes of local courts, and a financial one, for the collection of State taxes. The county officers (commissioners, assessor, collector, treasurer, superintendent of education, overseer of roads) have, besides the functions indicated by their names, the charge of the police and the poor of the county, and of the construction of public works, such as bridges and prisons. The county judges and the sheriff, and frequently the coroner, are also chosen by the people. The sheriff is the chief executive officer of the judicial machinery of the county. The most important local body in the Southern States is the school committee for each school district. In several States, such as Virginia and North Carolina, we now find townships. The school, someone truly says, is becoming the nucleus of local self-government in the South now, as the church was in New England two centuries ago.

However, all local authorities in the South and in the States which, like Nevada, Nebraska, and Oregon, may be said to have adopted the county system, are executive officers and nothing more.

The third type is less easy to characterize than either of the two preceding, and the forms under which it appears in the Middle and Northwestern States are even more various than those referable to the second type. Two features mark it. One is the importance and power of the county, which in the history of most of these States appears before any smaller division; the other is the activity of the township, which has more independence and a larger range of competence than under the system of the South. Now of these two features the former is the more conspicuous in one group of States—Pennsylvania, New Jersey, New York, Ohio, Indiana, Iowa; the latter in another group—Michigan, Illinois, Wisconsin, Minnesota, the difference being due to the proportion of New England settlers and influence. This reappearance of the New England town meeting, though in a somewhat less primitive and at the same time less perfect form, in Michigan and Illinois, is spreading. Legislation in California, Nebraska, and other Western States, permits its adoption.

In the proportion to the extent in which a State has adopted the township system the county has tended to decline in importance. It is nevertheless of more consequence in the West than in New England. The board of county commissioners consists in Michigan and Illinois of the supervisors of all the townships within the county; in Wisconsin and Minnesota the commissioners are directly chosen at a county election.

I pass to the mixed or compromise system as it appears in the other group of States, of which Pennsylvania, Ohio, Indiana, and Iowa may be taken as samples. In these States

we find no town meeting. Their township may have greater
or less power, but its members do not come together in a
primary assembly; it elects its local officers, and acts only
through and by them.

In most of these States the county overshadows the
township. Taking Pennsylvania as an example, we find
each county governed by a board of three commissioners,
elected for three years, upon a minority vote system, the
elector being allowed to vote for two candidates only. Besides these there are officers, also chosen by popular vote for
three years, *viz.*, a sheriff, coroner, prothonotary, registrar
of wills, recorder of deeds, treasurer, surveyor, three audi-
tors, clerk of the court, district attorney. The county, besides its judicial business and the management of the prisons
incident thereto, besides its duties as respects highways and
bridges, has educational and usually also poor law functions; and it levies its county tax and the State taxes through
a collector for each township whom it and not the township
appoints. Cities, even the smaller ones, are usually separated from the townships, while usually remaining members
of the counties, except where the city is made a county by
itself. Of villages and other minor municipalities there are
various forms in different States. The principles which
govern these organizations are generally the same; the details are infinite, and incapable of being summarized here.
Of minor incorporated bodies, therefore, I say no more.

Chapter XXXIV

CITY GOVERNMENT

THE growth of great cities has been among the most significant and least fortunate changes in the character of the population of the United States during the century that has passed since 1787. The census of 1790 showed only thirteen cities with more than 5000, and none with more than 40,000 inhabitants. In 1900 there were 38 exceeding 100,000, 838 over 5000. The ratio of persons living in cities exceeding 8000 inhabitants to the total population was, in 1790, 3.3 to every 100, in 1840, 8.5, in 1880, 22.5. And this change has gone on with accelerated speed, notwithstanding the enormous extension of settlement over the vast regions of the West. Needless to say that a still larger and increasing proportion of the wealth of the country is gathered into the larger cities. Their government is therefore a matter of high concern to America.

We find in all the larger cities:

A mayor, head of the executive, and elected directly by the voters within the city.

Certain executive officers or boards, some directly elected by the city voters, others nominated by the mayor or chosen by the city legislature.

A legislature, consisting usually of two, but sometimes of one chamber, directly elected by the city voters.

Judges, usually elected by the city voters, but sometimes appointed by the State.

What is this but the frame of a State government applied to the smaller area of a city? The mayor is by far the most conspicuous figure in city governments, much more important than the mayor of an English or Irish borough, or the provost of a Scotch one. He holds office, sometimes for one year, but now more frequently for two, three, or even five years. In some cities he is not reeligible. He is directly elected by the people of the whole city, and is usually not a member of the city legislature. He has, almost everywhere, a veto on all ordinances passed by that legislature, which, however, can be overridden by a two-thirds majority. In many cities he appoints some among the heads of departments and administrative boards, though usually the approval of the legislature or of one branch of it is required. Quite recently some city charters have gone so far as to make him generally responsible for all the departments, though limiting his initiative by the right of the legislature to give or withhold supplies, and making him liable to impeachment for misfeasance. He receives a considerable salary, varying with the size of the city, but sometimes reaching $10,000. It rests with him, as the chief executive officer, to provide for the public peace, to quell riots, and, if necessary, to call out the militia. He often exerts a pretty wide discretion as to the enforcement of the law; he may, for instance, put in force Sunday closing acts or regulations, or omit to do so.

The practical work of administration is carried on by a number of departments, sometimes under one head, sometimes constituted as boards or commissions. The most important of these are directly elected by the people, for a term of one, two, three, or four years. Some, however, are chosen by the city legislature, some by the mayor with the approval of the legislature or its upper chamber. In most cities the chief executive officers have been disconnected from one another, owing no common allegiance, except that which their financial dependence on the city legislature involves, and communicating less with the city legislature as a whole than with its committees, each charged with some one branch of administration, and each apt to job it.

Education has been generally treated as a distinct matter, with which neither the mayor nor the legislature has been suffered to meddle. It is committed to a Board of Education, whose members are separately elected by the people, or, as in New York, appointed by the mayor, and levy (though they do not themselves collect) a separate tax, and have an executive staff of their own at their disposal.

The city legislature usually consists in small cities of one chamber, in large ones of two, the upper of which generally bears the name of the Board of Aldermen, the lower that of the Common Council. All are elected by the citizens, generally in wards, but the upper house occasionally by districts or on what is called a " general ticket," *i. e.,* a vote over the whole city. Usually the common council is elected for one year, or at most for two years, the upper chamber frequently for a longer period. Both are usually unpaid in the smaller cities, sometimes paid in the larger. All city legislation, that is to say, ordinances, by-laws, and votes of money from the city treasury, are passed by the council or councils, subject in many cases to the mayor's veto. Except in a few cities governed by very recent charters, the councils have some control over at least the minor officials. Such control is exercised by committees, a method borrowed from the State and national legislatures, and suggested by the same reasons of convenience which have established it there, but proved by experience to have the evils of secrecy and irresponsibility as well as that of disconnecting the departments from one another.

The city judges are in so far a part of the municipal government that in most of the larger cities they are elected by the citizens, like the other chief officers. There are usually several superior judges, chosen for terms of five years and upwards, and a larger number of police judges or justices, generally for shorter terms. Occasionally, however, the State has prudently reserved to itself the appointment of judges.

It need hardly be said that all the above officers, from the mayor and judges downwards, are, like State officers, elected by manhood suffrage. Their election is usually made to coincide with that of State officers, perhaps also of Federal Congressmen. This saves expense and trouble. But as it not only bewilders the voter in his choice of men by distracting his attention between a large number of candidates and places, but also confirms the tendency, already strong, to vote for city officers on party lines, there has of late years been a movement in some few spots to have the municipal elections fixed for a different date from that of State or Federal elections, so that the undistracted and nonpartisan thought of the citizens may be given to the former.

At present the disposition to run and vote for candidates according to party is practically universal, although the duty of party loyalty is deemed less binding than in State or Federal elections. When both the great parties put forward questionable men, a nonpartisan list, or so-called " citizens' ticket," may be run by a combination of respectable men of both parties. Sometimes this attempt succeeds. However, though the tenets of Republicans and Democrats have absolutely nothing to do with the conduct of city affairs, though the sole object of the election, say of a city comptroller or auditor, may be to find an honest man of good business habits, four-fifths of the electors in nearly all cities give little thought to the personal qualifications of the candidates, and vote the " straight ticket."

The functions of city governments may be distributed into three groups—(a) those which are delegated by the State out of its general coercive and administrative powers, including the police power, the granting of licenses, the execution of laws relating to adulteration and explosives; (*b*) those which though done under general laws are properly matters of local charge and subject to local regulation, such as education and the care of the poor; and (*c*) those which are not so much of a political as of a purely business order, such as the paving and cleansing of streets, the maintenance of proper drains, the provision of water and light. All three sets of functions are dealt with by American legislation in the same way, and are alike given to officials and a legislature elected by persons of whom a large part pay no direct taxes. Education, however, is usually detached from the general city government and entrusted to a separate authority.

Taxes in cities, as in rural districts, are levied upon personal as well as real property; and the city tax is collected along with the county tax and State tax by the same collectors. Taxes are usually so much higher in the larger cities than in the country districts or smaller municipalities, that there is a strong tendency for rich men to migrate from the city to the suburbs to escape the city collector.

Pension Bureau, Washington, D. C.

Chapter XXXV

THE WORKING OF CITY GOVERNMENTS

TWO tests of practical efficiency may be applied to the government of a city: What does it provide for the people, and what does it cost the people? Space fails me to apply in detail the former of these tests, by showing what each city does or omits to do for its inhabitants; so I must be content with observing that in the United States generally constant complaints are directed against the bad paving and cleansing of the streets, the non-enforcement of the laws forbidding gambling and illicit drinking, and in some places against the sanitary arrangements and management of public buildings and parks.

The other test, that of expense, is easily applied. Both the debt and the taxation of American cities have risen with unprecedented rapidity, and now stand at an alarming figure. They have grown more swiftly than the population, and although it is true that much of this debt is represented by permanent improvements, yet for another large, and in some cities far larger, part there is nothing to show; it is due to simple waste or to malversation on the part of the municipal authorities.

There is no denying that the government of cities is the one conspicuous failure of the United States. The deficiencies of the national government tell but little for evil on the welfare of the people. The faults of the State governments are insignificant compared with the extravagance, corruption, and mismanagement which mark the administrations of most of the great cities. For these evils are not confined to one or two cities. There is not a city with a population exceeding 200,000 where the poison germs have not sprung into a vigorous life; and in some of the smaller ones, down to 70,000, it needs no microscope to note the results of their growth. Even in cities of the third rank similar phenomena may occasionally be discerned.

For evils which appear wherever a large population is densely aggregated, there must be some general and widespread causes. What are these causes? The party system has, not perhaps created, but certainly enormously aggravated them, and impressed on them their specific type. The chief sources of the malady, and the chief remedies that have been suggested for or applied to it have been summed up by the New York commissioners of 1876 appointed " to devise a plan for the government of cities in the State of New York," as follows:

1. The accumulation of a permanent municipal debt.

2. The excessive increase of the annual expenditure for ordinary purposes.

They suggest the following as the causes:

1. Incompetent and unfaithful governing boards and officers. As a corollary, corrupt promises must be redeemed by offices and contracts.

2. The introduction of State and national politics into municipal affairs.

" This obstacle to the union of good citizens paralyzes all ordinary efforts for good government."

3. The assumption by the legislature of the direct control of local affairs.

This last-mentioned cause of evil is no doubt a departure from the principle of local popular control and responsibility on which State governments and rural local governments have been based. It is a dereliction which has brought its punishment with it. But the resulting mischiefs have been immensely aggravated by the vices of the legislatures in a few of the States, such as New York and Pennsylvania. As regards the two former causes, they are largely due to what is called the Spoils System, whereby office becomes the reward of party service, and the whole machinery of party government made to serve, as its main object, the getting and keeping of places. Now the Spoils System, with the party machinery which it keeps oiled and greased and always working at high pressure, is far more potent and pernicious in great cities than in country districts. For in great cities we find an ignorant multitude, largely composed of recent immigrants, untrained in self-government; we find a great proportion of the voters paying no direct taxes, and therefore feeling no interest in moderate taxation and economical administration; we find able citizens absorbed in their private businesses, cultivated citizens unusually sensitive to the vulgarities of practical politics, and both sets therefore specially unwilling to sacrifice their time and tastes and comfort in the struggle with sordid wirepullers and noisy demagogues. In great cities the forces that attack and pervert democratic government are exceptionally numerous, the defensive forces that protect it exceptionally ill-placed for resistance. Satan has turned his heaviest batteries on the weakest part of the ramparts.

Besides these three causes on which the commissioners dwell, and the effects of which are felt in the great cities of other States as well as of New York, though perhaps to a less degree, there are what may be called mechanical defects in the structure of municipal governments, whose nature may be gathered from the account given in the last chapter. There is a want of methods for fixing public responsibility on the governing persons and bodies. The mayor can throw it on to the legislative body, and each branch of that on to the other. The various boards and officials have generally had little intercommunication; and the fact that some of them were directly elected by the people made these feel themselves independent both of the mayor and the city legislature. The mere multiplication of elective posts distracted the attention of the people, and deprived the voting at the polls of its efficiency as a means of reproof or commendation.

The remedies proposed by the New York commission were the following:

1. A restriction of the power of the State legislature to interfere by special legislation with municipal governments or the conduct of municipal affairs.

2. The holding of municipal elections at a different period of the year from State and national elections.

3. The vesting of the legislative powers of municipalities in two bodies: A board of aldermen, elected by the ordinary [manhood] suffrage, to be the common council of each city. A board of finance of from six to fifteen members, elected by voters who had for two years paid an annual tax or a rent. This board of finance was to have a practically exclusive control of the taxation and expenditure of each city.

4. Limitations on the borrowing powers of the municipality.

5. An extension of the general control and appointing power of the mayor, the mayor being himself subject to removal for cause by the governor of the State.

Among the other reforms in city government which I find canvassed in America are the following:

1. Civil service reform, i. e., the establishment of examinations as a test for admission to posts under the city, and the bestowal of these posts for a fixed term of years, or generally during good behavior.

2. The lengthening of the terms of service of the mayor and the heads of departments, so as to give them a

more assured position and diminish the frequency of elections.

3. The vesting of almost autocratic executive power in the mayor and restriction of the city legislature to purely legislative work and the voting of supplies.

4. The election of a city legislature, or one branch of it, or of a school committee, on a general ticket instead of by wards.

5. The limitation of taxing powers and borrowing powers by reference to the assessed value of the taxable property within the city.

Such restrictions are now often found embodied in State constitutions, and have, so far as I could ascertain, generally diminished the evil they are aimed at.

The question of city government is that which chiefly occupies practical publicists, and which newspapers and magazines incessantly discuss, because it is admittedly the weak point of the country. That adaptability of the institutions to the people and their conditions, which judicious strangers admire in the United States, and that consequent satisfaction of the people with their institutions, which contrasts so agreeably with the discontent of European nations, is wholly absent as regards municipal administration. Wherever there is a large city there are loud complaints, and Americans who deem themselves in other respects a model for the Old World are in this respect anxious to study Old World models, those particularly which the cities of Great Britain present. The best proof of dissatisfaction is to be found in the frequent changes of system and method. The newer frames of government are an improvement upon the older. Rogues are less audacious. Good citizens are more active. Party spirit is less and less permitted to dominate and pervert municipal politics,

Chapter XXXVI

POLITICAL PARTIES AND THEIR HISTORIES

IN America the great moving forces are the parties. The government counts for less than in Europe, the parties count for more; and the fewer have become their principles and the fainter their interest in those principles, the more perfect has become their organization. Although the early colonists carried with them across the sea some of the habits of English political life, and others may have been subsequently imitated from the old country, the parties of the United States are pure home growth, developed by the circumstances of the nation.

In the United States, the history of party begins with the Constitutional Convention of 1787 at Philadelphia. In its debates and discussions on the drafting of the Constitution there were revealed two opposite tendencies, which soon afterward appeared on a larger scale in the State conventions, to which the new instrument was submitted for acceptance. These were the centrifugal and centripetal tendencies—a tendency to maintain both the freedom of the individual citizen and the independence in legislation, in administration, in jurisdiction, indeed in everything except foreign policy and national defense, of the several States; an opposite tendency to subordinate the States to the nation and vest large powers in the central Federal authority. These tendencies found occasions for combating one another, not only in foreign policy and in current legislation, but also in the construction and application of the Constitution. The advocates of a central national authority had begun to receive the name of Federalists, and to act pretty constantly together; opposed to them were the Republicans.

Thus two parties grew up with tenets, leaders, impulse, sympathies, and hatreds, hatreds which soon became so bitter as not to spare the noble and dignified figure of Washington himself. At first the Federalists or centralizing party had the best of it. But they never recovered from the blow given in the election of 1800.

This period (1788-1824) may be said to constitute the first act in the drama of American party history. The people, accustomed hitherto to care only for their several commonwealths, learn to value and to work their new national institutions. Differences of view and feeling give rise to parties, yet parties are formed by no means solely on the basis of general principles, but owe much to the influence of prominent personalities, of transient issues, of local interests or prejudices. One remark is, however, needed as to the view which each party took of the Constitution. Although the Federalists were in general the advocates of a loose and liberal construction of the fundamental instrument, because such a construction opened a wider sphere to Federal power, they were ready, whenever their local interests stood in the way, to resist Congress and the Executive, alleging that the latter were overstepping their jurisdiction. On the other hand, the Republicans did not hesitate to stretch to their utmost, when they were themselves in power, all the authority which the Constitution could be construed to allow to the Executive and the Federal government generally.

The second period in the annals of American parties, which extends from about 1820 to 1856, includes the rise and fall of the Whig party. Most of the controversies which filled it have become matter for history only. But three large results, besides the general democratization of politics, stand out. One is the detachment of the United States from the affairs of the Old World. Another is the growth of a sense of national life, especially in the Northern and Western States, along with the growth at the same time of a secessionist spirit among the slaveholders. And the third is the development of the complex machinery of party organization, with the adoption of the principle on which that machinery so largely rests, that public office is to be enjoyed only by the adherents of the President for the time being.

The election of 1876 marks the close of the third period, which embraces the rise and overwhelming predominance of the Republican party. The old aims were accomplished, but new ones had not yet been substituted. Similarly the Democratic party had discharged its mission. The old parties still stood as organizations, and still claimed to be the exponents of principles. But their respective principles had, however, little direct application to the questions which confronted and divided the nation.

Two permanent oppositions may, I think, be discerned running through the history of the parties, sometimes openly recognized, sometimes concealed by the urgency of a transitory question. One of these is the opposition between a centralized or unified and a federalized government. In America the Federal form of government has made this permanent and natural opposition specially conspicuous. The latter has been the watchword of the Democratic party. The former was seldom distinctly avowed, but was generally in fact represented by the Federalists of the first period, the Whigs of the second, and the Republicans of the third.

The other opposition, though it goes deeper and is more pervasive, has been less clearly marked in America, and less consciously admitted by Americans themselves. It is the opposition between the tendency which makes some men prize the freedom of the individual as the first of social goods, and that which disposes others to insist on checking and regulating his impulses. The opposition of these two tendencies, the love of Liberty and the love of Order, is permanent and necessary, because it springs from differences in the intellect and feelings of men which one finds in all countries and at all epochs.

Each of these tendencies found among the fathers of the American Republic a brilliant and characteristic representative. Hamilton, who had a low opinion of mankind, but a gift and a passion for large constructive statesmanship, went so far in his advocacy of a strong government as to be suspected of wishing to establish a monarchy after the British pattern. Jefferson carried further than any other person set in an equally responsible place has ever done, his faith that government is either needless or an evil, and that with enough liberty, everything will go well.

Since 1876 American political parties have divided on three chief questions—the tariff, money, and imperialism, and yet the divisions have not been so great in fact as in protestation. The tariff question apparently ended for a time with the defeat of the Democrats in 1892; free silver was fought out and defeated in the elections of 1896 and 1900; imperialism may still be called a live issue. As time goes on, both parties seem to recede from advanced positions and take attitudes closer to each other. It cannot be charged, however, on the American parties that they have drawn toward one another by forsaking their old principles. It is time that has changed the circumstances of the country, and made those old principles inapplicable. The duty of a great party is to face these, to find answers and remedies, applying to the facts of the hour the doctrines it has lived by, so far as they are still applicable, and when they have ceased to be applicable, thinking out new doctrines conformable to the main principles and tendencies which it represents. This is a work to be accomplished by its ruling minds, while the habit of party loyalty to the leaders powerfully serves to diffuse through the mass of followers the conclusions of the leaders and the reasonings they have employed.

Chapter XXXVII

NOMINATING CONVENTIONS

IN every American election there are two acts of choice, two periods of contest. The first is the selection of the candidates from within the party by the party; the other is the struggle between the parties for the place. Frequently the former of these is more important, more keenly fought over, than the latter, for there are many districts in which the predominance of one party is so marked that its candidate is sure of success, and therefore the choice of a candidate is virtually the choice of the officer or representative.

The process of nominations is similar in every State of the Union, and through all elections to office, from the lowest to the highest, from that of common councilman for a city ward up to that of President of the United States. But, of course, the higher the office, and the larger the area over which the election extends, the greater are the efforts made to secure the nomination, and the hotter the passions it excites.

Like most political institutions, the system of nominating the President by a popular convention is the result of a long process of evolution.

In the first two elections, those of 1789 and 1792, there was no need for nominations of candidates, because the whole nation wished and expected George Washington to be elected. So too, when in 1796 Washington declared his retirement, the dominant feeling of one party was for John Adams, that of the other for Thomas Jefferson, and nobody thought of setting out formally what was so generally understood.

In 1800, however, the year of the fourth election, there was somewhat less unanimity. Jefferson and Adams were both expected to run again for President. For the Vice Presidency the Republicans called a congressional caucus. It was a small meeting and a secret meeting, but it is memorable not only as the first congressional caucus, but as the first attempt to arrange in any way a party nomination.

In 1804 a more regular gathering for the same purpose was held, and so down to 1816. But the objections which were from the first made to this action of the party in Congress, as being an arrogant usurpation of the rights of the people—for no one dreamed of leaving freedom to the Presidential electors—gained rather than lost strength on each successive occasion, so much so that in 1820 the few who met made no nomination, and in 1824, out of the Democratic members of both Houses of Congress summoned to the "nominating caucus," as it was called, only sixty-six attended, many of the remainder having announced their disapproval of the practice. The nominee of this caucus came in only third at the polls, and this failure gave the *coup de grâce* to a plan which the leveling tendencies of the time, and the disposition to refer everything to the arbitrament of the masses, would in any case have soon extinguished. No congressional caucus was ever again held for the choice of candidates.

A new method, however, was not at once discovered. In 1828 Jackson was recommended as candidate by the legislature of Tennessee and by a number of popular gatherings in different places, while his opponents accepted, without any formal nomination, the then President, J. Q. Adams, as their candidate. In 1831, however, and again in 1832, assemblies were held by two great parties (the Anti-Masons and the National Republicans, afterward called Whigs) consisting of delegates from most of the States; and each of these conventions nominated its candidates for the Presidency and Vice Presidency. A third "national convention" of young men, which met later in 1832, adopted the Whig nominations, and added to them a series of ten resolutions, constituting the first political platform ever put forth by a nominating body. The friends of Jackson followed suit by holding their convention which nominated him and Van Buren. For the election of 1836, a similar convention was held by the Jacksonian Democrats, none by their opponents. This precedent has been followed in every subsequent contest, so that the national nominating conventions of the great parties are now as much a part of the regular machinery of politics as the election rules contained in the Constitution itself. The establishment of the system coincides with and represents the complete social democratization of politics in Jackson's time and suits both the professionals and the ordinary citizen.

Thus from 1789 till 1800 there were no formal nominations; from 1800 till 1824, nominations were made by congressional caucuses; from 1824 till 1840, nominations irregularly made by State legislatures and popular meetings were gradually ripening toward the method of a special gathering of delegates from the whole country. This last plan has held its ground from 1840 till the present day, and is so exactly conformable to the political habits of the people that it is not likely soon to disappear.

Its perfection, however, was not reached at once. The early conventions were to a large extent mass meetings. The later and present ones are regularly-constituted representative bodies, composed exclusively of delegates, each of whom has been duly elected at a party meeting in his own State, and brings with him his credentials.

The Constitution provides that each State shall choose as many Presidential electors as it has persons representing it in Congress, *i. e.,* two electors to correspond to the two Senators from each State, and as many more as the State sends members to the House of Representatives.

Now in the nominating convention each State is allowed twice as many delegates as it has electoral votes. The delegates are chosen by local conventions in their several States, *viz.,* two for each congressional district by the party convention of that district, and four for the whole State (called delegates-at-large) by the State convention. As each convention is composed of delegates from primaries, it is the composition of the primaries which determines that of the local conventions, and the composition of the local conventions which determines that of the national. To every delegate there is added a person called his "alternate." Respecting the freedom of the delegate to vote for whom he will, there have been differences both of doctrine and of practice. Sometimes the local or State convention instructs how to vote, but often these instructions are broken.

Each State delegation has its chairman and is expected to keep together during the convention. Each delegation votes by its chairman, who announces how his delegates vote; but if his report is challenged the roll of delegates is called, and they vote individually. Whether the votes of a State delegation shall be given solid for the aspirant whom the majority of the delegation favors, or by the delegates individually according to their preferences, is a point which has excited bitter controversy. The present practice of the Republican party (so settled in 1876 and again in 1880) allows the delegates to vote individually, even when they have been instructed by a State convention to cast a solid vote. The Democratic party, on the other hand, sustains any such instruction given to the delegation, and records the vote of all the State delegates for the aspirant whom the majority among them approve. This is the so-called Unit

Rule. If, however, the State convention has not imposed the unit rule, the delegates vote individually.

For the sake of keeping up party life in the Territories and in the Federal District of Columbia, delegates from them are admitted to the national convention, although the Territories and District have no votes in a Presidential election. Delegations of States which are known to be in the hands of the opposite party, and whose preference of one aspirant to another will not really tell upon the result of the Presidential election, are admitted to vote equally with the delegations of the States sure to go for the party which holds the convention. This arrangement is justified on the ground that it sustains the interest and energy of the party in States where it is in a minority. But it permits the choice to be determined by districts whose own action will not tell in any way on the election itself.

So much for the composition of the national convention; we may now go on to describe its proceedings.

It is held in the summer immediately preceding a Presidential election, usually in June or July, the election falling in November. A large city is always chosen, in order to obtain adequate hotel accommodation, and easy railroad access.

Business begins by the " calling of the convention to order " by the chairman of the national party committee. Then a temporary chairman is nominated, and, if opposed, voted on, the vote sometimes giving an indication of the respective strength of the factions present. Then the secretaries and clerks are appointed, and the rules which are to govern the business are adopted. After this, the committees, particularly those on credentials and resolutions, are nominated, and the convention adjourns till their report can be presented.

The next sitting usually opens, after the customary

prayer, with the appointment of the permanent chairman, who opens the proceedings with a speech. Then the report of the committee on resolutions (if completed) is presented. It contains what is called the platform, a long series of resolutions embodying the principles and programme of the party, which has usually been so drawn as to conciliate every section, and avoid or treat with prudent ambiguity those questions on which opinion within the party is divided.

Next follows the nomination of aspirants for the post of party candidate. The roll of States is called, and when a State is reached to which an aspirant intended to be nominated belongs, a prominent delegate from that State mounts the platform, and proposes him in a speech extolling his merits and sometimes indirectly disparaging the other aspirants. Another delegate seconds the nomination, sometimes a third follows; and then the roll-call goes on till all the States have been dispatched, and all the aspirants nominated. The average number of nominations is seven or eight; it rarely exceeds twelve.

Thus the final stage is reached, for which all else has been but preparation—that of balloting between the aspirants. The clerks call the roll of States from Alabama to Wyoming, and as each is called the chairman of its delegation announces the votes, e. g., six for A, five for B, three for C, unless, of course, under the unit rule, the whole vote is cast for that one aspirant whom the majority of the delegation supports. When all have voted, the totals are made up and announced. If one competitor has an absolute majority of the whole number voting, according to the Republican rule, a majority of two-thirds of the number voting, according to the Democratic rule, he has been duly chosen, and nothing remains but formally to make his nomination unanimous. If, however, as has usually happened of late years, no one obtains the requisite majority, the roll is called again, in order that individual delegates and delegations (if the unit rule prevails) may have the opportunity of changing their votes; and the process is repeated until some one of the aspirants put forward has received the required number of votes. Sometimes many roll-calls take place.

When a candidate for the Presidency has been thus found, the convention proceeds to similarly determine its candidate for the Vice-Presidency. The work of the convention is then complete, and votes of thanks to the chairman and other officials conclude the proceedings. The two nominees are now entitled to the support of their parties, but not necessarily sure to receive it, for party discipline cannot compel an individual voter to cast his ballot for the party nominee. All that the convention can do is to recommend the candidate to the party; all that opinion can do is to brand as a kicker or bolter whoever breaks away; all that the local party organization can do is to strike the bolter off its lists. But how stands it, the reader will ask, with the delegates who have been present in the convention, have had their chance of carrying their man, and have been beaten? Are they not held absolutely bound to support the candidate chosen?

This is a question which has excited much controversy. The impulse and effort of the successful majority has always been to impose such an obligation on the defeated minority, and the chief motive which has prevented its always being formally enforced by a rule or resolution of the convention has been the fear that it might precipate hostilities, might induce men of independent character, or strongly opposed to some particular aspirant, to refuse to attend as delegates, or to secede early in the proceedings when they saw that a person whom they disapproved was likely to win.

Chapter XXXVIII

HOW PUBLIC OPINION RULES IN AMERICA

OF all the experiments which America has made, public opinion is that which best deserves study, for she has shown more boldness in trusting it, in recognizing and giving effect to it, than has yet been shown elsewhere. Towering over Presidents and State governors, over Congresses and State legislatures, over conventions and the vast machinery of party, public opinion stands out, in the United States, as the great source of power, the master of servants who tremble before it.

Congress sits for two years only. It is strictly limited by the Constitution, which is a fundamental law placed out of its reach, and by the coexistence of the State governments, which the Constitution protects. It has (except by way of impeachment) no control over the Federal Executive, who is directly named by and responsible to the people. So too the State legislatures sit for short periods, do not appoint the State Executives, are hedged in by the prohibitions of the State constitutions. The people frequently legislate directly by enacting or altering a constitution. The principle of popular sovereignty could hardly be expressed more unmistakably. Allowing for the differences to which the vast size of the country gives rise, the mass of citizens may be deemed as directly the supreme power in the United States as the Assembly was at Athens or Syracuse. The only check on the mass is that which they themselves have imposed, and which the ancient democracies did not possess, the difficulty of changing a rigid Constitution. And this difficulty is serious only as regards the Federal Constitution.

A consideration of the nature of the State governments as of the national government will show that legal theory as well as popular self-confidence gives birth to this rule of opinion. Supreme power resides in the whole mass of citizens. They have prescribed, in the strict terms of a legal document, the form of government. They alone have the right to change it, and that only in a particular way. They have committed only a part of their sovereignty to their executive and legislative agents, reserving the rest to themselves. Hence their will, or in other words, public opinion, is constantly felt by these agents to be, legally as well as practically, the controlling authority. In England, Parliament is the nation, not merely by a legal fiction, but because the nation looks to Parliament only, having neither reserved any authority to itself nor bestowed any elsewhere. In America, Congress is not the nation, and does not claim to be so.

The ordinary functions and business of government, the making of laws, the imposing of taxes, the interpretation of laws, and their execution, the administration of justice, the conduct of foreign relations, are parceled out among a number of bodies and persons whose powers are so carefully balanced and touch at so many points that there is a constant risk of conflicts, even of deadlocks. Some of the difficulties thence arising are dealt with by the courts, as questions of the interpretation of the Constitution. But in many cases the intervention of the courts, which can act only in a suit between parties, comes too late to deal with the matter, which may be an urgent one; and in some cases there is nothing for the courts to decide, because each of the conflicting powers is within its legal right. The Senate, for instance, may refuse the measures which the House thinks necessary. The President may veto bills passed by both Houses, and the Houses may not have a two-thirds majority to pass them over his veto. Congress may urge the President to adopt a certain course of action, and the President may refuse. The President may propose a treaty to the Senate and the Senate may reject it. In such cases there is a stoppage of governmental action which may involve loss to the country. The master, however, is at hand to settle the quarrels of his servants. If the question be a grave one, and the mind of the country clear upon it, public opinion throws its weight into one or other scale, and its weight is decisive. Should opinion be nearly balanced, it is no doubt difficult to ascertain, till the next election arrives, which of many discordant cries is really the prevailing voice. This difficulty must, in a large country, where frequent plebiscites are impossible, be endured, and it may be well, when the preponderance of opinion is not great, that serious decisions should not be quickly taken. The general truth remains that a system of government by checks and balances specially needs the presence of an arbiter to incline the scale in favor of one or other of the balanced authorities, and that public opinion must therefore be more frequently invoked and more constantly active in America than in other countries.

Those who invented this machinery of checks and balances were anxious not so much to develop public opinion as to resist and build up breakwaters against it. No men were less revolutionary in spirit than the heroes of the American Revolution. They made a revolution in the name of Magna Charta and the Bill of Rights: they were penetrated by a sense of the dangers incident to democracy. As an able American writer says, " the prevalent conception of popular opinion was that it was aggressive, revolutionary, unreasoning, passionate, futile, and a breeder of mob violence." We may presently inquire whether this conception has been verified. Meantime be it noted that the efforts made in 1787 to divide authority and, so to speak, force the current of the popular will into many small channels instead of permitting it to rush down one broad bed, have really tended to exalt public opinion above the regular legally-appointed organs of government. Each of these organs is too small to form opinion, too narrow to express it, too weak to give effect to it. It grows up not in Congress, not in State legislatures, not in those great conventions which frame platforms and choose candidates, but at large among the people. It is expressed in voices everywhere. It rules as a prevading and impalpable power, like the ether which, as physicists say, passes through all things. It binds all the parts of the complicated system together and gives them whatever unity of aim and action they possess.

In the United States public opinion is the opinion of the whole nation, with little distinction of social classes. The politicians, including the members of Congress and of State legislatures, are, perhaps not (as Americans sometimes insinuate) below, yet certainly not above the average level of their constituents. They find no difficulty in keeping touch with outside opinion. Washington or Albany may corrupt them, but not in the way of modifying their political ideas. They do not aspire to the function of forming opinion. They are like the Eastern slave who says " I hear and obey." Nor is there any one class or set of men, or any one " social layer," which more than another originates ideas and builds up political doctrine for the mass. The opinion of the nation is the resultant of the views, not of a number of classes, but of a multitude of individuals, diverse, no doubt, from one another, but, for the purpose of politics far less diverse than if they were members of groups defined by social rank or by property. The consequences are noteworthy. One is, that statesmen cannot, as in Europe, declare any sentiment, which they find telling on their friends or their opponents in politics to be confined to the rich, or to those occupied with government, and to be opposed to the general sentiment of the people. In America you cannot appeal from the classes to the masses. What the employer thinks, his workmen think. What the wholesale merchant feels, the retail storekeeper feels, and the poorer customers feel. Divisions of opinion are vertical and not horizontal. Obviously this makes opinion more easily ascertained, while increasing its force as a governing power, and gives the people, that is to say, all classes in the community, a clearer and stronger consciousness of being the rulers of their country than European peoples have. Every man knows that he is himself a part of the government, bound by duty as well as by self-interest to devote part of his time and thoughts to it. He may neglect this duty, but he admits it to be a duty. So the system of party organizations already described is built upon this theory; and as this system is more recent, and is the work of practical politicians, it is even better evidence of the general acceptance of the doctrine than are the provisions of Constitutions. Compare European countries, or compare the other states of the New World. In the so-called republics of Central and South America a small section of the inhabitants pursue politics, while the rest follow their ordinary vocations, indifferent to elections and *pronunciamentos* and revolutions. In Germany, and in the German and Slavonic parts of the Austro-Hungarian monarchy, people think of the government as a great machine which will go on, whether they put their hand to it or not, a few persons working it, and all the rest paying and looking on. The same thing is largely true of republican France, and of semi-republican Italy, where free government is still a novelty, and local self-government in its infancy. Even in England, though the seventy-five years that have passed over her since the great Reform Act have brought many new ideas with them, the ordinary voter is still far from feeling, as the American does, that the government is his own, and he individually responsible for its conduct.

APPENDIX

APPENDIX

I

FIRST CHARTER OF VIRGINIA, 1606

I. *JAMES,* by the Grace of God, King of *England, Scotland, France,* and *Ireland,* Defender of the Faith, &c WHEREAS our loving and well-disposed Subjects, Sir *Thomas Gates,* and Sir *George Somers,* Knights, *Richard Hackluit,* Prebendary of *Westminster,* and *Edward-Maria Wing-field, Thomas Hanham,* and *Ralegh Gilbert,* Esqrs. *William Parker,* and *George Popham,* Gentlemen, and divers others of our loving Subjects, have been humble Suitors unto us, that We would vouchsafe unto them our Licence to make Habitation, Plantation, and to deduce a Colony of sundry of our People into that Part of *America,* commonly called VIR-GINIA, and other Parts and Territories in *America,* either appertaining unto us, or which are not now actually possessed by any *Christian* Prince or People, situate, lying, and being all along the Sea Coasts, between four and thirty Degrees of *Northerly* Latitude from the Equinoctial Line, and five and forty Degrees of the same Latitude, and in the main Land between the same four and thirty and five and forty Degrees, and the Islands thereunto adjacent, or within one hundred Miles of the Coasts thereof;

II. And to that End, and for the more speedy Accomplishment of their said intended Plantation and Habitation there, are desirous to divide themselves into two several Colonies and Companies; The one consisting of certain Knights, Gentlemen, Merchants, and other Adventurers, of our City of *London* and elsewhere, which are, and from time to time shall be, joined unto them, which do desire to begin their Plantation and Habitation in some fit and convenient Place, between four and thirty and one and forty Degrees of the said Latitude, along the Coasts of *Virginia* and Coasts of *America* aforesaid, And the other consisting of sundry Knights, Gentlemen, Merchants, and other Adventurers, of our Cities of *Bristol* and *Exeter,* and of our Town of *Plimouth,* and of other Places, which do join themselves unto that Colony, which do desire to begin their Plantation and Habitation in some fit and convenient Place, between eight and thirty Degrees and five and forty Degrees of the said Latitude, all alongst the said Coast of *Virginia* and *America,* as that Coast lyeth;

III. We, greatly commending, and graciously accepting of, their Desires for the Furtherance of so noble a Work, which may, by the Providence of Almighty God, hereafter tend to the Glory of his Divine Majesty, in propagating of *Christian* Religion to such People, as yet live in Darkness and miserable Ignorance of the true Knowledge and Worship of God, and may in time bring the Infidels and Savages, living in those Parts, to human Civility, and to a settled and quiet Government; DO, by these our Letters Patents, graciously accept of, and agree to, their humble and well-intended Desires;

IV. And do therefore, for Us, our Heirs, and Successors, GRANT and agree, that the said Sir *Thomas Gates,* Sir *George Somers, Richard Hackluit,* and *Edward-Maria Wingfield,* Adventurers of and for our City of *London,* and all such others, as are, or shall be, joined unto them of that Colony, shall be called the *first Colony;* And they shall and may begin their said first Plantation and Habitation, at any Place upon the said Coast of *Virginia* and *America,* where they shall think fit and convenient, between the said four and thirty and one and forty Degrees of the said Latitude; And that they shall have all the Lands, Woods, Soil, Grounds, Havens, Ports, Rivers, Mines, Marshes, Waters, Fishings, Commodities, and Hereditaments whatsoever, from the said first Seat of their Plantation and Habitation by the Space of fifty Miles of *English* Statute Measure, and along the said Coast of *Virginia* and *America,* towards the *West* and *Southwest,* as the Coast lyeth, with all the Islands within one hundred Miles directly over against the same Sea Coast, And also all the Lands, Soil, Ground, Havens, Ports, Rivers, Mines, Minerals, Woods, Waters, Marshes, Fishings, Commodities and Hereditaments, whatsoever, from the said Place of their first Plantation and Habitation for the space of fifty like *English* Miles, all alongst the said Coast of *Virginia* and *America,* towards the *East* and *Northeast,* or towards the *North,* as the Coast lyeth, together with all the Islands within one hundred Miles, directly over against the said Sea Coast; And also all the Lands, Woods, Soil, Grounds, Havens, Ports, Rivers, Mines, Minerals, Marshes, Waters, Fishings, Commodities, and Hereditaments, whatsoever, from the same fifty Miles every way on the Sea Coast, directly into the main Land by the Space of one hundred like *English* Miles, And shall and may inhabit and remain there; And shall and may also build and fortify within any the same, for their better Safeguard and Defence, according to their best Discretion, and the Discretion of the Council of that Colony, And that no other of our Subjects shall be permitted, or suffered, to plant or inhabit behind, or on the Backside of them, towards the main Land, without the Express Licence or Consent of the Council of that Colony, thereunto in Writing first had and obtained;

V. And we do likewise, for Us, our Heirs, and Successors, by these Presents, GRANT and agree, that the said *Thomas Hanham*, and *Ralegh Gilbert, William Parker*, and *George Popham*, and all others of the Town of *Plimouth* in the County of *Devon*, or elsewhere, which are, or shall be, joined unto them of that Colony, shall be called the *second Colony;* And that they shall and may begin their said Plantation and Seat of their first Abode and Habitation, at any Place upon the said Coast of *Virginia* and *America*, where they shall think fit and convenient, between eight and thirty Degrees of the said Latitude, and five and forty Degrees of the same Latitude; And that they shall have all the Lands, Soils, Grounds, Havens, Ports, Rivers, Mines, Minerals, Woods, Marshes, Waters, Fishings, Commodities, and Hereditaments, whatsoever, from the first Seat of their Plantation and Habitation by the Space of fifty like *English* Miles, as is aforesaid, all alongst the said Coast of *Virginia* and *America*, towards the *West* and *Southwest*, or towards the *South*, as the Coast lyeth, and all the Islands within one hundred Miles, directly over against the said Sea Coast, (etc , etc., as above, Art IV.),

VI. Provided always, and our Will and Pleasure herein is, that the Plantation and Habitation of such of the said Colonies, as shall last plant themselves, as aforesaid, shall not be made within one hundred like *English* Miles of the other of them, that first began to make their Plantation, as aforesaid;

VII. And we do also ordain, establish, and agree, for Us, our Heirs, and Successors, that each of the said Colonies shall have a Council, which shall govern and order all Matters and Causes, which shall arise, grow, or happen, to or within the same several Colonies, according to such Laws, Ordinances, and Instructions, as shall be, in that behalf, given and signed with Our Hand or Sign Manual, and pass under the Privy Seal of our Realm of *England;* Each of which Councils shall consist of thirteen Persons, to be ordained, made, and removed, from time to time, according as shall be directed, and comprised in the same instructions; And shall have a several Seal, for all Matters that shall pass or concern the same several Councils, Each of which Seals shall have the King's Arms engraven on the one Side thereof, and his Portraiture on the other; And that the Seal for the Council of the said first Colony shall have engraven round about,

on the one Side, these Words; *Sigillum Regis Magnæ Britanniæ, Franciæ,
& Hiberniæ;* on the other Side this Inscription, round about, *Pro Concilio
primæ Coloniæ Virginiæ;* And the Seal for the Council of the said second
Colony shall also have engraven, round about the one Side thereof, the
aforesaid Words; *Sigillum Regis Magnæ, Britanniæ, Franciæ, & Hiberniæ;* and on the other Side; *Pro Concilio secundæ Coloniæ Virginiæ;*

VIII. And that also there shall be a Council established here in
England, which shall, in like Manner, consist of thirteen Persons, to be,
for that Purpose, appointed by Us, our Heirs, and Successors, which shall
be called our *Council of Virginia,* And shall, from time to time, have the
superior Managing and Direction, only of and for all Matters, that shall
or may concern the Government, as well of the said several Colonies, as
of and for any other Part or Place, within the aforesaid Precincts of four
and thirty and five and forty Degrees, above mentioned, Which Council
shall, in like manner, have a Seal, for Matters concerning the Council or
Colonies, with the like Arms and Portraiture, as aforesaid, with this Inscription, engraven round about on the one Side; *Sigillum Regis Magnæ
Britanniæ, Franciæ, & Hiberniæ;* and round about the other Side, *Pro
Concilio suo Virginiæ,*

IX. And moreover, we do GRANT and agree, for Us, our Heirs, and
Successors, that the said several Councils, of and for the said several Colonies, shall and lawfully may, by Virtue hereof, from time to time, without any Interruption of Us, our Heirs, or Successors, give and take Order,
to dig, mine, and search for all Manner of Mines of Gold, Silver, and
Copper, as well within any part of their said several Colonies, as for the
said main Lands on the Backside of the same Colonies; And to HAVE and
enjoy the Gold, Silver and Copper, to be gotten thereof, to the Use and
Behoof of the same Colonies, and the Plantations thereof, YIELDING therefore, to Us, our Heirs, and Successors, the fifth Part only of all the same
Gold and Silver, and the fifteenth Part of all the same Copper, so to be
gotten or had, as is aforesaid, without any other Manner or Profit or Account, to be given or yielded to Us, our Heirs, or Successors, for or in
Respect of the same;

X. And that they shall, or lawfully may, establish and cause to be
made a Coin, to pass current there between the People of those several
Colonies, for the more Ease of Traffick and Bargaining between and
amongst them and the Natives there, of such Metal, and in such Manner
and Form, as the said several Councils there shall limit and appoint;

XI. And we do likewise, for Us, our Heirs, and Successors, by these
Presents, give full Power and Authority to the said Sir *Thomas Gates,*

(etc.), and to every of them, and to the said several Companies, Plantations, and Colonies, that they, and every of them, shall and may, at all and every time and times hereafter, have, take, and lead in the said Voyage, and for and towards the said several Plantations and Colonies, and to travel thitherward, and to abide and inhabit there, in every the said Colonies and Plantations, such and so many of our Subjects, as shall willingly accompany them, or any of them, in the said Voyages and Plantations, With sufficient Shipping and Furniture of Armour, Weapons, Ordenance, Powder, Victual, and all other things, necessary for the said Plantations, and for their Use and Defence there PROVIDED always, that none of the said Persons be such, as shall hereafter be specially restrained by Us, our Heirs, and Successors,

XII. Moreover, we do, by these Presents, for Us, our Heirs, and Successors, GIVE AND GRANT Licence unto the said Sir *Thomas Gates,* (etc.), and to every of the said Colonies, that they, and every of them, shall and may, from time to time, and at all times for ever hereafter, for their several Defences, encounter, expulse, repel, and resist, as well by Sea as by Land, by all Ways and Means whatsoever, all and every such Person and Persons, as without the especial Licence of the said several Colonies and Plantations, shall attempt to inhabit within the said several Precincts and Limits of the said several Colonies and Plantations, or any of them, or that shall enterprise or attempt, at any time hereafter, the Hurt, Detriment, or Annoyance, of the said several Colonies or Plantations;

XIII. Giving and granting, by these Presents, unto the said Sir *Thomas Gates,* Sir *George Somers, Richard Hackluit, Edward-Maria Wingfield,* and their Associates of the said first Colony, and unto the said *Thomas Hanham, Ralegh Gilbert, William Parker,* and *George Popham,* and their Associates of the said second Colony, and to every of them, from time to time, and at all times for ever hereafter, Power and Authority to take and surprise, by all Ways and Means whatsoever, all and every Person and Persons, with their Ships, Vessels, Goods, and other Furniture, which shall be found trafficking, into any Harbour or Harbours, Creek or Creeks, or Place, within the Limits or Precincts of the said several Colonies and Plantations, not being of the same Colony, until such time, as they, being of any Realms or Dominions under our Obedience, shall pay, or agree to pay, to the Hands of the Treasurer of that Colony, within whose Limits and Precincts they shall so traffick, two and a half upon every Hundred, of any thing, so by them trafficked, bought, or sold; And being Strangers, and not Subjects under our Obeysance, until they shall pay five upon every Hundred, of such Wares and Merchandise, as they shall traffick, buy, or sell, within the Precincts of the said several Colonies, wherein they shall so traffick, buy, or sell, as aforesaid, WHICH, Sums of Money, or Benefit, as aforesaid, for and during the Space of one and twenty Years, next ensuing the Date hereof, shall be wholly emploied to the Use, Benefit, and Behoof of the said several Plantations, where such Traffick shall be made; And after the said one and twenty Years ended, the same shall be taken to the Use of Us, our Heirs, and Successors, by such Officers and Ministers, as by Us, our Heirs, and Successors, shall be thereunto assigned or appointed;

XIV. And we do further, by these Presents, for Us, our Heirs, and Successors, GIVE AND GRANT unto the said Sir *Thomas Gates,* Sir *George Somers, Richard Hackluit,* and *Edward-Maria Wingfield,* and to their Associates of the said first Colony and Plantation, and to the said *Thomas Hanham, Ralegh Gilbert, William Parker,* and *George Popham,* and their Associates of the said second Colony and Plantation, that they, and every of them, by their Deputies, Ministers, and Factors, may transport the Goods, Chattels, Armour, Munition, and Furniture, needful to be used by them, for their said Apparel, Food, Defence, or otherwise in Respect of the said Plantations, out of our Realms of *England* and *Ireland,* and all other our Dominions, from time to time, for and during the Time of seven Years, next ensuing the Date hereof, for the better Relief of the said several Colonies and Plantations, without any Custom, Subsidy, or other Duty, unto Us, our Heirs, or Successors, to be yielded or paid for the same,

XV Also we do, for Us, our Heirs, and Successors, DECLARE, by these Presents, that all and every the Persons, being our Subjects, which shall dwell and inhabit within every or any of the said several Colonies and Plantations, and every of their children, which shall happen to be born within any of the Limits and Precincts of the said several Colonies and Plantations, shall HAVE and enjoy all Liberties, Franchises, and Immunities, within any of our other Dominions, to all Intents and Purposes, as if they had been abiding and born, within this our Realm of *England,* or any other of our said Dominions;

XVI Moreover, our gracious Will and Pleasure is, and we do, by these Presents, for Us, our Heirs, and Successors, declare and set forth, that if any Person or Persons, which shall be of any of the said Colonies and Plantations, or any other, which shall traffick to the said Colonies and Plantations, or any of them, shall, at any time or times hereafter, transport any Wares, Merchandises, or Commodities, out of any of our Dominions, with a Pretence to land, sell, or otherwise dispose of the same, within any the Limits and Precincts of any the said Colonies and Plantations, and yet nevertheless, being at Sea, or after he hath landed the same within any of the said Colonies and Plantations, shall carry the same into any other Foreign Country, with a Purpose there to sell or dispose of the same, without the Licence of Us, our Heirs, and Successors, in that Behalf first had and obtained; That then, all the Goods and Chattels of such Person or Persons, so offending and transporting, together with the said Ship or Vessel, wherein such Transportation was made, shall be forfeited to Us, our Heirs, and Successors;

XVII Provided always, and our Will and Pleasure is, and we do hereby declare to all *Christian* Kings, Princes, and States, that if any Person or Persons, which shall hereafter be of any of the said several Colonies and Plantations, or any other, by his, their or any of their Licence and Appointment, shall, at any time or times hereafter, rob or spoil, by Sea or by Land, or do any Act of unjust and unlawful Hostility, to any the Subjects of Us, our Heirs, or Successors, or any the Subjects of any King, Prince, Ruler, Governor, or State, being then in League or Amity with Us, our Heirs, or Successors, and that upon such Injury, or upon just Complaint of such Prince, Ruler, Governor, or State, or their Subjects, We, our Heirs, or Successors, shall make open Proclamation, within any of the Ports of our Realm of *England,* commodious for that Purpose, That the said Person or Persons, having committed any such Robbery or Spoil, shall, within the Term to be limited by such Proclamations, make full Restitution or Satisfaction of all such Injuries done, so as the said Princes, or others, so complaining, may hold themselves fully satisfied and contented; And that, if the said Person or Persons, having committed such Robbery or Spoil, shall not make, or cause to be made, Satisfaction accordingly, within such Time so to be limited, That then it shall be lawful to Us, our Heirs, and Successors, to put the said Person or Persons, having committed such Robbery or Spoil, and their Procurers, Abetters, or Comforters, out of our Allegiance and Protection; And that it shall be lawful and free, for all Princes and others, to pursue with Hostility the said Offenders, and every of them, and their and every of their Procurers, Aiders, Abetters, and Comforters in that Behalf;

XVIII And Finally, we do, for Us, our Heirs, and Successors, GRANT and agree, to and with the said Sir *Thomas Gates,* Sir *George Somers, Richard Hackluit,* and *Edward-Maria Wingfield,* and all others of the said first Colony, that We, our Heirs, and Successors, upon Petition in that Behalf to be made, shall, by Letters-patent under the Great Seal of *England,* Give and Grant unto such Persons, their Heirs, and Assigns, as the Council of that Colony, or the most Part of them, shall, for that Purpose nominate and assign, all the Lands, Tenements, and Hereditaments, which shall be within the Precincts limited for that Colony, as is aforesaid, To be holden of Us, our Heirs, and Successors, as of our Manor at *East-Greenwich* in the County of *Kent,* in free and common Soccage only, and not in Capite;

XIX And do, in like Manner, Grant and agree, for Us, our Heirs, and Successors, to and with the said *Thomas Hanham, Ralegh Gilbert, William Parker,* and *George Popham,* and all others of the said second Colony, That We, our Heirs, and Successors, upon Petition in that Behalf to be made, shall, by Letters-patent under the Great Seal of *England,* Give and Grant unto such Persons, their Heirs, and Assigns, as the Council of that Colony, or the most Part of them, shall, for that Purpose, nominate and assign, all the Lands, Tenements, and Hereditaments, which shall be within the Precincts limited for that Colony, as is aforesaid, To be holden of Us, our Heirs, and Successors, as of our Manour of *East-Greenwich* in the County of *Kent,* in free and common Soccage only, and not in Capite;

XX All which Lands, Tenements, and Hereditaments, so to be passed by the said several Letters-patent, shall be sufficient Assurance from the said Patentees, so distributed and divided amongst the Undertakers for the Plantation of the said several Colonies, and such as shall make their Plantations in either of the said several Colonies, in such Manner and Form, and for such Estates, as shall be ordered and set down by the Council of the said Colony, or the most Part of them, respectively, within which the same Lands, Tenements, and Hereditaments shall lye or be; Although express Mention of the true yearly Value or Certainty of the Premises, or any of them, or of any other Gifts or Grants, by Us or any of our Progenitors or Predecessors, to the aforesaid Sir *Thomas Gates,* Knt. Sir *George Somers,* Knt *Richard Hackluit, Edward-Maria Wingfield, Thomas Hanham, Ralegh Gilbert, William Parker,* and *George Popham,* or any of them, heretofore made, in these Presents, is not made; Or any Statute, Act, Ordinance, or Provision, Proclamation, or Restraint, to the contrary hereof had, made, ordained, or any other Thing, Cause, or Matter whatsoever, in any wise notwithstanding In Witness Whereof we have caused these our Letters to be made Patents; Witness Ourself at *Westminster,* the tenth Day of *April,* in the fourth Year of our Reign of *England, France,* and *Ireland,* and of *Scotland* the nine and thirtieth.

II

THE MAYFLOWER COMPACT, 1620

In the name of God, Amen. We, whose names are underwritten, the loyal subjects of our dread sovereigne Lord, King James, by the grace of God, of Great Britaine, France, and Ireland king, defender of the faith, etc , having undertaken, for the glory of God, and advancement of the Christian faith, and honour of our king and country, a voyage to plant the first colony in the Northerne parts of Virginia, doe, by these presents solemnly and mutually in the presence of God, and one of another, covenant and combine ourselves together into a civill body politick, for our better ordering and preservation and furtherance of the ends aforesaid; and by virtue hereof to enact, constitute, and frame such just and equall laws, ordinances, acts, constitutions, and offices, from time to time, as shall be thought most meete and convenient for the generall good of the Colonie, unto which we promise all due submission and obedience. In Witness Whereof we have hereunder subscribed our names at Cap-Codd the 11 of November, in the year of the raigne of our sovereigne Lord, King James, of England, France, and Ireland, the eighteenth, and of Scotland the fiftie-fourth, Anno. Dom. 1620.

III

ARTICLES OF CONFEDERATION OF THE NEW ENGLAND COLONIES, 1643

Articles of Confederation between the Plantations under the Government of Massachusetts, the Plantations under the Government of New Plymouth, the Plantations under the Government of Connecticut, and the Government of New Haven with the Plantations in Combination therewith·

Whereas we all came into these parts of America with one and the same end and aim, namely, to advance the kingdom of our Lord Jesus Christ and to enjoy the liberties of the Gospel in purity with peace; and whereas in our settling (by a wise providence of God) we are further dispersed upon the sea coasts and rivers than was at first intended, so that we can not according to our desire with convenience communicate in one government and jurisdiction; and whereas we live encompassed with people of several nations and strange languages which hereafter may prove injurious to us or our posterity; and forasmuch as the natives have formerly committed sundry insolences and outrages upon several plantations of the English and have of late combined themselves against us; and seeing, by reason of those sad distractions in England (which they have heard of) and by which they know we are hindered from that humble way of seeking advice or reaping those comfortable fruits of protection which at other times we might well expect; we therefore do conceive it our bounden duty, without delay to enter into a present consociation amongst ourselves, for mutual help and strength in all our future concernments. That, as in nation and religion, so in other respects, we be and continue one according to the tenor and true meaning of the ensuing articles. 1. Wherefore it is fully agreed and concluded by and between the parties or jurisdictions above named, and they jointly and severally do by these presents agree and conclude, that they all be and henceforth be called by the name of the United Colonies of New England.

2. The said United Colonies, for themselves and their posterities, do jointly and severally hereby enter into a firm and perpetual league of friendship and amity, for offence and defence, mutual advice and succor upon all just occasions, both for preserving and propagating the truth and liberties of the Gospel, and for their own mutual safety and welfare.

3. It is further agreed that the plantations which at present are or hereafter shall be settled with[in] the limits of the Massachusetts shall be forever under the Massachusetts, and shall have peculiar jurisdiction among themselves in all cases, as an entire body. And that Plymouth, Connecticut, and New Haven shall each of them have like peculiar jurisdiction and government within their limits and in reference to the plantations which already are settled, or shall hereafter be erected, or shall settle within their limits, respectively; provided no other jurisdiction shall hereafter be taken in, as a distinct head or member of this confederation, nor shall any other plantation or jurisdicton in present being, and not already in combination or under the jurisdiction of any of these confederates, be received by any of them; nor shall any two of the confederates join in one jurisdiction without consent of the rest, which consent to be interpreted as is expressed in the 6 article ensuing.

4. It is by these confederates agreed, that the charge of all just wars, whether offensive or defensive, upon what part or member of this confederation soever they fall, shall both in men, provisions, and all other

disbursements be borne by all the parts of this confederation in different proportions according to their different abilities, in manner following: namely, that the commissioners for each jurisdiction from time to time, as there shall be occasion, bring a true account and number of all their males in every plantation, or any way belonging to or under their several jurisdictions, of what quality or condition soever they be, from 16 years old to 60, being inhabitants there; and that according to the different numbers which from time to time shall be found in each jurisdiction upon a true and just account, the service of men and all charges of the war be borne by the poll; each jurisdiction or plantation being left to their own just course and custom of rating themselves and people according to their different estates with due respects to their qualities and exemptions amongst themselves though the confederates take no notice of any such privilege. And that according to their different charge of each jurisdiction and plantation, the whole advantage of the war (if it please God so to bless their endeavours,) whether it be in lands, goods, or persons, shall be proportionably divided among the said confederates.

5. It is further agreed, that if these jurisdictions, or any plantation under or in combination with them, be invaded by any enemy whomsoever, upon notice and request of any 3 magistrates of that jurisdiction so invaded, the rest of the confederates, without any further meeting or expostulation, shall forthwith send aid to the confederate in danger, but in different proportions; namely, the Massachusetts an hundred men sufficiently armed and provided for such a service and journey, and each of the rest, forty-five so armed and provided, or any lesser number, if less be required according to this proportion. But if such confederate in danger may be supplied by their next confederates, not exceeding the number hereby agreed, they may crave help there, and seek no further for the present, the charge to be borne as in this article is expressed, and at the return to be victualled and supplied with powder and shot for their journey (if there be need) by that jurisdiction which employed or sent for them. But none of the jurisdictions to exceed these numbers till, by a meeting of the commissioners for this confederation, a greater aid appear necessary And this proportion to continue till upon knowledge of greater numbers in each jurisdiction, which shall be brought to the next meeting, some other proportion be ordered. But in any such case of sending men for present aid, whether before or after such order or alteration, it is agreed that at the meeting of the commissioners for this confederation, the cause of such war or invasion be duly considered; and if it appear that the fault lay in the parties so invaded then that jurisdiction

or plantation make just satisfaction, both to the invaders whom they have injured, and bear all the charges of the war themselves, without requiring any allowance from the rest of the confederates towards the same. And further, that if any jurisdiction see any danger of invasion approaching, and there be time for a meeting, that in such a case 3 magistrates of that jurisdiction may summon a meeting at such convenient place as themselves shall think meet, to consider and provide against the threatened danger, provided when they are met, they may remove to what place they please; only whilst any of these four confederates have but three magistrates in their jurisdiction, their requests, or summons, from any 2 of them shall be accounted of equal force with the 3 mentioned in both the clauses of this article, till there be an increase of magistrates there.

6. It is also agreed that, for the managing and concluding of all affairs proper, and concerning the whole confederation, two commissioners shall be chosen by and out of each of these 4 jurisdictions: namely, 2 for the Massachusetts, 2 for Plymouth, 2 for Connecticut, and 2 for New Haven, being all in Church-fellowship with us, which shall bring full power from their several General Courts respectively to hear, examine, weigh, and determine all affairs of war, or peace, leagues, aids, charges, and numbers of men for war, division of spoils, and whatsoever is gotten by conquest, receiving of more confederates, or plantations into combination with any of the confederates, and all things of like nature, which are the proper concomitants or consequents of such a confederation for amity, offence, and defence; not intermeddling with the government of any of the jurisdictions, which by the third article is preserved entirely to themselves. But if these 8 commissioners when they meet shall not all agree yet it [is] concluded that any 6 of the 4 agreeing shall have power to settle and determine the business in question. But if 6 do not agree, that then such propositions, with their reasons, so far as they have been debated, be sent and referred to the 4 General Courts; namely, the Massachusetts, Plymouth, Connecticut, and New Haven, and if at all the said General Courts the business so referred be concluded, then to be prosecuted by the confederates and all their members It is further agreed that these 8 commissioners shall meet once every year, besides extraordinary meetings (according to the fifth article), to consider, treat, and conclude of all affairs belonging to this confederation, which meeting shall ever be the first Thursday in September. And that the next meeting after the date of these presents, which shall be accounted the 2 meeting, shall be at Boston in the Massachusetts, the 3. at Hartford, the 4. at New Haven, the 5. at Plymouth, and so in course successively, if in the meantime some

middle place be not found out and agreed on, which may be commodious for all the jurisdictions

7 It is further agreed, that at each meeting of these 8 Commissioners, whether ordinary or extraordinary, they or 6 of them agreeing as before, may choose their President out of themselves whose office and work shall be to take care and direct for order and a comely carrying on of all proceedings in the present meeting but he shall be invested with no such power or respect, as by which he shall hinder the propounding or progress of any business, or any way cast the scales otherwise than in the precedent article is agreed

8 It is also agreed, that the commissioners for this confederation hereafter at their meetings, whether ordinary or extraordinary, as they may have commission or opportunity, do endeavor to frame and establish agreements and orders in general cases of a civil nature, wherein all the plantations are interested, for the preserving of peace among themselves, and preventing as much as may be all occasion of war or differences with others; as about the free and speedy passage of justice, in every jurisdiction, to all the confederates equally as to their own; not receiving those that remove from one plantation to another without due certificate; how all the jurisdictions may carry it towards the Indians, that they neither grow insolent, nor be injured without due satisfaction, lest war break in upon the confederates through such miscarriages. It is also agreed that if any servant run away from his master into any other of these confederated jurisdictions, that in such case, upon the certificate of one magistrate in the jurisdiction out of which the said servant fled, or upon other due proof, the said servant shall be delivered, either to his master, or any other that pursues and brings such certificate or proof And that upon the escape of any prisoner whatsoever, or fugitive for any criminal cause, whether breaking prison, or getting from the officer, or otherwise escaping, upon the certificate of 2 magistrates of the jurisdiction out of which the escape is made, that he was a prisoner, or such an offender at the time of the escape, they, magistrates, some of them of that jurisdiction where for the present the said prisoner or fugitive abideth, shall forthwith grant such a warrant as the case will bear, for the apprehending of any such person, and the delivering of him into the hands of the officer or other person who pursues him. And if there be help required, for the safe returning of any such offender, then it shall be granted to him that craves the same, he paying the charges thereof.

9 And for that the justest wars may be of dangerous consequence, especially to the smaller plantations in these United Colonies, it is agreed

that neither the Massachusetts, Plymouth, Connecticut, nor New Haven, nor any of the members of them, shall at any time hereafter begin, undertake, or engage themselves, or this confederation, or any part thereof in any war whatsoever (sudden exigencies, with the necessary consequents thereof excepted, which are also to be moderated as much as the case will permit), without the consent and agreement of the forementioned 8 commissioners or at least 6 of them, as in the 6 article is provided. And that no charge be required of any of the confederates, in case of a defensive war, till the said commissioners have met, and approved the justice of the war, and have agreed upon the sum of money to be levied, which sum is then to be paid by the several confederates in proportion according to the fourth article.

10. That in extraordinary occasions, when meetings are summoned by 3 magistrates of any jurisdiction, or 2 as in the 5 article, if any of the commissioners come not, due warning being given or sent, it is agreed that 4 of the commissioners shall have power to direct a war which cannot be delayed, and to send for due proportions of men out of each jurisdiction, as well as 6 might do if all met; but not less than 6 shall determine the justice of the war, or allow the demands or bills of charges, or cause any levies to be made for the same.

11 It is further agreed that if any of the confederates shall hereafter break any of these present articles, or be any other way injurious to any one of the other jurisdictions, such breach of agreement or injury shall be duly considered and ordered by the commissioners for the other jurisdictions, that both peace and this present confederation may be entirely preserved without violation

12. Lastly, this perpetual confederation, and the several articles and agreements thereof being read, and seriously considered, both by the General Court for the Massachusetts, and by the commissioners for Plymouth, Connecticut, and New Haven, were fully allowed and confirmed by three of the forenamed confederates, namely, the Massachusetts, Connecticut, and New Haven; only the commissioners for Plymouth having no commission to conclude, desired respite until they might advise with their General Court; whereupon it was agreed and concluded by the said Court of the Massachusetts, and the commissioners for the other two confederates, that, if Plymouth consent, then the whole treaty as it stands in these present articles is, and shall continue, firm and stable without alteration   But if Plymouth come not in, yet the other 3 confederates do by these presents confirm the whole confederation, and all the articles thereof; only in September next when the 2. meeting of the com-

missioners is to be at Boston, new consideration may be taken of the 6. article, which concerns number of commissioners for meeting and concluding the affairs of this confederation to the satisfaction of the Court of the Massachusetts, and the commissioners for the other 2 confederates, but the rest to stand unquestioned   In the testimony whereof, the General Court of the Massachusetts, by their Secretary, and the commissioners for Connecticut and New Haven, have subscribed these present articles this 19. of the 3. month, commonly called May, Anno Dom 1643

At a meeting of the commissioners for the confederation held at Boston the 7. of September, it appearing that the General Court of New Plymouth and the several townships thereof have read, considered, and approved these Articles of confederation, as appeareth by commission of their General Court, bearing date the 29 of August, 1643, to Mr. Edward Winslow and Mr. William Collier, to ratify and confirm the same on their behalf. We therefore, the commissioners for the Massachusetts, Connecticut, and New Haven, do also for our several Governments subscribe unto them.

John Winthrop, Governor of the Massachusetts,
Tho. Dudley,   Edwa. Hopkins,
Geo. Fenwick,   Thomas Gregson.
Theoph. Eaton.

IV

FRANKLIN'S PLAN OF UNION, 1754[1]

Plan of a proposed Union of the several Colonies of Massachusetts-Bay, New-Hampshire, Connecticut, Rhode Island, New-York, New-Jersey, Pennsylvania, Maryland, Virginia, North-Carolina and South-Carolina for their mutual Defence and Security, and for the Extending the British Settlements in North America.

That humble application be made for an Act of Parliament of Great Britain, by virtue of which one general government may be formed in America, including all the said Colonies, within and under which government each Colony may retain its present constitution, except in the particulars wherein a change may be directed by the said Act, as hereafter follows:

[1] Proposed at the Albany Congress.

PRESIDENT-GENERAL AND GRAND COUNCIL.

That the said general government be administered by a President-General, to be appointed and supported by the Crown; and a Grand Council to be chosen by the several Colonies met in their respective assemblies

ELECTION OF MEMBERS.

That within ——— months after the passing such Act, the House of Representatives that happens to be sitting within that time, or that shall be especially for that purpose convened, may and shall choose members for the Grand Council, in the following proportion, that is to say,

Massachusetts-Bay	7
New-Hampshire	2
Connecticut	5
Rhode Island	2
New-York	4
New-Jersey	3
Pennsylvania	6
Maryland	4
Virginia	7
North Carolina	4
South Carolina	4
	48

PLACE OF FIRST MEETING.

Who shall meet for the first time at the city of Philadelphia in Pennsylvania, being called by the President-General as soon as conveniently may be after his appointment.

NEW ELECTION.

That there shall be a new election of the members of the Grand Council every three years, and on the death or resignation of any member, his place shall be supplied by a new choice at the next sitting of the Assembly of the Colony he represented

PROPORTION OF MEMBERS AFTER THE FIRST THREE YEARS.

That after the first three years, when the proportion of money arising out of each Colony to the general treasury can be known, the number of members to be chosen for each Colony shall, from time to time, in all ensuing elections, be regulated by that proportion, yet so as that the number to be chosen by any one Province be not more than seven, nor less than two.

MEETINGS OF THE GRAND COUNCIL AND CALL.

That the Grand Council shall meet once in every year, and oftener if occasion require, at such time and place as they shall adjourn to at the last preceding meeting, or as they shall be called to meet at by the President-General on any emergency, he having first obtained in writing the consent of seven of the members to such call, and sent due and timely notice to the whole.

CONTINUANCE.

That the Grand Council have power to choose their speaker; and shall neither be dissolved, prorogued, nor continued sitting longer than six weeks at one time, without their own consent, or the special command of the crown.

MEMBERS' ALLOWANCE.

That the members of the Grand Council shall be allowed for their service ten shillings per diem, during their session and journey to and from the place of meeting, twenty miles to be reckoned a day's journey.

ASSENT OF PRESIDENT-GENERAL AND HIS DUTY.

That the assent of the President-General be requisite to all acts of the Grand Council, and that it be his office and duty to cause them to be carried into execution.

POWER OF PRESIDENT-GENERAL AND GRAND COUNCIL, TREATIES OF PEACE AND WAR.

That the President-General, with the advice of the Grand Council, hold or direct all Indian treaties, in which the general interest of the Colonies may be concerned, and make peace or declare war with Indian nations.

INDIAN TRADE.

That they make such laws as they judge necessary for regulating all Indian trade.

INDIAN PURCHASES.

That they make all purchases from Indians, for the Crown, of lands not now within the bounds of particular Colonies, or that shall not be within their bounds when some of them are reduced to more convenient dimensions.

NEW SETTLEMENTS.

That they make new settlements on such purchases by granting lands in the King's name, reserving a quit-rent to the Crown for the use of the general treasury.

LAWS TO GOVERN THEM.

That they make laws for regulating and governing such new settlements, till the Crown shall think fit to form them into particular governments.

RAISE SOLDIERS, AND EQUIP VESSELS, ETC.

That they raise and pay soldiers and build forts for the defence of any of the Colonies, and equip vessels of force to guard the coasts and protect the trade on the ocean, lakes, or great rivers; but they shall not impress men in any colony, without the consent of the legislature.

POWER TO MAKE LAWS, LAY DUTIES, ETC.

That for these purposes they have power to make laws and lay and levy such general duties, imposts, or taxes, as to them shall appear most equal and just (considering the ability and other circumstances of the inhabitants in the several colonies), and such as may be collected with the least inconvenience to the people, rather discouraging luxury, than loading industry with unnecessary burdens.

GENERAL TREASURER AND PARTICULAR TREASURER.

That they may appoint a General Treasurer, and Particular Treasurer in government when necessary; and, from time to time, may order the sums in the treasuries of each government into the general treasury, or draw on them for special payments, as they find most convenient.

MONEY, HOW TO ISSUE.

Yet no money to issue but by the joint orders of the President-General and Grand Council, except where sums have been appointed to particular purposes, and the President-General is previously empowered by an act to draw such sums

ACCOUNTS.

That the general accounts shall be yearly settled and reported to the several Assemblies.

QUORUM

That a quorum of the Grand Council, empowered to act with the President-General, do consist of twenty-five members, among whom there shall be one or more from a majority of the Colonies.

LAWS TO BE TRANSMITTED.

That the laws made by them for the purposes aforesaid shall not be repugnant, but, as near as may be, agreeable to the laws of England, and shall be transmitted to the King in Council for approbation, as soon as may be after their passing; and if not disapproved within three years after presentation, to remain in force.

DEATH OF THE PRESIDENT-GENERAL.

That, in case of the death of the President-General, the Speaker of the Grand Council for the time being shall succeed, and be vested with the same powers and authorities, to continue till the King's pleasure be known.

OFFICERS, HOW APPOINTED.

That all military commission officers, whether for land or sea service, to act under this general constitution, shall be nominated by the President-General, but the approbation of the Grand Council is to be obtained, before they receive their commission. And all civil officers are to be nominated by the Grand Council, and to receive the President-General's approbation before they officiate.

VACANCIES, HOW SUPPLIED.

But, in case of vacancy by death or removal of any officer, civil or military, under this constitution, the Governor of the province in which such vacancy happens, may appoint, till the pleasure of the President-General and Grand Council can be known.

EACH COLONY MAY DEFEND ITSELF IN EMERGENCY, ETC.

That the particular military as well as civil establishments in each Colony remain in their present state, the general constitution notwithstanding; and that on sudden emergencies any Colony may defend itself, and lay the accounts of expense thence arising before the President-General and Grand Council, who may allow and order payment of the same, as far as they judge such accounts just and reasonable.

V

THE DECLARATION OF INDEPENDENCE, 1776

When in the Course of human events, it becomes necessary for one people to dissolve the political bands which have connected them with another, and to assume among the Powers of the earth, the separate and equal station to which the Laws of Nature and of Nature's God entitle them, a decent respect to the opinions of mankind requires that they should declare the causes which impel them to the separation

We hold these truths to be self-evident, that all men are created equal, that they are endowed by their Creator with certain unalienable Rights, that among these are Life, Liberty, and the pursuit of Happiness That to secure these rights, Governments are instituted among Men, deriving their just powers from the consent of the governed, That whenever any Form of Government becomes destructive of these ends, it is the Right of the People to alter or to abolish it, and to institute new Government, laying its foundation on such principles, and organizing its powers in such form, as to them shall seem most likely to effect their Safety and Happiness. Prudence, indeed, will dictate that Governments long established should not be changed for light and transient causes, and accordingly all experience hath shown, that mankind are more disposed to suffer, while evils are sufferable, than to right themselves by abolishing the forms to which they are accustomed. But when a long train of abuses and usurpations, pursuing invariably the same Object evinces a design to reduce them under absolute Despotism, it is their right, it is their duty, to throw off such Government, and to provide new Guards for their future security—Such has been the patient sufferance of these Colonies; and such is now the necessity which constrains them to alter their former Systems of Government. The history of the present King of Great Britain is a history of repeated injuries and usurpations, all having in direct object the establishment of an absolute Tyranny over these States. To prove this, let Facts be submitted to a candid world

He has refused his Assent to Laws, the most wholesome and necessary for the public good.

He has forbidden his Governors to pass Laws of immediate and pressing importance, unless suspended in their operation till his Assent should be obtained; and when so suspended, he has utterly neglected to attend to them.

He has refused to pass other Laws for the accommodation of large districts of people, unless those people would relinquish the right of Representation in the Legislature, a right inestimable to them and formidable to tyrants only.

He has called together legislative bodies at places unusual, uncomfortable, and distant from the depository of their Public Records, for the sole purpose of fatiguing them into compliance with his measures.

He has dissolved Representative Houses repeatedly, for opposing with manly firmness his invasions on the rights of the people.

He has refused for a long time, after such dissolutions, to cause others to be elected, whereby the Legislative Powers, incapable of Annihilation, have returned to the People at large for their exercise; the State remaining in the mean time exposed to all the dangers of invasion from without, and convulsions within.

He has endeavoured to prevent the population of these States; for that purpose obstructing the Laws of Naturalization of Foreigners; refusing to pass others to encourage their migration hither, and raising the conditions of new Appropriations of Lands.

He has obstructed the Administration of Justice, by refusing his Assent to Laws for establishing Judiciary Powers.

He has made Judges dependent on his Will alone for the tenure of their offices, and the amount and payment of their salaries.

He has erected a multitude of New Offices, and sent hither swarms of Officers to harass our People, and eat out their substance

He has kept among us, in times of peace, Standing Armies without the Consent of our Legislature.

He has affected to render the Military independent of and superior to the Civil Power.

He has combined with others to subject us to a jurisdiction foreign to our constitution, and unacknowledged by our laws, giving his Assent to their acts of pretended legislation:

For quartering large bodies of armed troops among us·

For protecting them, by a mock Trial, from Punishment for any Murders which they should commit on the Inhabitants of these States.

For cutting off our Trade with all parts of the world:

For imposing taxes on us without our Consent:

For depriving us in many cases, of the benefits of Trial by Jury:

For transporting us beyond Seas to be tried for pretended offences:

For abolishing the free System of English Laws in a neighbouring Province, establishing therein an Arbitrary government, and enlarging its Boundaries so as to render it at once an example and fit instrument for introducing the same absolute rule into these Colonies:

For taking away our Charters, abolishing our most valuable Laws, and altering fundamentally the Forms of our Governments·

For suspending our own Legislature, and declaring themselves invested with Power to legislate for us in all cases whatsoever.

He has abdicated Government here, by declaring us out of his Protection and waging War against us.

He has plundered our seas, ravaged our Coasts, burnt our towns, and destroyed the lives of our people.

He is at this time transporting large armies of foreign mercenaries to compleat the works of death, desolation, and tyranny, already begun with circumstances of Cruelty & Perfidy scarcely paralleled in the most barbarous ages, and totally unworthy the Head of a civilized nation.

He has constrained our fellow Citizens taken Captive on the high Seas to bear Arms against their Country, to become the executioners of their friends and Brethren, or to fall themselves by their Hands

He has excited domestic insurrection amongst us, and has endeavoured to bring on the inhabitants of our frontiers, the merciless Indian Savages, whose known rule of warfare, is an undistinguished destruction of all ages, sexes, and conditions.

In every stage of these Oppressions We have Petitioned for Redress in the most humble terms: Our repeated Petitions have been answered only by repeated injury. A Prince whose character is thus marked by every act which may define a Tyrant, is unfit to be the ruler of a free People.

Nor have We been wanting in attention to our British brethren We have warned them from time to time of attempts by their legislature to extend an unwarrantable jurisdiction over us We have reminded them of the circumstances of our emigration and settlement here. We have appealed to their native justice and magnanimity, and we have conjured them by the ties of our common kindred to disavow these usurpations, which, would inevitably interrupt our connections and correspondence. They too have been deaf to the voice of justice and of consanguinity. We must, therefore, acquiesce in the necessity, which denounces our Separation, and hold them, as we hold the rest of mankind, Enemies in War, in Peace, Friends

We, therefore, the Representatives of the United States of America, in General Congress, Assembled, appealing to the Supreme Judge of the world for the rectitude of our intentions, do, in the Name, and by Authority of the good People of these Colonies, solemnly publish and declare, That these United Colonies are, and of Right ought to be Free and Independent States; that they are Absolved from all Allegiance to the British Crown, and that all political connection between them and the State of Great Britain, is and ought to be totally dissolved, and that as Free and Independent States, they have full Power to levy War, conclude Peace, contract Alliances, establish Commerce, and to do all other Acts and Things which Independent States may of right do. And for the support of this Declaration, with a firm reliance on the Protection of Divine Providence, we mutually pledge to each other our Lives, our Fortunes, and our sacred Honor.

JOHN HANCOCK.

New Hampshire

JOSIAH BARTLETT   MATTHEW THORNTON
WM. WHIPPLE

Massachusetts Bay

SAML. ADAMS   ROBT TREAT PAINE
JOHN ADAMS   ELBRIDGE GERRY

Rhode Island

STEP. HOPKINS   WILLIAM ELLERY

Connecticut

ROGER SHERMAN   WM. WILLIAMS
SAM'EL HUNTINGTON   OLIVER WOLCOTT

New York

WM. FLOYD

PHIL. LIVINGSTON

FRANS. LEWIS

LEWIS MORRIS

New Jersey

RICHD. STOCKTON ·

JNO. WITHERSPOON

FRAS. HOPKINSON

JOHN HART

ABRA. CLARK

Pennsylvania

ROBT MORRIS

BENJAMIN RUSH

BENJA. FRANKLIN,

JOHN MORTON

GEO. CLYMER

JAS. SMITH

GEO TAYLOR

JAMES WILSON

GEO. ROSS

Delaware

CÆSAR RODNEY

GEO. READ

THO. M'KEAN

Maryland

SAMUEL CHASE

WM. PACA

THOS STONE

CHARLES CARROLL of Carrollton

Virginia

GEORGE WYTHE

RICHARD HENRY LEE

TH JEFFERSON

BENJA. HARRISON

THOS. NELSON, jr.

FRANCIS LIGHTFOOT LEE

CARTER BRAXTON

North Carolina

WM. HOOPER

JOSEPH HEWES

JOHN PENN

South Carolina

EDWARD RUTLEDGE

THOS. HEYWARD, junr

THOMAS LYNCH, junr

ARTHUR MIDDLETON

Georgia

BUTTON GWINNETT

LYMAN HALL

GEO. WALTON

VI.

ARTICLES OF CONFEDERATION, 1777

To all to whom these Presents shall come, we the undersigned Delegates of the States affixed to our Names send greeting

Whereas the Delegates of the United States of America in Congress assembled did on the fifteenth day of November in the year of our Lord One Thousand Seven Hundred and Seventyseven, and in the Second Year of the Independence of America agree to certain articles of Confederation and perpetual Union between the States of Newhampshire, Massachusetts-bay, Rhodeisland and Providence Plantations, Connecticut, New-York, New-Jersey, Pennsylvania, Delaware, Virginia, North-Carolina, South-Carolina and Georgia in the Words following, viz.

"Articles of Confederation and perpetual Union between the States of Newhampshire, Massachusetts-bay, Rhodeisland, and Providence Plantations, Connecticut, New-York, New-Jersey, Pennsylvania, Delaware, Maryland, Virginia, North-Carolina, South-Carolina and Georgia.

ARTICLE I. The stile of this confederacy shall be "The United States of America."

ARTICLE II. Each State retains its sovereignty, freedom and independence, and every power, jurisdiction and right, which is not by this confederation expressly delegated to the United States, in Congress assembled.

ARTICLE III The said States hereby severally enter into a firm league of friendship with each other, for their common defence, the security of their liberties, and their mutual and general welfare, binding themselves to assist each other, against all force offered to, or attacks made upon them, or any of them, on account of religion, sovereignty, trade, or any other pretence whatever.

ARTICLE IV. The better to secure and perpetuate mutual friendship and intercourse among the people of the different States in this Union, the free inhabitants of each of these States, paupers, vagabonds and fugitives from justice excepted, shall be entitled to all privileges and immunities of free citizens in the several States; and the people of each State shall have free ingress and regress to and from any other State, and shall enjoy therein all the privileges of trade and commerce, subject to the same duties, impositions and restrictions as the inhabitants thereof respectively, provided that such restrictions shall not extend so far as to prevent the removal of property imported into any State, to any other State of which the owner is an inhabitant; provided also that no imposition, duties or restriction shall be laid by any State, on the property of the United States, or either of them.

If any person guilty of, or charged with treason, felony, or other high misdemeanor in any State, shall flee from justice, and be found in any of the United States, he shall upon demand of the Governor or Executive power, of the State from which he fled, be delivered up and removed to the State having jurisdiction of his offence.

Full faith and credit shall be given in each of these States to the records, acts and judicial proceedings of the courts and magistrates of every other State

Article V. For the more convenient management of the general interest of the United States, delegates shall be annually appointed in such manner as the legislature of each State shall direct, to meet in Congress on the first Monday in November, in every year, with a power reserved to each State, to recall its delegates, or any of them, at any time within the year, and to send others in their stead, for the remainder of the year.

No State shall be represented in Congress by less than two, nor by more than seven members; and no person shall be capable of being a delegate for more than three years in any term of six years; nor shall any person, being a delegate, be capable of holding any office under the United States, for which he, or another for his benefit receives any salary, fees or emolument of any kind.

Each State shall maintain its own delegates in a meeting of the States, and while they act as members of the committee of the States

In determining questions in the United States, in Congress assembled, each State shall have one vote.

Freedom of speech and debate in Congress shall not be impeached or questioned in any court, or place out of Congress, and the members of Congress shall be protected in their persons from arrests and imprisonments, during the time of their going to and from, and attendance on Congress, except for treason, felony, or breach of the peace.

Article VI. No State without the consent of the United States in Congress assembled, shall send any embassy to, or receive any embassy from, or enter into any conference, agreement, alliance or treaty with any king, prince or state; nor shall any person holding any office of profit or trust under the United States, or any of them, accept of any present, emolument, office or title of any kind whatever from any king, prince or foreign state; nor shall the United States in Congress assembled, or any of them, grant any title of nobility.

No two or more States shall enter into any treaty, confederation or alliance whatever between them, without the consent of the United States in Congress assembled, specifying accurately the purposes for which the same is to be entered into, and how long it shall continue.

No State shall lay any imposts or duties, which may interfere with any stipulations in treaties, entered into by the United States in Congress assembled, with any king, prince or state, in pursuance of any treaties already proposed by Congress, to the courts of France and Spain.

No vessels of war shall be kept up in time of peace by any State, except such number only, as shall be deemed necessary by the United States in Congress assembled, for the defence of such State, or its trade; nor shall any body of forces be kept up by any State, in time of peace, except such number only, as in the judgment of the United States, in Congress assembled, shall be deemed requisite to garrison the forts necessary for the defence of such State, but every State shall always keep up a well regulated and disciplined militia, sufficiently armed and accoutered, and shall provide and constantly have ready for use, in public stores, a due number of field pieces and tents, and a proper quantity of arms, ammunition and camp equipage.

No State shall engage in any war without the consent of the United States in Congress assembled, unless such State be actually invaded by enemies, or shall have received certain advice of a resolution being formed by some nation of Indians to invade such State, and the danger is so imminent as not to admit of a delay, till the United States in Congress assembled can be consulted: nor shall any State grant commissions to any ships or vessels of war, nor letters of marque or reprisal, except it be after a declaration of war by the United States in Congress assembled, and then only against the kingdom or state and the subjects thereof, against which war has been so declared, and under such regulations as shall be established by the United States in Congress assembled, unless such State be infested by pirates, in which case vessels of war may be fitted out for that occasion, and kept so long as the danger shall continue, or until the United States in Congress assembled shall determine otherwise.

ARTICLE VII. When land-forces are raised by any State for the common defence, all officers of or under the rank of colonel, shall be appointed by the Legislature of each State respectively by whom such forces shall be raised, or in such manner as such State shall direct, and all vacancies shall be filled up by the State which first made the appointment.

ARTICLE VIII. All charges of war, and all other expenses that shall be incurred for the common defence or general welfare, and allowed by the United States in Congress assembled, shall be defrayed out of a common treasury, which shall be supplied by the several States, in proportion to the value of all land within each State, granted to or surveyed for any person, as such land and the buildings and improvements thereon shall be estimated according to such mode as the United States in Congress assembled, shall from time to time direct and appoint.

The taxes for paying the proportion shall be laid and levied by the authority and direction of the Legislatures of the several States within the time agreed upon by the United States in Congress assembled.

ARTICLE IX. The United States in Congress assembled, shall have the sole and exclusive right and power of determining on peace and war, except in the cases mentioned in the sixth article—of sending and receiving ambassadors—entering into treaties and alliances, provided that no treaty of commerce shall be made whereby the legislative power of the respective States shall be restrained from imposing such imposts and duties on foreigners, as their own people are subjected to, or from prohibiting the exportation or importation of any species of goods or commodities whatsoever—of establishing rules for deciding in all cases, what captures on land or water shall be legal, and in what manner prizes taken by land or naval forces in the service of the United States shall be divided or appropriated—of granting letters of marque and reprisal in times of peace—appointing courts for the trial of pirates and felonies committed on the high seas and establishing courts for receiving and determining finally appeals in all cases of captures, provided that no member of Congress shall be appointed a judge of any of the said courts.

The United States in Congress assembled shall also be the last resort on appeal in all disputes and differences now subsisting or that hereafter may arise between two or more States concerning boundary, jurisdiction or any other cause whatever; which authority shall always be exercised in the manner following. Whenever the legislative or executive authority or lawful agent of any State in controversy with another shall present a petition to Congress, stating the matter in question and praying for a hearing, notice thereof shall be given by order of Congress to the legislative or executive authority of the other State in controversy, and a day assigned for the appearance of the parties by their lawful agents, who shall then be directed to appoint by joint consent, commissioners or judges to constitute a court for hearing and determining the matter in question: but if they cannot agree, Congress shall name three persons out of each of the United States, and from the list of such persons each party shall alternately strike out one, the petitioners beginning, until the number shall be reduced to thirteen, and from that number not less than seven, nor more than nine names as Congress shall direct, shall in the presence of Congress be drawn out by lot, and the persons whose names shall be so drawn or any five of them, shall be commissioners or judges, to hear and finally determine the controversy, so always as a major part of the judges who shall hear the cause shall agree in the determination and if either party shall neglect to attend at the day appointed, without showing reasons, which Congress shall judge sufficient, or being present shall refuse to strike, the Congress shall proceed to nominate three persons out of each State, and the Secretary of Congress shall strike in behalf of such party absent or refusing; and the judgment and sentence of the court to be appointed, in the manner before prescribed, shall be final and conclusive; and if any of the parties shall refuse to submit to the authority of such court, or to appear or defend their claim or cause, the court shall nevertheless proceed to pronounce sentence, or judgment, which shall in like manner be final and decisive, the judgment or sentence and other proceedings being in either case transmitted to Congress, and lodged among the acts of Congress for the security of the parties concerned: provided that every commissioner, before he sits in judgment, shall take an oath to be administered by one of the judges of the supreme or superior court of the State, where the cause shall be tried, " well and truly to hear and determine the matter in question, according to the best of his judgment, without favour, affection or hope of reward: " provided also that no State shall be deprived of territory for the benefit of the United States

All controversies concerning the private right of soil claimed under different grants of two or more States, whose jurisdiction as they may respect such lands, and the States which passed such grants are adjusted, the said grants or either of them being at the same time claimed to have originated antecedent to such settlement of jurisdiction, shall on the petition of either party to the Congress of the United States, be finally determined as near as may be in the same manner as is before prescribed for deciding disputes respecting territorial jurisdiction between different States.

The United States in Congress assembled shall also have the sole and exclusive right and power of regulating the alloy and value of coin struck by their own authority, or by that of the respective States—fixing the standard of weights and measures throughout the United States—regulating the trade and managing all affairs with the Indians, not members of any of the States, provided that the legislative right of any State within its own limits be not infringed or violated—establishing and regulating post-offices from one State to another, throughout all the United States, and exacting such postage on the papers passing thro' the same as may be requisite to defray the expenses of the said office—appointing all officers of the land forces, in the service of the United States, excepting regimental officers—appointing all the officers of the naval forces, and commissioning all officers whatever in the service of the United States—making rules for the government and regulation of the said land and naval forces, and directing their operations

The United States in Congress assembled shall have authority to appoint a committee, to sit in the recess of Congress, to be denominated " a Committee of the States," and to consist of one delegate from each State, and to appoint such other committees and civil officers as may be necessary for managing the general affairs of the United States under their direction—to appoint one of their number to preside, provided that no person be allowed to serve in the office of president more than one year in any term of three years, to ascertain the necessary sums of money to be raised for the service of the United States, and to appropriate and apply the same for defraying the public expenses—to borrow money, or emit bills on the credit of the United States, transmitting every half year to the respective States an account of the sums of money so borrowed or emitted,—to build and equip a navy—to agree upon the number of land forces, and to make requisitions from each State for its quota, in proportion to the number of white inhabitants in such State; which requisition shall be binding, and thereupon the Legislature of each State shall appoint the regimental officers, raise the men and cloath, arm and equip them in a soldier like manner, at the expense of the United States; and the officers and men so cloathed, armed and equipped shall march to the place appointed, and within the time agreed on by the United States in Congress assembled: but if the United States in Congress assembled shall, on consideration of circumstances judge proper that any State should not raise men, or should raise a smaller number than its quota, and that any other State should raise a greater number of men than the quota thereof, such extra number shall be raised. officered, cloathed, armed and equipped in the same as the quota of such State, unless the legislature of such State shall judge that such extra number cannot be safely spared outside of the same, in which case they shall raise, officer, cloath, arm and equip as many of such extra number as they judge can be safely spared. And the officers and men so cloathed, armed and equipped, shall march to the place appointed, and within the time agreed on by the United States in Congress assembled.

The United States in Congress assembled shall never engage in a war, nor grant letters of marque and reprisal in time of peace, nor enter into any treaties or alliances, nor coin money, nor regulate the value thereof, nor ascertain the sums and expenses necessary for the defence and welfare of the United States, or any of them, nor emit bills, nor borrow money on the credit of the United States, nor appropriate money, nor agree upon the number of vessels of war, to be built or purchased, or the number of land or sea forces to be raised, nor appoint a commander in chief of the army or navy, unless nine States assent to the same: nor shall a question on any other point, except for adjourning from day to day be determined, unless by the votes of a majority of the United States in Congress assembled

The Congress of the United States shall have power to adjourn to any time within the year, and to any place within the United States, so that no period of adjournment be for a longer duration than the space of six months, and shall publish the journal of their proceedings monthly, except such parts thereof relating to treaties, alliances or military operations, as in their judgment require secrecy; and the yeas and nays of the delegates of each State on any question shall be entered on the journal, when it is desired by any delegate, and the delegates of a State, or any of them, at his or their request shall be furnished with a transcript of the said journal, except such parts as are above excepted, to lay before the Legislatures of the several States.

ARTICLE X The committee of the States, or any nine of them, shall be authorized to execute, in the recess of Congress, such of the powers of Congress as the United States in Congress assembled, by the consent of nine States, shall from time to time think expedient to vest them with; provided that no power be delegated to the said committee, for the exercise of which, by the articles of confederation, the voice of nine States in the Congress of the United States assembled is requisite

ARTICLE XI Canada acceding to this confederation, and joining in the measures of the United States, shall be admitted into, and entitled to all the advantages of this Union but no other colony shall be admitted into the same, unless such admission be agreed to by nine States.

ARTICLE XII. All bills of credit emitted, monies borrowed and debts contracted by, or under the authority of Congress, before the assembling of the United States, in pursuance of the present confederation, shall be deemed and considered as a charge against the United States, for payment and satisfaction whereof the said United States, and the public faith are hereby solemnly pledged

ARTICLE XIII. Every State shall abide by the determinations of the United States in Congress assembled, on all questions which by this confederation are submitted to them. And the articles of this confederation shall be inviolably observed by every State, and the Union shall be perpetual, nor shall any alteration at any time hereafter be made in any of them; unless such alteration be agreed to in a Congress of the United States, and be afterwards confirmed by the Legislatures of every State.

And whereas it hath pleased the Great Governor of the World to incline the hearts of the Legislatures we respectively represent in Congress, to approve of, and to authorize us to ratify the said articles of confederation and perpetual union. Know ye that we the undersigned delegates, by virtue of the power and authority to us given for that purpose, do by these presents, in the name and in behalf of our respective constituents, fully and entirely ratify and confirm each and every of the said articles of confederation and perpetual union, and all and singular the matters and things therein contained: and we do further solemnly plight and engage the faith of our respective constituents, that they shall abide by the determinations of the United States in Congress assembled, on all questions, which by the said confederation are submitted to them. And that the articles thereof shall be inviolably observed by the States we respectively represent, and that the Union shall be perpetual.

IN WITNESS WHEREOF we have hereunto set our hands in Congress Done at Philadelphia in the State of Pennsylvania the ninth day of July in the year of our Lord one thousand seven hundred and seventy-eight, and in the third year of the independence of America.

On the part & behalf of the State of New Hampshire

JOSIAH BARTLETT   JOHN WENTWORTH, Junr
                                            August 8th, 1778

On the part and behalf of the State of Massachusetts Bay

JOHN HANCOCK   FRANCIS DANA
SAMUEL ADAMS   JAMES LOVELL
ELBRIDGE GERRY   SAMUEL HOLTEN

On the part and behalf of the State of Rhode Island and Providence
Plantations

WILLIAM ELLERY   JOHN COLLINS
HENRY MARCHANT

On the part and behalf of the State of Connecticut

ROGER SHERMAN   TITUS HOSMER
SAMUEL HUNTINGTON   ANDREW ADAMS
OLIVER WOLCOTT

On the part and behalf of the State of New York

JAS. DUANE   WM DUER
FRA LEWIS   GOUV. MORRIS

On the part and in behalf of the State of New Jersey, Novr. 26, 1778

JNO. WITHERSPOON   NATHL SCUDDER

On the part and behalf of the State of Pennsylvania

ROBT. MORRIS   WILLIAM CLINGAN
DANIEL ROBERDEAU   JOSEPH REED, 22d July,
JNO BAYARD SMITH   1778

On the part & behalf of the State of Delaware

THOS. M'KEAN, Feby. 12,   JOHN DICKINSON, May 5th,
  1779   1779
NICHOLAS VAN DYKE

On the part and behalf of the State of Maryland

JOHN HANSON, March 1,   DANIEL CARROLL, Mar. 1,
  1781   1781

On the part and behalf of the State of Virginia

RICHARD HENRY LEE   JNO HARVIE
JOHN BANISTER   FRANCIS LIGHTFOOT LEE
THOMAS ADAMS

On the part and behalf of the State of No. Carolina

JOHN PENN, July 21, 1778   JNO. WILLIAMS
CORNS. HARTNETT

On the part & behalf of the State of South Carolina

HENRY LAURENS   RICHD HUTSON
WILLIAM HENRY DRAYTON   THOS. HEYWARD, Junr
JNO. MATTHEWS

On the part & behalf of the State of Georgia

JNO. WALTON, 24th July,   EDWD. LANGWORTHY
    1778
EDWD. TELFAIR

VII

THE NORTHWEST TERRITORIAL GOVERNMENT, 1787

An Ordinance for the government of the territory of the United States northwest of the river Ohio

SECTION 1 *Be it ordained by the United States in Congress assembled,* That the said territory, for the purposes of temporary government, be one district, subject, however, to be divided into two districts, as future circumstances may, in the opinion of Congress, make it expedient.

SEC. 2. *Be it ordained by the authority aforesaid,* That the estates both of resident and non-resident proprietors in the said territory, dying intestate, shall descend to, and be distributed among, their children and the descendants of a deceased child in equal parts, the descendants of a deceased child or grandchild to take the share of their deceased parent in equal parts among them; and where there shall be no children or descendants, then in equal parts to the next of kin, in equal degree; and among collaterals, the children of a deceased brother or sister of the intestate shall have, in parts among them, their deceased parent's share; and there shall, in no case, be a distinction between kindred of the whole and half blood, saving in all cases to the widow of the intestate, her third part of the real estate for life, and one-third part of the personal estate; and this law relative to descents and dower, shall remain in full force until altered by the legislature of the district. And until the governor and judges shall adopt laws as hereinafter mentioned, estates in the said territory may be devised or bequeathed by wills in writing, signed and sealed by him or her in whom the estate may be, (being of full age,) and attested by three witnesses; and real estates may be conveyed by lease and release, or bargain and sale, signed, sealed, and delivered by the person, being of full age, in whom the estate may be, and attested by two witnesses, provided such wills be duly proved, and such conveyances be acknowledged, or the execution thereof duly proved, and be recorded within one year after proper magistrates, courts, and registers shall be appointed for that purpose; and personal property may be transferred by delivery, saving, however, to the French and Canadian inhabitants, and other settlers of the Kaskaskies, Saint Vincents, and the neighboring villages, who have heretofore professed themselves citizens of Virginia, their laws and customs now in force among them, relative to the descent and conveyance of property.

SEC. 3. *Be it ordained by the authority aforesaid,* That there shall be appointed, from time to time, by Congress, a governor, whose commission shall continue in force for the term of three years unless sooner revoked by Congress; he shall reside in the district, and have a freehold estate therein, in five hundred acres of land, while in the exercise of his office.

SEC. 4. There shall be appointed from time to time, by Congress, a secretary, whose commission shall continue in force for four years, unless sooner revoked; he shall reside in the district, and have a freehold estate therein, in five hundred acres of land, while in the exercise of his office. It shall be his duty to keep and preserve the acts and laws passed by the legislature, and the public records of the district, and the proceedings of the governor in his executive department, and transmit authentic copies of such acts and proceedings every six months to the Secretary of Congress. There shall also be appointed a court, to consist of three judges, any two of whom to form a court, who shall have a common-law jurisdiction, and reside in the district, and have each therein a freehold estate, in five hundred acres of land, while in the exercise of their offices; and their commissions shall continue in force during good behavior.

SEC. 5. The governor and judges, or a majority of them, shall adopt and publish in the district such laws of the original States, criminal and civil, as may be necessary and best suited to the circumstances of the district, and report them to Congress from time to time, which laws shall be in force in the district until the organization of the general assembly therein, unless disapproved of by Congress; but afterwards the legislature shall have authority to alter them as they shall think fit

SEC. 6. The governor, for the time being, shall be commander-in-chief of the militia, appoint and commission all officers in the same below the rank of general officers; all general officers shall be appointed and commissioned by Congress.

SEC. 7. Previous to the organization of the general assembly the governor shall appoint such magistrates, and other civil officers, in each county or township, as he shall find necessary for the preservation of the peace and good order in the same After the general assembly shall be organized the powers and duties of magistrates and other civil officers shall be regulated and defined by the said assembly; but all magistrates and other civil officers, not herein otherwise directed, shall, during the continuance of this temporary government, be appointed by the governor.

SEC. 8. For the prevention of crimes and injuries, the laws to be adopted or made shall have force in all parts of the district, and for the execution of process, criminal and civil, the governor shall make proper divisions thereof; and he shall proceed, from time to time, as circumstances may require, to lay out the parts of the district in which the Indian titles shall have been extinguished, into counties and townships, subject however, to such alterations as may thereafter be made by the legislature.

SEC. 9. So soon as there shall be five thousand free male inhabitants, of full age, in the district, upon giving proof thereof to the governor, they shall receive authority, with time and place, to elect representatives from their counties or townships, to represent them in the general assembly: *Provided,* That for every five hundred free male inhabitants there shall be one representative, and so on, progressively, with the number of free male inhabitants, shall the right of representation increase, until the number of representatives shall amount to twenty-five; after which the number and proportion of representatives shall be regulated by the legislature *Provided,* That no person be eligible or qualified to act as a representative, unless he shall have been a citizen of one of the United States three years, and be a resident in the district, or unless he shall have resided in the district three years, and, in either case, shall likewise hold in his own right, in fee-simple, two hundred acres of land within the same: *Provided, also,* That a freehold in fifty acres of land in the district, having been a citizen of one of the States, and being resident in the district, or the like freehold and two years' residence in the district, shall be necessary to qualify a man as an elector of a representative

SEC. 10. The representatives thus elected shall serve for the term of two years; and in case of the death of a representative, or removal from office, the governor shall issue a writ to the county or township, for which he was a member, to elect another in his stead, to serve for the residue of the term.

SEC. 11. The general assembly, or legislature, shall consist of the governor, legislative council, and a house of representatives The legislative council shall consist of five members, to continue in office five years, unless sooner removed by Congress, any three of whom to be a quorum; and the members of the council shall be nominated and appointed in the following manner, to wit As soon as representatives shall be elected the governor shall appoint a time and place for them to meet together, and when met they shall nominate ten persons, residents in the district, and each possessed of a freehold in five hundred acres of land, and return their names to Congress, five of whom Congress shall appoint and commission to serve as aforesaid, and whenever a vacancy shall happen in the council, by death or removal from office, the house of representatives shall nominate two persons, qualified as aforesaid, for each vacancy, and return their names to Congress, one of whom Congress shall appoint and commission for the residue of the term, and every five years, four months at least before the expiration of the time of service of the members of the council, the said house shall nominate ten persons, qualified as aforesaid, and return their names to Congress, five of whom Congress shall appoint and commission to serve as members of the council five years, unless sooner removed. And the governor, legislative council, and house of representatives shall have authority to make laws in all cases for the good government of the district, not repugnant to the principles and articles in this ordinance established and declared. And all bills, having passed by a majority in the house, and by a majority in the council, shall be referred to the governor for his assent; but no bill, or legislative act whatever, shall be of any force without his assent. The governor shall have power to convene, prorogue, and dissolve the general assembly when, in his opinion, it shall be expedient.

SEC. 12 The governor, judges, legislative council, secretary, and such other officers as Congress shall appoint in the district, shall take an oath or affirmation of fidelity, and of office, the governor before the President of Congress, and all other officers before the governor. As soon as a legislature shall be formed in the district, the council and house assembled, in one room, shall have authority, by joint ballot, to elect a delegate to Congress, who shall have a seat in Congress, with a right of debating, but not of voting, during this temporary government.

SEC. 13 And for extending the fundamental principles of civil and religious liberty, which form the basis whereon these republics, their laws and constitutions, are erected; to fix and establish those principles as the basis of all laws, constitutions, and governments, which forever hereafter shall be formed in the said territory; to provide, also, for the establishment of States, and permanent government, therein, and for their admission to a share in the Federal councils on an equal footing with the original States, at as early periods as may be consistent with the general interest

SEC. 14. It is hereby ordained and declared, by the authority aforesaid, that the following articles shall be considered as articles of compact, between the original States and the people and States in the said territory, and forever remain unalterable, unless by common consent, to wit.

ARTICLE I.

No person, demeaning himself in a peaceable and orderly manner, shall ever be molested on account of his mode of worship, or religious sentiments, in the said territories.

ARTICLE II.

The inhabitants of the said territory shall always be entitled to the benefits of the writ of *habeas corpus*, and of the trial by jury; of a proportionate representation of the people in the legislature, and of judicial proceedings according to the course of common law. All persons shall be bailable, unless for capital offences, where the proof shall be evident, or the presumption great. All fines shall be moderate; and no cruel or unusual punishments shall be inflicted. No man shall be deprived of his liberty or property, but by the judgment of his peers, or the law of the land, and should the public exigencies make it necessary, for the common preservation, to take any person's property, or to demand his particular services, full compensation shall be made for the same. And, in the just preservation of rights and property, it is understood and declared, that no law ought ever to be made or have force in the said territory, that shall, in any manner whatever, interfere with or affect private contracts, or engagements, *bona fide*, and without fraud previously formed.

ARTICLE III.

Religion, morality, and knowledge being necessary to good government and the happiness of mankind, schools and the means of education shall forever be encouraged. The utmost good faith shall always be observed towards the Indians; their lands and property shall never be taken from them without their consent, and in their property, rights, and liberty they never shall be invaded or disturbed, unless in just and lawful wars authorized by Congress, but laws founded in justice and humanity shall, from time to time, be made, for preventing wrongs being done to them, and for preserving peace and friendship with them.

ARTICLE IV.

The said territory, and the States which may be formed therein, shall forever remain a part of this confederacy of the United States of America, subject to the Articles of Confederation, and to such alterations therein as shall be constitutionally made; and to all the acts and ordinances of the United States in Congress assembled, conformable thereto. The inhabitants and settlers in the said territory shall be subject to pay a part of the Federal debts, contracted, or to be contracted, and a proportional part of the expenses of government to be apportioned on them by Congress, according to the same common rule and measure by which apportionments thereof shall be made on the other States; and the taxes for paying their proportion shall be laid and levied by the authority and direction of the legislature of the district, or districts, or new States, as in the original States, within the time agreed upon by the United States in Congress assembled. The legislatures of those districts, or new States, shall never interfere with the primary disposal of the soil by the United States in Congress assembled, nor with any regulations Congress may find necessary for securing the title in such soil to the *bona fide* purchasers. No tax shall be imposed on lands the property of the United States; and in no case shall non-resident proprietors be taxed higher than residents The navigable waters leading into the Mississippi and Saint Lawrence, and the carrying places between the same, shall be common highways, and forever free, as well to the inhabitants of the said territory as to the citizens of the United States, and those of any other States that may be admitted into the confederacy, without any tax, impost, or duty therefor.

ARTICLE V.

There shall be formed in the said territory not less than three nor more than five States; and the boundaries of the States, as soon as Virginia shall alter her act of cession and consent to the same, shall become fixed and established as follows, to wit: The western State in the said territory, shall be bounded by the Mississippi, the Ohio, and the Wabash Rivers; a direct line drawn from the Wabash and Post Vincents, due north, to the territorial line between the United States and Canada, and by the said territorial lines to the Lake of the Woods and Mississippi. The middle State shall be bounded by the said direct line, the Wabash from Post Vincents to the Ohio, by the Ohio, by a direct line drawn due north from the mouth of the Great Miami to the said territorial line, and by the said territorial line. The eastern State shall be bounded by the last-mentioned direct line, the Ohio, Pennsylvania, and the said territorial line: *Provided, however,* And it is further understood and declared, that the boundaries of these three States shall be subject so far to be altered, that, if Congress shall hereafter find it expedient, they shall have authority to form one or two States in that part of the said territory which lies north of an east and west line drawn through the southerly bend or extreme of Lake Michigan. And whenever any of the said States shall have sixty thousand free inhabitants therein, such State shall be admitted, by its delegates, into the Congress of the United States, on an equal footing with the original States, in all respects whatever, and shall be at liberty to form a permanent constitution and State government: *Provided,* The constitution and government, so to be formed, shall be republican, and in conformity to the principles contained in these articles, and, so far as it can be consistent with the general interest of the confederacy, such admission shall be allowed at an earlier period, and when there may be a less number of free inhabitants in the State than sixty thousand

ARTICLE VI.

There shall be neither slavery nor involuntary servitude in the said territory, otherwise than in the punishment of crimes, whereof the party shall have been duly convicted· *Provided always,* That any person escaping into the same, from whom labor or service is lawfully claimed in any one of the original States, such fugitive may be lawfully reclaimed, and conveyed to the person claiming his or her service as aforesaid

Be it ordained by the authority aforesaid, That the resolutions of the 23d of April, 1784, relative to the subject of this ordinance, be, and the same are hereby, repealed, and declared null and void

Done by the United States, in Congress assembled, the 13th day of July, in the year of our Lord 1787, and of their sovereignty and independence the twelfth.

VIII

CONSTITUTION OF THE UNITED STATES, 1787

We the People of the United States, in Order to form a more perfect Union, establish Justice, insure domestic Tranquillity, provide for the common defence, promote the general Welfare, and secure the Blessings of Liberty to ourselves and our Posterity, do ordain and establish this CONSTITUTION for the United States of America.

ARTICLE I.

SECTION 1. All legislative Powers herein granted shall be vested in a Congress of the United States, which shall consist of a Senate and House of Representatives.

SECTION 2. (1) The House of Representatives shall be composed of Members chosen every second Year by the People of the several States, and the Electors in each State shall have the Qualifications requisite for Electors of the most numerous Branch of the State Legislature.

(2) No person shall be a Representative who shall not have attained to the Age of Twenty-five years, and been seven Years a Citizen of the United States, and who shall not, when elected, be an inhabitant of that State in which he shall be chosen.

(3) Representatives and direct Taxes shall be apportioned among the several States which may be included within this Union, according to their respective Numbers, which shall be determined by adding to the whole Number of free Persons, including those bound to Service for a Term of Years, and excluding Indians not taxed, three fifths of all other Persons The actual Enumeration shall be made within three Years after the first Meeting of the Congress of the United States, and within every subsequent Term of ten Years, in such Manner as they shall by Law direct. The Number of Representatives shall not exceed one for every thirty Thousand, but each State shall have at Least one Representative;

and until such enumeration shall be made, the State of New-Hampshire shall be entitled to chuse three, Massachusetts eight, Rhode-Island and Providence Plantations one, Connecticut five, New-York six, New-Jersey four, Pennsylvania eight, Delaware one, Maryland six, Virginia ten, North-Carolina five, South-Carolina five, and Georgia three.

(4) When vacancies happen in the Representation from any State, the Executive Authority thereof shall issue Writs of Election to fill such Vacancies

(5) The House of Representatives shall chuse their Speaker and other Officers, and shall have the sole Power of Impeachment

SECTION 3 (1) The Senate of the United States shall be composed of two Senators from each State, chosen by the Legislature thereof, for six Years; and each Senator shall have one Vote.

(2) Immediately after they shall be assembled in Consequence of the first Election, they shall be divided as equally as may be into three Classes. The Seats of the Senators of the first Class shall be vacated at the Expiration of the second year, of the second Class at the Expiration of the fourth Year, and of the third Class at the Expiration of the sixth Year, so that one third may be chosen every second Year; and if Vacancies happen by Resignation, or otherwise, during the Recess of the Legislature of any State, the Executive thereof may make temporary Appointments until the next Meeting of the Legislature, which shall then fill such Vacancies.

(3) No Person shall be a Senator who shall not have attained to the Age of thirty Years, and been nine Years a Citizen of the United States, and who shall not, when elected, be an Inhabitant of that State for which he shall be chosen.

(4) The Vice President of the United States shall be President of the Senate, but shall have no Vote, unless they be equally divided

(5) The Senate shall chuse their other Officers, and also a President pro tempore, in the Absence of the Vice President, or when he shall exercise the Office of President of the United States

(6) The Senate shall have the sole Power to try all Impeachments When sitting for that Purpose, they shall be on Oath or Affirmation. When the President of the United States is tried, the Chief Justice shall preside And no Person shall be convicted without the Concurrence of two-thirds of the Members present.

(7) Judgment in Cases of Impeachment shall not extend further than to removal from Office, and disqualification to hold and enjoy any Office of Honor, Trust or Profit under the United States; but the Party

convicted shall nevertheless be liable and subject to Indictment, Trial, Judgment and Punishment, according to Law.

Section 4. (1) The Times, Places and Manner of holding Elections for Senators and Representatives, shall be prescribed in each State by the Legislature thereof; but the Congress may at any time by Law make or alter such Regulations, except as to the Places of chusing Senators

(2) The Congress shall assemble at least once in every Year, and such Meeting shall be on the first Monday in December, unless they shall by Law appoint a different Day.

Section 5. (1) Each House shall be the Judge of the Elections, Returns and Qualifications of its own Members, and a Majority of each shall constitute a Quorum to do Business; but a smaller Number may adjourn from day to day, and may be authorized to compel the Attendance of absent Members, in such Manner, and under such Penalties as each House may provide.

(2) Each House may determine the Rules of its Proceedings, punish its Members for disorderly Behaviour, and, with the Concurrence of two thirds, expel a Member

(3) Each House shall keep a Journal of its Proceedings, and from time to time publish the same, excepting such Parts as may in their Judgment require Secrecy, and the Yeas and Nays of the Members of either House on any question shall, at the Desire of one fifth of those present, be entered on the Journal

(4) Neither House, during the Session of Congress, shall, without the Consent of the other, adjourn for more than three days, nor to any other Place than that in which the two Houses shall be sitting.

Section 6 (1) The Senators and Representatives shall receive a Compensation for their Services, to be ascertained by Law, and paid out of the Treasury of the United States. They shall in all Cases, except Treason, Felony and Breach of the Peace, be privileged from Arrest during their Attendance at the Session of their respective Houses, and in going to and returning from the same; and for any Speech or Debate in either House they shall not be questioned in any other Place

(2) No Senator or Representative shall, during the Time for which he was elected, be appointed to any civil Office under the Authority of the United States, which shall have been created, or the Emoluments whereof shall have been encreased during such time; and no Person holding any Office under the United States, shall be a Member of either House during his Continuance in Office.

Section 7. (1) All Bills for Raising Revenue shall originate in the

House of Representatives; but the Senate may propose or concur with Amendments as on other Bills.

(2) Every Bill which shall have passed the House of Representatives and the Senate, shall, before it becomes a Law, be presented to the President of the United States; If he approve he shall sign it, but if not he shall return it, with his Objections to that House in which it shall have originated, who shall enter the Objections at large on their Journal, and proceed to reconsider it. If after such Reconsideration two thirds of that House shall agree to pass the Bill, it shall be sent, together with the Objections, to the other House, by which it shall likewise be reconsidered, and if approved by two thirds of that House, it shall become a Law. But in all such Cases the Votes of both Houses shall be determined by Yeas and Nays, and the Names of the Persons voting for and against the Bill shall be entered on the Journal of each House respectively. If any Bill shall not be returned by the President within ten Days (Sundays excepted) after it shall have been presented to him, the Same shall be a law, in like Manner as if he had signed it, unless the Congress by their Adjournment prevent its Return, in which Case it shall not be a Law.

(3) Every Order, Resolution, or Vote to which the Concurrence of the Senate and House of Representatives may be necessary (except on a question of Adjournment) shall be presented to the President of the United States, and before the Same shall take Effect, shall be approved by him, or being disapproved by him shall be passed by two-thirds of the Senate and House of Representatives, according to the Rules and Limitations prescribed in the Case of a Bill.

SECTION 8. (1) The Congress shall have Power To lay and collect Taxes, Duties, Imposts and Excises, to pay the Debts and provide for the common Defence and general Welfare of the United States, but all Duties, Imposts and Excises shall be uniform throughout the United States;

(2) To borrow money on the Credit of the United States;

(3) To regulate Commerce with foreign Nations, and among the several States, and with the Indian Tribes,

(4) To establish an uniform Rule of Naturalization, and uniform Laws on the subject of Bankruptcies throughout the United States;

(5) To coin Money, regulate the Value thereof, and of foreign Coin, and to fix the Standard of Weights and Measures;

(6) To provide for the Punishment of counterfeiting the Securities and current Coin of the United States;

(7) To establish Post Offices and post Roads;

(8) To promote the Progress of Science and useful Arts, by securing for limited Times to Authors and Inventors the exclusive Right to their respective Writings and Discoveries,

(9) To constitute Tribunals inferior to the Supreme Court;

(10) To define and Punish Piracies and Felonies committed on the high Seas, and Offences against the Law of Nations;

(11) To declare War, grant Letters of Marque and Reprisal, and make Rules concerning Captures on Land and Water;

(12) To raise and support Armies, but no Appropriation of Money to that Use shall be for a longer Term than two Years;

(13) To provide and maintain a Navy;

(14) To make Rules for the Government and Regulation of the land and naval Forces·

(15) To provide for calling forth the Militia to execute the Laws of the Union, suppress Insurrections and repel Invasions;

(16) To provide for organizing, arming, and disciplining, the Militia, and for governing such Part of them as may be employed in the Service of the United States, reserving to the States respectively, the Appointment of the Officers, and the Authority of training the Militia according to the discipline prescribed by Congress;

(17) To exercise exclusive Legislation in all Cases whatsoever, over such District (not exceeding ten Miles square) as may, by Cession of particular States, and the Acceptance of Congress, become the Seat of the Government of the United States, and to exercise like Authority over all Places purchased by the Consent of the Legislature of the State in which the Same shall be, for the Erection of Forts, Magazines, Arsenals, dock-Yards, and other needful Buildings;—And

(18) To make all Laws which shall be necessary and proper for carrying into Execution the foregoing Powers, and all other Powers vested by this Constitution in the Government of the United States, or in any Department or Officer thereof ·

Section 9. (1) The Migration or Importation of such Persons as any of the States now existing shall think proper to admit, shall not be prohibited by the Congress prior to the Year one thousand eight hundred and eight, but a Tax or Duty may be imposed on such Importation, not exceeding ten dollars for each Person.

(2) The Privilege of the Writ of Habeas Corpus shall not be suspended, unless when in Cases of Rebellion or Invasion the public Safety may require it

(3) No Bill of Attainder or ex post facto Law shall be passed.

(4) No Capitation, or other direct, tax shall be laid, unless in Proportion to the Census or Enumeration herein before directed to be taken.

(5) No Tax or Duty shall be laid on Articles exported from any State.

(6) No preference shall be given by any Regulation of Commerce or Revenue to the Ports of one State over those of another. nor shall Vessels bound to, or from, one State, be obliged to enter, clear, or pay Duties in another.

(7) No Money shall be drawn from the Treasury, but in Consequence of Appropriations made by Law; and a regular Statement and Account of the Receipts and Expenditures of all public Money shall be published from time to time.

(8) No Title of Nobility shall be granted by the United States · And no Person holding any Office of Profit or Trust under them, shall, without the Consent of the Congress, accept of any present, Emolument, Office, or Title, of any kind whatever, from any King, Prince, or foreign State

SECTION 10. (1) No State shall enter into any Treaty, Alliance, or Confederation; grant Letters of Marque and Reprisal, coin Money; emit Bills of Credit; make any Thing but gold and silver Coin a Tender in Payment of Debts; pass any Bill of Attainder, ex post facto Law, or Law impairing the Obligation of Contracts. or grant any Title of Nobility.

(2) No State shall, without the Consent of the Congress, lay any Imposts or Duties on Imports or Exports, except what may be absolutely necessary for executing its inspection Laws: and the net Produce of all Duties and Imposts, laid by any State on Imports or Exports, shall be for the Use of the Treasury of the United States, and all such Laws shall be subject to the revision and Controul of the Congress

(3) No State shall, without the Consent of Congress, lay any Duty of Tonnage, keep Troops, or Ships of War in time of Peace, enter into any Agreement or Compact with another State, or with a foreign Power, or engage in War, unless actually invaded, or in such imminent Danger as will not admit of Delay.

ARTICLE II.

SECTION 1 (1) The executive Power shall be vested in a President of the United States of America. He shall hold his Office during the Term of four Years, and, together with the Vice President, chosen for the same Term, be elected, as follows ·

(2) Each State shall appoint, in such Manner as the Legislature

thereof may direct, a Number of Electors, equal to the whole Number of Senators and Representatives to which the State may be entitled in the Congress. but no Senator or Representative, or Person holding an Office of Trust or Profit under the United States, shall be appointed an Elector.

The Electors shall meet in their respective States, and vote by ballot for two Persons, of whom one at least shall be an Inhabitant of the same State with themselves. And they shall make a List of all the Persons voted for, and of the Number of Votes for each; which List they shall sign and certify, and transmit sealed to the Seat of Government of the United States, directed to the President of the Senate. The President of the Senate shall, in the Presence of the Senate and House of Representatives, open all the Certificates, and the Votes shall then be counted. The Person having the greatest Number of Votes shall be the President, if such Number be a Majority of the whole Number of Electors appointed; and if there be more than one who have such Majority and have an equal Number of Votes, then the House of Representatives shall immediately chuse by Ballot one of them for President; and if no person have a Majority, then from the five highest on the List the said House shall in like Manner chuse the President. But in chusing the President, the Votes shall be taken by States, the Representation from each State having one Vote; A quorum for this Purpose shall consist of a Member or Members from two-thirds of the States, and a Majority of all the States shall be necessary to a Choice. In every Case, after the Choice of the President, the person having the greatest Number of Votes of the Electors shall be the Vice President. But if there should remain two or more who have equal Votes, the Senate shall chuse from them by Ballot the Vice President.

(3) The Congress may determine the Time of chusing the Electors, and the Day on which they shall give their Votes; which Day shall be the same throughout the United States

(4) No Person except a natural born Citizen, or a Citizen of the United States, at the time of the Adoption of this Constitution, shall be eligible to the Office of President, neither shall any Person be eligible to that Office who shall not have attained to the Age of thirty-five Years, and been fourteen Years a Resident within the United States.

(5) In Case of the Removal of the President from Office, or of his Death, Resignation, or Inability to discharge the Powers and Duties of the said Office, the same shall devolve on the Vice President, and the Congress may by Law provide for the Case of Removal, Death, Resignation, or Inability, of both the President and Vice President, declaring what

Officer shall then act as President, and such Officer shall act accordingly, until the Disability be removed, or a President shall be elected

(6) The President shall, at stated Times, receive for his Services, a Compensation, which shall neither be encreased nor diminished during the Period for which he shall have been elected, and he shall not receive within that Period any other Emolument from the United States, or any of them.

(7) Before he enter on the Execution of his Office, he shall take the following Oath or Affirmation—" I do solemnly swear (or affirm) that I will faithfully execute the Office of President of the United States, and will to the best of my Ability, preserve, protect and defend the Constitution of the United States."

Section 2. (1) The President shall be Commander in Chief of the Army and Navy of the United States, and of the Militia of the several States, when called into the actual Service of the United States; he may require the Opinion, in writing, of the principal Officer in each of the executive Departments, upon any Subject relating to the Duties of their respective Offices, and he shall have Power to grant Reprieves and Pardons for Offences against the United States, except in Cases of Impeachment.

(2) He shall have Power, by and with the Advice and Consent of the Senate, to make Treaties, provided two-thirds of the Senators present concur; and he shall nominate, and by and with the Advice and Consent of the Senate, shall appoint Ambassadors, other public Ministers and Councils, Judges of the Supreme Court, and all other Officers of the United States, whose Appointments are not herein otherwise provided for, and which shall be established by Law· but the Congress may by Law vest the Appointment of such inferior Officers, as they think proper, in the President alone, in the Courts of Law, or in the Heads of Departments.

(3) The President shall have Power to fill up all Vacancies that may happen during the Recess of the Senate, by granting Commissions which shall expire at the End of their next Session.

Section 3. He shall from time to time give to the Congress Information of the State of the Union, and recommend to their Consideration such Measures as he shall judge necessary and expedient; he may, on extraordinary Occasions, convene both Houses, or either of them, and in Case of Disagreement between them, with Respect to the Time of Adjournment, he may adjourn them to such Time as he shall think proper; he shall receive Ambassadors and other public Ministers; he shall take Care that the

Laws be faithfully executed, and shall Commission all the Officers of the United States.

Section 4. The President, Vice President and all civil Officers of the United States, shall be removed from Office on Impeachment for, and Conviction of, Treason, Bribery, or other high Crimes and Misdemeanors.

ARTICLE III.

Section 1. The judicial Power of the United States, shall be vested in one supreme Court, and in such inferior Courts as the Congress may from time to time ordain and establish. The Judges, both of the supreme and inferior Courts, shall hold their Offices during good Behavior, and shall, at stated Times, receive for their Services, a Compensation, which shall not be diminished during their Continuance in Office.

Section 2. (1) The judicial Power shall extend to all Cases, in Law and Equity, arising under this Constitution, the Laws of the United States, and Treaties made, or which shall be made, under their Authority;—to all Cases affecting Ambassadors, other public Ministers and Consuls;—to all Cases of admiralty and maritime Jurisdiction;—to Controversies to which the United States shall be a Party;—to Controversies between two or more States;—between a State and Citizens of another State;—between Citizens of different States,—between Citizens of the same State claiming Lands under Grants of different States, and between a State, or the Citizens thereof, and foreign States, Citizens or Subjects.

(2) In all Cases affecting Ambassadors, other public Ministers and Consuls, and those in which a State shall be a Party, the supreme Court shall have original Jurisdiction. In all the other Cases before mentioned, the supreme Court shall have appellate Jurisdiction, both as to Law and Fact, with such Exceptions, and under such Regulations as the Congress shall make

(3) The Trial of all Crimes, except in Cases of Impeachment, shall be by Jury; and such Trial shall be held in the State where the said Crimes shall have been committed; but when not committed within any State, the Trial shall be at such Place or Places as the Congress may by Law have directed.

Section 3. (1) Treason against the United States, shall consist only in levying War against them, or in adhering to their Enemies, giving them Aid and Comfort. No Person shall be convicted of Treason unless on the Testimony of two Witnesses to the same overt Act, or on Confession in Open Court.

(2) The Congress shall have Power to declare the Punishment of Treason, but no Attainder of Treason shall work Corruption of Blood, or Forfeiture except during the Life of the Person attainted.

ARTICLE IV.

SECTION 1. Full Faith and Credit shall be given in each State to the public Acts, Records, and judicial Proceedings of every other State. And the Congress may by general Laws prescribe the Manner in which such Acts, Records and Proceedings shall be proved, and the Effect thereof.

SECTION 2. (1) The Citizens of each State shall be entitled to all Privileges and Immunities of Citizens in the several States.

(2) A person charged in any State with Treason, Felony, or other Crime, who shall flee from Justice, and be found in another State, shall on Demand of the executive Authority of the State from which he fled, be delivered up to be removed to the State having Jurisdiction of the Crime.

(3) No Person held to Service or Labour in one State, under the Laws thereof, escaping into another, shall, in Consequence of any Law or Regulation therein, be discharged from such Service or Labour, but shall be delivered up on Claim of the Party to whom such Service or Labour may be due.

SECTION 3. (1) New States may be admitted by the Congress into this Union; but no new State shall be formed or erected within the Jurisdiction of any other State; nor any State be formed by the Junction of two or more States, or Parts of States, without the Consent of the Legislatures of the States concerned as well as of the Congress.

(2) The Congress shall have Power to dispose of and make all needful Rules and Regulations respecting the Territory or other Property belonging to the United States; and nothing in this Constitution shall be so construed as to Prejudice any Claims of the United States or of any particular State.

SECTION 4. The United States shall guarantee to every State in this Union a Republican Form of Government, and shall protect each of them against Invasion; and on Application of the Legislature, or of the Executive (when the Legislature cannot be convened) against domestic Violence.

ARTICLE V.

The Congress, whenever two-thirds of both Houses shall deem it necessary, shall propose Amendments to this Constitution, or, on the Application of the Legislatures of two-thirds of the several States, shall call a Convention for proposing Amendments, which, in either Case, shall be valid to all Intents and Purposes, as Part of this Constitution, when ratified by the Legislatures of three-fourths of the several States, or by Conventions in three-fourths thereof, as the one or the other Mode of Ratification may be proposed by the Congress, Provided that no Amendment which may be made prior to the Year One thousand eight hundred and eight shall in any Manner affect the first and fourth Clauses in the Ninth Section of the first Article; and that no State, without its Consent, shall be deprived of its equal Suffrage in the Senate.

ARTICLE VI.

(1) All Debts contracted and Engagements entered into, before the Adoption of this Constitution, shall be as valid against the United States under this Constitution, as under the Confederation.

(2) This Constitution, and the Laws of the United States which shall be made in pursuance thereof; and all Treaties made, or which shall be made, under the Authority of the United States, shall be the supreme Law of the Land; and the Judges in every State shall be bound thereby, any Thing in the Constitution or Laws of any State to the Contrary notwithstanding.

(3) The Senators and Representatives before mentioned, and the Members of the several State Legislatures, and all executive and judicial Officers, both of the United States and of the several States, shall be bound by Oath or Affirmation, to support this Constitution; but no religious Test shall ever be required as a Qualification to any Office or public Trust under the United States.

ARTICLE VII.

The Ratification of the Conventions of nine States, shall be sufficient for the Establishment of this Constitution between the States so ratifying the Same.

Done in Convention by the Unanimous Consent of the States present the Seventeenth Day of September in the Year of our Lord one thousand seven hundred and Eighty seven and of the Independence of the United States of America the Twelfth   In Witness Whereof We have hereunto subscribed our Names,

Go WASHINGTON
Presidt. and Deputy from Virginia

New Hampshire

JOHN LANGDON   NICHOLAS GILMAN

Massachusetts

NATHANIEL GORHAM   RUFUS KING

Connecticut

WM. SAML. JOHNSON   ROGER SHERMAN

New York

ALEXANDER HAMILTON

New Jersey

WIL· LIVINGSTON   WM. PATTERSON
DAVID BREARLEY   JONA: DAYTON

Pennsylvania

B. FRANKLIN   THOS. FITZSIMONS
THOMAS MIFFLIN   JARED INGERSOLL
ROBT. MORRIS   JAMES WILSON
GEO. CLYMER   GOUV. MORRIS

Delaware

GEO. READ   RICHARD BASSETT
GUNNING BEDFORD, JUN   JACO· BROOM
JOHN DICKINSON

Maryland

JAMES MCHENRY   DANL. CARROLL
DAN OF ST THOS. JENIFER

Virginia

JOHN BLAIR   JAMES MADISON, Jr

North Carolina

WM. BLOUNT   HU. WILLIAMSON
RICHD DOBBS SPAIGHT

South Carolina

J. RUTLEDGE   CHARLES PINCKNEY
CHARLES COTESWORTH   PIERCE BUTLER
    PINCKNEY

Georgia

WILLIAM FEW   ABR. BALDWIN

Attest   WILLIAM JACKSON *Secretary*

AMENDMENTS

Articles in Addition to, and Amendment of, the Constitution of the United States of America, Proposed by Congress, and Ratified by the Legislatures of the Several States Pursuant to the Fifth Article of the Original Constitution.

ARTICLE I.

Congress shall make no law respecting an establishment of religion, or prohibiting the free exercise thereof; or abridging the freedom of speech, or of the press, or the right of the people peaceably to assemble, and to petition the Government for a redress of grievances.

ARTICLE II.

A well regulated Militia, being necessary to the security of a free State, the right of the people to keep and bear Arms, shall not be infringed.

ARTICLE III.

No Soldier shall, in time of peace be quartered in any house, without the consent of the Owner, nor in time of war, but in a manner to be prescribed by law.

ARTICLE IV.

The right of the people to be secure in their persons, houses, papers, and effects, against unreasonable searches and seizures, shall not be violated, and no Warrants shall issue, but upon probable cause, supported by Oath or Affirmation and particularly describing the place to be searched, and the persons or things to be seized.

ARTICLE V.

No person shall be held to answer for a capital, or otherwise infamous crime, unless on a presentment or indictment of a Grand Jury, except in cases arising in the land or naval forces, or in the Militia, when in actual service in time of War or in public danger; nor shall any person be subject for the same offence to be twice put in jeopardy of life or limb; nor shall be compelled in any Criminal Case to be a witness against himself, nor be deprived of life, liberty, or property, without due process of law;

nor shall private property be taken for public use, without just compensation

ARTICLE VI.

In all criminal prosecutions, the accused shall enjoy the right to a speedy and public trial, by an impartial jury of the State and district wherein the crime shall have been committed, which district shall have been previously ascertained by law, and to be informed of the nature and cause of the accusation; to be confronted with the witnesses against him, to have compulsory process for obtaining Witnesses in his favor, and to have the Assistance of Counsel for his defence.

ARTICLE VII

In suits at common law, where the value in controversy shall exceed twenty dollars, the right of trial by jury shall be preserved, and no fact tried by a jury shall be otherwise re-examined in any Court of the United States, than according to the rules of the common law.

ARTICLE VIII.

Excessive bail shall not be required, nor excessive fines imposed, nor cruel and unusual punishments inflicted.

ARTICLE IX.

The enumeration in the Constitution, of certain rights, shall not be construed to deny or disparage others retained by the people.

ARTICLE X

The powers not delegated to the United States by the Constitution, nor prohibited by it to the States, are reserved to the States respectively, or to the people.

ARTICLE XI.

The Judicial power of the United States shall not be construed to extend to any suit in law or equity, commenced or prosecuted against one of the United States by Citizens of another State, or by Citizens or Subjects of any Foreign State.

ARTICLE XII.

The Electors shall meet in their respective States, and vote by ballot for President and Vice President, one of whom, at least, shall not be an inhabitant of the same State with themselves; they shall name in their ballots the person voted for as President, and in distinct ballots the person voted for as Vice President, and they shall make distinct lists of all persons voted for as President, and of all persons voted for as Vice President, and of the number of votes for each, which lists they shall sign and certify, and transmit sealed to the seat of the government of the United States, directed to the President of the Senate;—The President of the Senate shall, in presence of the Senate and House of Representatives, open all the certificates and the votes shall then be counted,—The person having the greatest number of votes for President, shall be the President, if such number be a majority of the whole number of Electors appointed; and if no person have such majority, then from the persons having the highest numbers not exceeding three on the list of those voted for as President, the House of Representatives shall choose immediately, by ballot, the President. But in choosing the President, the votes shall be taken by States, the representation from each State having one vote; a quorum for this purpose shall consist of a Member or Members from two-thirds of the States, and a majority of all the States shall be necessary to a choice. And if the House of Representatives shall not choose a President whenever the right of choice shall devolve upon them, before the fourth day of March next following, then the Vice President shall act as President, as in the case of the death or other constitutional disability of the President. The person having the greatest number of votes as Vice President, shall be the Vice President, if such number be a majority of the whole number of Electors appointed, and if no person have a majority, then from the two highest numbers on the list, the Senate shall choose the Vice President; a quorum for the purpose shall consist of two-thirds of the whole number of Senators, and a majority of the whole number shall be necessary to a choice. But no person constitutionally ineligible to the Office of President shall be eligible to that of Vice President of the United States.

ARTICLE XIII.

Section 1 Neither slavery nor involuntary servitude, except as a punishment for crime whereof the party shall have been duly convicted,

shall exist within the United States, or any place subject to their jurisdiction

SECTION 2 Congress shall have power to enforce this article by
appropriate legislation.

ARTICLE XIV.

SECTION 1. All persons born or naturalized in the United States, and
subject to the jurisdiction thereof, are citizens of the United States and
of the State wherein they reside. No State shall make or enforce any law
which shall abridge the privileges or immunities of citizens of the United
States; nor shall any State deprive any person of life, liberty, or property,
without due process of law; nor deny to any person within its jurisdiction
the equal protection of the laws.

SECTION 2. Representatives shall be apportioned among the several
States according to their respective numbers, counting the whole number
of persons in each State, excluding Indians not taxed. But when the
right to vote at any election for the choice of Electors for President and
Vice President of the United States, Representatives in Congress, the
Executive and Judicial officers of a State, or the members of the Legislature thereof, is denied to any of the male inhabitants of such State,
being twenty-one years of age, and citizens of the United States, or in
any way abridged, except for participation in rebellion, or other crime,
the basis of representation therein shall be reduced in the proportion
which the number of such male citizens shall bear to the whole number
of male citizens twenty-one years of age in such State.

SECTION 3. No person shall be a Senator or Representative in Congress, or Elector of President and Vice President, or hold any office, civil
or military, under the United States, or under any State, who, having
previously taken an oath, as a member of Congress, or as an officer of the
United States, or as a member of any State legislature, or as an executive
or judicial officer of any State, to support the Constitution of the United
States, shall have engaged in insurrection or rebellion against the same,
or given aid or comfort to the enemies thereof. But Congress may by a
vote of two-thirds of each House, remove such disability

SECTION 4. The validity of the public debt of the United States,
authorized by law, including debts incurred for payment of pensions and
bounties for services in suppressing insurrection or rebellion, shall not
be questioned. But neither the United States nor any State shall assume
or pay any debt or obligation incurred in aid of insurrection or rebellion
against the United States, or any claim for the loss or emancipation of

any slave; but all such debts, obligations and claims shall be held illegal and void

SECTION 5 The Congress shall have power to enforce, by appropriate legislation, the provisions of this article.

ARTICLE XV.

SECTION 1. The right of citizens of the United States to vote shall not be denied or abridged by the United States or by any State on account of race, color, or previous condition of servitude

SECTION 2 The Congress shall have power to enforce this article by appropriate legislation.

IX

CONSTITUTION OF THE CONFEDERATE STATES OF AMERICA, 1861

We, the people of the Confederate States, each State active in its sovereign and independent character, in order to form a permanent federal government, establish justice, insure domestic tranquillity, and secure the blessings of liberty to ourselves and our posterity—invoking the favor and guidance of Almighty God—do ordain and establish this Constitution for the Confederate States of America.

ARTICLE I.

SECTION 1. All legislative powers herein delegated shall be vested in a Congress of the Confederate States, which shall consist of a Senate and a House of Representatives.

SECTION 2. (1) The House of Representatives shall be composed of members chosen every second year by the people of the several States; and the electors in each State shall be citizens of the Confederate States, and have the qualifications requisite for electors of the most numerous branch of the State Legislature; but no person of foreign birth, not a citizen of the Confederate States, shall be allowed to vote for any officer, civil or political, State or Federal.

(2) No person shall be a Representative who shall not have attained the age of twenty-five years, and be a citizen of the Confederate States, and who shall not, when elected, be an inhabitant of that State in which he shall be chosen.

(3) Representatives and direct taxes shall be apportioned among the several States, which may be included within this Confederacy, according to their respective numbers, which shall be determined, by adding to the whole number of free persons, including those bound to service for a term of years, and excluding Indians not taxed, three-fifth of all slaves. The actual enumeration shall be made within three years after the first meeting of the Congress of the Confederate States, and within every subsequent term of ten years, in such manner as they shall by law direct. The number of Representatives shall not exceed one for every fifty thousand, but each State shall have at least one Representative; and until such enumeration shall be made, the State of South Carolina shall be entitled to choose six; the State of Georgia ten; the State of Alabama nine; the State of Florida two, the State of Mississippi seven, the State of Louisiana six; and the State of Texas six.

(4) When vacancies happen in the representation from any State, the Executive authority thereof shall issue writs of election to fill such vacancies

(5) The House of Representatives shall choose their Speaker and other officers; and shall have the sole power of impeachment; except that any judicial or other Federal officer, resident and acting solely within the limits of any State, may be impeached by a vote of two-thirds of both branches of the Legislature thereof.

SECTION 3. (1) The Senate of the Confederate States shall be composed of two Senators from each State, chosen for six years by the Legislature thereof, at the regular session next immediately preceding the commencement of the term of service; and each Senator shall have one vote.

(2) Immediately after they shall be assembled, in consequence of the first election, they shall be divided as equally as may be into three classes. The seats of the Senators of the first class shall be vacated at the expiration of the second year, of the second class at the expiration of the fourth year, and of the third class at the expiration of the sixth year, so that one-third may be chosen every second year; and if vacancies happen by resignation, or otherwise, during the recess of the Legislature of any State, the Executive thereof may make temporary appointments until the next meeting of the Legislature which shall then fill such vacancies.

(3) No person shall be a Senator who shall not have attained to the age of thirty years, and be a citizen of the Confederate States; and who shall not, when elected, be an inhabitant of the State for which he shall be chosen.

(4) The Vice President of the Confederate States shall be President of the Senate, but shall have no vote unless they be equally divided.

(5) The Senate shall choose their other officers; and also a President *pro tempore* in the absence of the Vice President, or when he shall exercise the office of President of the Confederate States.

(6) The Senate shall have power to try all impeachments. When sitting for that purpose, they shall be on oath or affirmation. When the President of the Confederate States is tried, the Chief Justice shall preside; and no persons shall be convicted without the concurrence of two-thirds of the members present

(7) Judgment in cases of impeachment shall not extend further than to removal from office, and disqualification to hold and enjoy any office of honor, trust, or profit, under the Confederate States; but the party convicted shall, nevertheless, be liable and subject to indictment, trial, judgment and punishment according to law.

SECTION 4. (1) The times, places and manner of holding elections for Senators and Representatives, shall be prescribed in each State by the Legislature thereof, subject to the provisions of this Constitution, but the Congress may, at any time, by law, make or alter such regulations, except as to the times and places of choosing Senators.

(2) The Congress shall assemble at least once in every year; and such meeting shall be on the first Monday in December, unless they shall, by law, appoint a different day.

SECTION 5. (1) Each House shall be the judge of the elections, returns, and qualifications of its own members, and a majority of each shall constitute a quorum to do business; but a smaller number may adjourn from day to day, and may be authorized to compel the attendance of absent members, in such manner and under such penalties as each House may provide.

(2) Each House may determine the rules of its proceedings, punish its members for disorderly behavior, and with the concurrence of two-thirds of the whole number, expel a member.

(3) Each House shall keep a journal of its proceedings, and from time to time publish the same, excepting such parts as may in their judgment require secrecy; and the yeas and nays of the members of either House, on any question, shall, at the desire of one-fifth of those present, be entered on the journal.

(4) Neither House, during the session of Congress, shall, without the consent of the other, adjourn for more than three days, nor to any other place than that in which the two Houses shall be sitting.

SECTION 6. (1) The Senators and Representatives shall receive a compensation for their services, to be ascertained by law, and paid out of the treasury of the Confederate States. They shall, in all cases, except treason, felony, and breach of the peace, be privileged from arrest during their attendance at the session of their respective Houses, and in going to and returning from the same; and for any speech or debate in either House, they shall not be questioned in any other place.

(2) No Senator or Representative shall, during the time for which he was elected, be appointed to any civil office under the authority of the Confederate States, which shall have been created, or the emoluments whereof shall have been increased during such time; and no person holding any office under the Confederate States shall be a member of either House during his continuance in office. But Congress may, by law, grant to the principal officer in each of the Executive Departments a seat upon the floor of either House, with the privilege of discussing any measure appertaining to his department

SECTION 7 (1) All bills for raising revenue shall originate in the House of Representatives; but the Senate may propose or concur with the amendments, as on other bills.

(2) Every bill which shall have passed both Houses, shall, before it becomes a law be presented to the President of the Confederate States; if he approve, he shall sign it; but if not, he shall return it, with his objections, to that House in which it shall have originated, who shall enter the objections at large on their journal, and proceed to reconsider it. If, after such reconsideration, two-thirds of that House shall agree to pass the bill, it shall be sent, together with the objections, to the other House, by which it shall likewise be reconsidered, and if approved by two-thirds of that House, it shall become a law. But in all such cases, the votes of both Houses shall be determined by yeas and nays, and the names of the persons voting for and against the bill shall be entered on the journal of each House respectively If any bill shall not be returned by the President within ten days (Sundays excepted) after it shall have been presented to him the same shall be a law, in like manner as if he had signed it, unless the Congress by their adjournment prevent its return; in which case it shall not be a law. The President may approve any appropriation and disapprove any other appropriation in the same bill. In such case he shall, in signing the bill, designate the appropriations disapproved; and shall return a copy of such appropriations, with his objections, to the House in which the bill shall have originated; and the

same proceedings shall then be had as in case of other bills disapproved by the President.

(3) Every order, resolution, or vote, to which the concurrence of both Houses may be necessary (except on a question of adjournment), shall be presented to the President of the Confederate States; and before the same shall take effect, shall be approved by him; or being disapproved by him, shall be repassed by two-thirds of both Houses, according to the rules and limitations prescribed in case of a bill.

SECTION 8. The Congress shall have power—

(1) To lay and collect taxes, duties, imposts, and excises, for revenue necessary to pay the debts, provide for the common defence, and carry on the government of the Confederate States; but no bounties shall be granted from the treasury; nor shall any duties or taxes on importations from foreign nations be laid to promote or foster any branch of industry; and all duties, imposts, and excises shall be uniform throughout the Confederate States:

(2) To borrow money on the credit of the Confederate States:

(3) To regulate commerce with foreign nations, and among the several States, and with the Indian tribes; but neither this, nor any other clause contained in the constitution, shall ever be construed to delegate the power to Congress to appropriate money for any internal improvement intended to facilitate commerce, except for the purpose of furnishing lights, beacons, and buoys, and other aids to navigation upon the coasts, and the improvement of harbors and the removing of obstructions in river navigation, in all which cases, such duties shall be laid on the navigation facilitated thereby, as may be necessary to pay the costs and expenses thereof:

(4) To establish uniform laws of naturalization, and uniform laws on the subject of bankruptcies, throughout the Confederate States, but no law of Congress shall discharge any debt contracted before the passage of the same

(5) To coin money, regulate the value therof and of foreign coin, and fix the standard of weights and measures:

(6) To provide for the punishment of counterfeiting the securities and current coin of the Confederate States:

(7) To establish post-offices and post-routes; but expenses of the Post-Office Department, after the first day of March in the year of our Lord eighteen hundred and sixty-three, shall be paid out of its own revenue·

(8) To promote the progress of science and useful arts, by securing

for limited times to authors and inventors the exclusive right to their respective writings and discoveries·

(9) To constitute tribunals inferior to the Supreme Court.

(10) To define and punish piracies and felonies committed on the high seas, and offences against the law of nations:

(11) To declare war, grant letters of marque and reprisal, and make rules concerning captures on land and water:

(12) To raise and support armies; but no appropriation of money to that use shall be for a longer term than two years.

(13) To provide and maintain a navy:

(14) To make rules for the government and regulation of the land and naval forces:

(15) To provide for calling forth the militia to execute the laws of the Confederate States, suppress insurrections, and repel invasions:

(16) To provide for organizing, arming, and disciplining the militia, and for governing such part of them as may be employed in the service of the Confederate States, reserving to the States, respectively, the appointment of the officers, and the authority of training the militia according to the discipline prescribed by Congress:

(17) To exercise exclusive legislation, in all cases whatsoever, over such district (not exceeding ten miles square) as may, by cession of one or more States and the acceptance of Congress, become the seat of the Government of the Confederate States: and to exercise like authority over all places purchased by the consent of the legislature of the State in which the same shall be, for the erection of forts, magazines, arsenals, dockyards, and other needful buildings. and

(18) To make all laws which shall be necessary and proper for carrying into execution the foregoing powers, and all other powers vested by this Constitution in the Government of the Confederate States, or in any department or officer thereof.

SECTION 9. (1) The importation of negroes of the African race, from any foreign country other than the slave-holding States or Territories of the United States of America, is hereby forbidden; and Congress is required to pass such laws as shall effectually prevent the same

(2) Congress shall also have power to prohibit the introduction of slaves from any State not a member of, or Territory not belonging to this Confederacy.

(3) The privilege of the writ of *habeas corpus* shall not be suspended, unless when in case of rebellion or invasion the public safety may require it.

(4) No bill of attainder, or *ex post facto* law, or law denying or impa[i]ring the right if property in negro slaves shall be passed

(5) No capitation or other direct tax shall be laid, unless in proportion to the census or enumeration hereinbefore directed to be taken

(6) No tax or duty shall be laid upon articles exported from any State, except by a vote of two-thirds of both Houses

(7) No preference shall be given by any regulation of commerce or revenue to the ports of one State over those of another

(8) No money shall be drawn from the treasury, but in consequence of appropriations made by law; and a regular statement and account of the receipts and expenditures of all public money shall be published from time to time.

(9) Congress shall appropriate no money from the treasury except by a vote of two-thirds of both Houses, taken by yeas and nays, unless it be asked and estimated for by some one of the heads of departments, and submitted to Congress by the President, or for the purpose of paying its own expenses and contingencies; or for the payment of claims against the Confederate States, the justice of which shall have been judicially declared by a tribunal for the investigation of claims against the government, which it is hereby made the duty of Congress to establish.

(10) All bills appropriating money shall specify in federal currency the exact amount of each appropriation and the purposes for which it is made; and Congress shall grant no extra compensation to any public contractor, officer, agent or servant, after such contract shall have been made or such service rendered.

(11) No title of nobility shall be granted by the Confederate States; and no person holding any office of profit or trust under them shall, without the consent of Congress, accept of any present, emolument, office or title of any kind whatever, from any king, prince, or foreign state.

(12) Congress shall make no law respecting an establishment of religion, or prohibiting the free exercise thereof, or abridging the freedom of speech, or of the press; or the right of the people peaceably to assemble and petition the government for a redress of grievances.

(13) A well regulated militia being necessary to the security of a free State, the right of the people to keep and bear arms shall not be infringed

(14) No soldier shall, in time of peace, be quartered in any house, without the consent of the owner, nor in time of war, but in a manner to be prescribed by law.

(15) The right of the people to be secure in their persons, houses,

papers, and effects, against unreasonable searches and seizures, shall not be violated; and no warrants shall issue but upon probable cause, supported by oath or affirmation, and particularly describing the place to be searched, and the persons or things to be seized

(16) No person shall be held to answer for a capital or otherwise infamous crime, unless on a presentment or indictment of a grand jury, except in cases arising in the land or naval forces, or in the militia, when in actual service in time of war or public danger; nor shall any person be subject for the same offence to be twice put in jeopardy of life or limb; nor be compelled, in any criminal case, to be a witness against himself; nor to be deprived of life, liberty, or property without due process of law; nor shall private property be taken for public use, without just compensation.

(17) In all criminal prosecutions, the accused shall enjoy the right to a speedy and public trial, by an impartial jury of the State and district wherein the crime shall have been committed, which district shall have been previously ascertained by law, and to be informed of the nature and cause of the accusation, to be confronted with the witnesses against him; to have compulsory process for obtaining witnesses in his favor; and to have the assistance of counsel for his defence.

(18) In suits at common law, where the value in controversy shall exceed twenty dollars, the right of trial by jury shall be preserved; and no fact so tried by a jury shall be otherwise re-examined in any court of the Confederacy, than according to the rules of common law.

(19) Excessive bail shall not be required, nor excessive fines imposed, nor cruel and inhuman punishment inflicted.

(20) Every law, or resolution having the force of law, shall relate to but one subject, and that shall be expressed in the title.

SECTION 10 (1) No State shall enter into any treaty, alliance, or confederation, grant letters of marque and reprisal; coin money; make anything but gold and silver coin a tender in payment of debts; pass any bill of attainder, *ex post facto* law, or law impairing the obligation of contracts, or grant any title of nobility.

(2) No State shall, without the consent of Congress, lay any imposts or duties on imports or exports, except what may be absolutely necessary for executing its inspection laws, and the net produce of all duties and imposts, laid by any State on imports or exports, shall be for the use of the Treasury of the Confederate States; and all such laws shall be subject to the revision and control of Congress

(3) No State shall, without the consent of Congress, lay any duty

on tonnage, except on sea-going vessels, for the improvement of its rivers and harbors navigated by the said vessels; but such duties shall not conflict with any treaties of the Confederate States with foreign nations, and any surplus revenue, thus derived, shall, after making such improvement, be paid into the common treasury. Nor shall any State keep troops or ships-of-war in time of peace, enter into any agreement or compact with another State, or with a foreign power, or engage in war, unless actually invaded, or in such imminent danger as will not admit of delay. But when any river divides or flows through two or more States, they may enter into compacts with each other to improve the navigation thereof.

ARTICLE II.

Section 1. (1) The executive power shall be vested in a President of the Confederate States of America. He and the Vice President shall hold their offices for the term of six years, but the President shall not be re-eligible The President and the Vice President shall be elected as follows.

(2) Each State shall appoint, in such manner as the legislature thereof may direct, a number of electors equal to the whole number of Senators and Representatives to which the State may be entitled in the Congress; but no Senator or Representative or person holding an office of trust or profit under the Confederate States, shall be appointed an elector.

(3) The electors shall meet in their respective States and vote by ballot for President and Vice President, one of whom, at least, shall not be an inhabitant of the same State with themselves; they shall name in their ballots the person voted for as President, and in distinct ballots the person voted for as Vice President, and they shall make distinct lists of all persons voted for as President, and of all persons voted for as Vice President, and of the number of votes for each, which list they shall sign and certify, and transmit, sealed, to the seat of the Government of the Confederate States, directed to the President of the Senate; the President of the Senate shall, in the presence of the Senate and House of Representatives, open all the certificates, and the votes shall then be counted, the person having the greatest number of votes for President shall be the President, if such number be a majority of the whole number of electors appointed; and if no person have such a majority, then, from the persons having the highest number, not exceeding three, on the list of those voted for as President, the House of Representatives shall choose

immediately, by ballot, the President. But in choosing the President, the votes shall be taken by States—the representation from each State having one vote; a quorum for this purpose shall consist of a member or members from two-thirds of the States, and a majority of all the States shall be necessary to the choice. And if the House of Representatives shall not choose a President, whenever the right of choice shall devolve upon them, before the fourth day of March next following, then the Vice President shall act as President, as in the case of the death, or other constitutional disability of the President.

(4) The person having the greatest number of votes as Vice President, shall be the Vice President, if such number be a majority of the whole number of electors appointed, and if no person have a majority, then, from the two highest numbers on the list, the Senate shall choose the Vice President; a quorum for the purpose shall consist of two-thirds of the whole number of Senators, and a majority of the whole number shall be necessary to a choice.

(5) But no person constitutionally ineligible to the office of President shall be eligible to that of Vice President of the Confederate States.

(6) The Congress may determine the time of choosing the electors, and the day on which they shall give their votes; which day shall be the same throughout the Confederate States.

(7) No person except a natural born citizen of the Confederate States, or a citizen thereof at the time of the adoption of this Constitution, or a citizen thereof born in the United States prior to the 20th of December, 1860, shall be eligible to the office of President; neither shall any person be eligible to that office who shall not have attained the age of thirty-five years, and been fourteen years a resident within the limits of the Confederate States, as they may exist at the time of his election.

(8) In case of the removal of the President from office, or of his death, resignation, or inability to discharge the powers and duties of the said office, the same shall devolve on the Vice President, and Congress may, by law, provide for the case of removal, death, resignation, or inability, both of the President and Vice President, declaring what officer shall then act as President; and such officer shall act accordingly, until the disability be removed or a President shall be elected.

(9) The President shall, at stated times, receive for his services a compensation, which shall neither be increased nor diminished during the period for which he shall have been elected, and he shall not receive within that period any other emolument from the Confederate States, or any of them.

(10) Before he enters on the execution of his office, he shall take the following oath or affirmation:

" I do solemnly swear (or affirm) that I will faithfully execute the office of President of the Confederate States, and will, to the best of my ability, preserve, protect, and defend the Constitution thereof "

SECTION 2 (1) The President shall be Commander-in-chief of the army and navy of the Confederate States, and of the militia of the several States, when called into the actual service of the Confederate States; he may require the opinion, in writing, of the principal officer in each of the executive departments, upon any subject relating to the duties of their respective offices, and he shall have power to grant reprieves and pardons for offences against the Confederate States, except in cases of impeachment.

(2) He shall have power, by and with the advice and consent of the Senate, to make treaties; provided two-thirds of the Senators present concur; and he shall nominate, and by and with the advice and consent of the Senate, shall appoint ambassadors, other public ministers and consuls, judges of the Supreme Court, and all other officers of the Confederate States whose appointments are not herein otherwise provided for, and which shall be established by law; but the Congress may, by law, vest the appointment of such inferior officers, as they think proper, in the President alone, in the courts of law, or in the heads of departments

(3) The principal officer in each of the executive departments, and all persons connected with the diplomatic service, may be removed from office at the pleasure of the President. All other civil officers of the executive department may be removed at any time by the President, or other appointing power, when their services are unnecessary, or for dishonesty, incapacity, inefficiency, misconduct, or neglect of duty; and when so removed, the removal shall be reported to the Senate, together with the reasons therefor.

(4) The President shall have power to fill all vacancies that may happen during the recess of the Senate, by granting commissions which shall expire at the end of their next session, but no person rejected by the Senate shall be re-appointed to the same office during their ensuing recess.

SECTION 3. (1) The President shall, from time to time, give to the Congress information of the state of the Confederacy, and recommend to their consideration such measures as he shall judge necessary and expedient; he may, on extraordinary occasions, convene both Houses, or either of them, and in case of disagreement between them, with respect to the time of adjournment, he may adjourn them to such time as he shall think proper; he shall receive ambassadors and other public ministers, he shall take care that the laws be faithfully executed, and shall commission all the officers of the Confederate States.

SECTION 4. (1) The President, Vice President, and all civil officers of the Confederate States, shall be removed from office on impeachment, for and conviction of, treason, bribery, or other high crimes and misdemeanors.

ARTICLE III.

SECTION 1. (1) The judicial power of the Confederate States shall be vested in one Supreme Court, and in such inferior courts as the Congress may, from time to time, ordain and establish. The judges, both of the supreme and inferior courts, shall hold their offices during good behavior, and shall, at stated times, receive for their services, a compensation which shall not be diminished during their continuance in office

SECTION 2. (1) The judicial power shall extend to all cases arising under this Constitution, the laws of the Confederate States, and treaties made, or which shall be made, under their authority; to all cases affecting ambassadors, other public ministers and consuls; to all cases of admiralty and maritime jurisdiction; to controversies to which the Confederate States shall be a party; to controversies between two or more States; between a State and citizens of another State, where the State is plaintiff; between citizens claiming lands under grants of different States; and between a State or the citizens thereof, and foreign states, citizens or subjects; but no State shall be sued by a citizen or subject of any foreign state.

(2) In all cases affecting ambassadors, other public ministers and consuls, and those in which a State shall be a party, the Supreme Court shall have original jurisdiction In all the other cases before mentioned, the Supreme Court shall have appellate jurisdiction both as to law and fact, with such exceptions and under such regulations as the Congress shall make.

(3) The trial of all crimes, except in cases of impeachment, shall be by jury; and such trial shall be held in the State where the said crimes shall have been committed, but when not committed within any State, the trial shall be at such place or places as the Congress may by law have directed.

SECTION 3. (1) Treason against the Confederate States shall consist only in levying war against them, or in adhering to their enemies, giving them aid and comfort. No person shall be convicted of treason unless on the testimony of two witnesses to the same overt act, or on confession in open court.

(2) The Congress shall have power to declare the punishment of treason; but no attainder of treason shall work corruption of blood, or forfeiture, except during the life of the person attainted.

ARTICLE IV.

SECTION 1. (1) Full faith and credit shall be given in each State to the public acts, records, and judicial proceedings of every other State. And the Congress may, by general laws, prescribe the manner in which such acts, records, and proceedings shall be proved, and the effect thereof.

SECTION 2. (1) The citizens of each State shall be entitled to all the privileges and immunities of citizens in the several States; and shall have the right of transit and sojourn in any State of this Confederacy, with their slaves and other property; and the right of property in said slaves shall not be thereby impaired.

(2) A person charged in any State with treason, felony, or other crime against the laws of such State, who shall flee from justice, and be found in another State, shall, on demand of the Executive authority of the State from which he fled, be delivered up, to be removed to the State having jurisdiction of the crime.

(3) No slave or other person held to service or labor in any State or Territory of the Confederate States, under the laws thereof, escaping or lawfully carried into another, shall, in consequence of any law or regulation therein, be discharged from such service or labor; but shall be delivered up on claim of the party to whom such slave belongs, or to whom such service or labor may be due.

SECTION 3. (1) Other States may be admitted into this Confederacy by a vote of two-thirds of the whole House of Representatives and two-thirds of the Senate, the Senate voting by States; but no new State shall be formed or erected within the jurisdiction of any other State; nor any State be formed by the junction of two or more States, or parts of States, without the consent of the legislatures of the States concerned, as well as of the Congress.

(2) The Congress shall have power to dispose of and make all needful rules and regulations concerning the property of the Confederate States, including the lands thereof.

(3) The Confederate States may acquire new territory; and Congress shall have power to legislate and provide governments for the inhabitants

of all territory belonging to the Confederate States, lying without the limits of the several States; and may permit them, at such times, and in such manner as it may by law provide, to form States to be admitted into the Confederacy. In all such territory, the institution of negro slavery, as it now exists in the Confederate States, shall be recognized and protected by Congress and by the territorial government: and the inhabitants of the several Confederate States and Territories shall have the right to take to such territory any slaves lawfully held by them in any of the States or Territories of the Confederate States.

(4) The Confederate States shall guarantee to every State that now is, or hereafter may become, a member of this Confederacy, a republican form of government; and shall protect each of them against invasion; and on application of the legislature (or of the executive, when the legislature is not in session), against domestic violence.

ARTICLE V.

Section 1. (1) Upon the demand of any three States, legally assembled in their several conventions, the Congress shall summon a convention of all the States, to take into consideration such amendments to the Constitution as the said States shall concur in suggesting at the time when the said demand is made; and should any of the proposed amendments to the Constitution be agreed on by the said convention—voting by States —and the same be ratified by the legislatures of two-thirds of the several States, or by conventions in two-thirds thereof—as the one or the other mode of ratification may be proposed by the general convention—they shall henceforward form a part of the Constitution. But no State shall, without its consent, be deprived of its equal representation in the Senate.

ARTICLE VI.

(1) The Government established by this Constitution is the successor of the Provisional Government of the Confederate States of America, and all the laws passed by the latter shall continue in force until the same shall be repealed or modified; and all the officers appointed by the same shall remain in office until their successors are appointed and qualified, or the offices abolished

(2) All debts contracted and engagements entered into before the adoption of this Constitution shall be as valid against the Confederate States under this Constitution, as under the Provisional Government.

(3) This Constitution, and the laws of the Confederate States made in pursuance thereof, and all treaties made, or which shall be made, under

the authority of the Confederate States, shall be the supreme law of the land; and the judges in every State shall be bound thereby, anything in the Constitution or laws of any State to the contrary notwithstanding.

(4) The Senators and Representatives before mentioned, and the members of the several State legislatures, and all executive and judicial officers, both of the Confederate States and of the several States, shall be bound by oath or affirmation to support this Constitution; but no religious test shall ever be required as a qualification to any office or public trust under the Confederate States

(5) The enumeration, in the Constitution, of certain rights, shall not be construed to deny or disparage others retained by the people of the several States.

(6) The powers not delegated to the Confederate States by the Constitution, nor prohibited by it to the States, are reserved to the States, respectively, or to the people thereof.

ARTICLE VII.

(1) The ratification of the conventions of five States shall be sufficient for the establishment of this Constitution between the States so ratifying the same.

(2) When five States shall have ratified this Constitution, in the manner before specified, the Congress under the Provisional Constitution shall prescribe the time for holding the election of President and Vice President, and for the meeting of the Electoral College, and for counting the votes, and inaugurating the President   They shall, also, prescribe the time for holding the first election of members of Congress under this Constitution, and the time for assembling the same   Until the assembling of such Congress, the Congress under the Provisional Constitution shall continue to exercise the legislative powers granted them; not extending beyond the time limit by the Constitution of the Provisional Government.

Adopted unanimously by the Congress of the Confederate States of South Carolina, Georgia, Florida, Alabama, Mississippi, Louisiana, and Texas, sitting in convention at the capitol, in the city of Montgomery, Alabama, on the Eleventh day of March, in the year Eighteen Hundred and Sixty-one.

HOWELL COBB
President of the Congress

X

EMANCIPATION PROCLAMATION, 1863

Whereas, on the twenty-second day of September, in the year of our Lord one thousand eight hundred and sixty-two, a proclamation was issued by the President of the United States, containing, among other things, the following, to wit:

" That on the first day of January, in the year of our Lord one thousand eight hundred and sixty-three, all persons held as slaves within any State, or designated part of a State, the people whereof shall then be in rebellion against the United States, shall be then, thenceforward, and forever free; and the Executive Government of the United States, including the military and naval authority thereof, will recognize and maintain the freedom of such persons, and will do no act or acts to repress such persons, or any of them, in any efforts they may make for their actual freedom.

" That the Executive will, on the first day of January aforesaid, by proclamation, designate the States and parts of States, if any, in which the people thereof respectively, shall then be in rebellion against the United States; and the fact that any State, or the people thereof, shall on that day be in good faith represented in the Congress of the United States by members chosen thereto at elections wherein a majority of the qualified voters of such State shall have participated, shall in the absence of strong countervailing testimony, be deemed conclusive evidence that such State, and the people thereof, are not then in rebellion against the United States "

Now, therefore, I, Abraham Lincoln, President of the United States, by virtue of the power in me vested as commander-in-chief of the Army and Navy of the United States, in time of actual armed rebellion against authority and government of the United States, and as a fit and necessary war measure for suppressing said rebellion, do, on this first day of January, in the year of our Lord one thousand eight hundred and sixty-three, and in accordance with my purpose so to do, publicly proclaim for the full period of one hundred days from the day first above mentioned, order and designate as the States and parts of States wherein the people thereof, respectively, are this day in rebellion against the United States, the following, to wit.

Arkansas, Texas, Lousiana (except the parishes of St. Bernard, Plaquemines, Jefferson, St. John, St. Charles, St James, Ascension,

Assumption, Terrebonne, Lafourche, St Mary, St. Martin, and Orleans, including the city of New Orleans), Mississippi, Alabama, Florida, Georgia, South Carolina, North Carolina, and Virginia (except the forty-eight counties designated as West Virginia, and also the counties of Berkley, Accomac, Northampton, Elizabeth City, York, Princess Ann, and Norfolk, including the cities of Norfolk and Portsmouth), and which excepted parts are, for the present, left precisely as if this proclamation were not issued.

And by virtue of the power and for the purpose aforesaid, I do order and declare that all persons held as slaves within said designated States and parts of States are, and henceforward shall be, free; and that the Executive government of the United States including the military and naval authorities thereof, will recognize and maintain the freedom of said persons.

And I hereby enjoin upon the people so declared to be free to abstain from all violence, unless in necessary self-defence; and I recommend to them that, in all cases when allowed, they labor faithfully for reasonable wages.

And I further declare and make known, that such persons of suitable condition, will be received into the armed service of the United States to garrison forts, positions, stations, and other places, and to man vessels of all sorts in said service

And upon this act, sincerely believed to be an act of justice, warranted by the Constitution, upon military necessity, I invoke the considerate judgment of mankind and the gracious favor of Almighty God.

In witness whereof, I have hereunto set my hand, and caused the seal of the United States to be affixed.

Done at the city of Washington, this first day of January, in the year of our Lord one thousand eight hundred and sixty-three, and of the Independence of the United States of America the eighty-seventh.

ABRAHAM LINCOLN

L. S.

By the President:

WILLIAM H. SEWARD,
        Secretary of State.

PRESIDENTS AND CABINETS OF THE UNITED STATES AND OF THE CONFEDERATE STATES

PRESIDENTS AND CABINETS OF THE
UNITED STATES

George Washington, 1789-1797,
  Vice President
    John Adams
  Secretary of State
    Thomas Jefferson, Virginia, September 26, 1789
    Edmund Randolph, Virginia, January 2, 1794
    Timothy Pickering, Pennsylvania, December 10,
      1795
  Secretary of the Treasury
    Alexander Hamilton, New York, September 11, 1789
    Oliver Wolcott, Connecticut, February 2, 1795
  Secretary of War
    Henry Knox, Massachusetts, September 12, 1789
    Timothy Pickering, Pennsylvania, January 2, 1795
    James McHenry, Maryland, January 27, 1796
  Attorney-General
    Edmund Randolph, Virginia, September 26, 1789
    William Bradford, Pennsylvania, January 27, 1794
    Charles Lee, Virginia, December 10, 1795
  Postmaster-General (not regularly a member of the
      Cabinet until 1829)
    Samuel Osgood, Massachusetts, September 26, 1789
    Timothy Pickering, Pennsylvania, August 12, 1791
    Joseph Habersham, Georgia, February 25, 1795

John Adams, 1797-1801
  Vice President
    Thomas Jefferson

Secretary of State
    Timothy Pickering, Pennsylvania, continued
    John Marshall, Virginia, May 13, 1800
Secretary of the Treasury
    Oliver Wolcott, Connecticut, continued
    Samuel Dexter, Massachusetts, January 1, 1801
Secretary of War
    James McHenry, Maryland, continued
    Samuel Dexter, Massachusetts, May 13, 1800
    Roger Griswold, Connecticut, February 3, 1801
Secretary of the Navy
    George Cabot, Massachusetts, May 3, 1798
    Benjamin Stoddert, Maryland, May 21, 1798
Attorney-General
    Charles Lee, Virginia, continued
    Theophilus Parsons, Massachusetts, February 20, 1801
Postmaster-General
    Joseph Habersham, Georgia, continued

Thomas Jefferson, 1801-1809
    Vice President
        Aaron Burr, 1801-1805
        George Clinton, 1805-1809
    Secretary of State
        James Madison, Virginia, March 5, 1801
    Secretary of the Treasury
        Samuel Dexter, Massachusetts, continued
        Albert Gallatin, Pennsylvania, May 14, 1801
    Secretary of War
        Henry Dearborn, Massachusetts, March 5, 1801
    Secretary of the Navy
        Benjamin Stoddert, Maryland, continued
        Robert Smith, Maryland, July 23, 1801

Jacob Crowninshield, Massachusetts, nominal only
 from March 3, 1805, to his death, April 15,
 1808
Attorney-General
  Levi Lincoln, Massachusetts, March 5, 1801'
  Robert Smith, Maryland, March 3, 1805
  John Breckinridge, Kentucky, August 7, 1805
  Cæsar A. Rodney, Pennsylvania, January 20, 1807
Postmaster-General
  Joseph Habersham, Georgia, continued
  Gideon Granger, Connecticut, November 28, 1801

James Madison, 1809-1817.
  Vice President
    George Clinton, 1809-April 20, 1812
    Elbridge Gerry, 1813-November 23, 1814
  Secretary of State
    Robert Smith, Maryland, March 6, 1809
    James Monroe, Virginia, April 2, 1811
  Secretary of the Treasury
    Albert Gallatin, Pennsylvania, continued
    George W. Campbell, Tennessee, February 9, 1814
    A. J. Dallas, Pennsylvania, October 6, 1814
    William H. Crawford, Georgia, October 22, 1816
  Secretary of War
    William Eustis, Massachusetts, March 7, 1809
    John Armstrong, New York, January 13, 1813
    James Monroe (acting), September 27, 1814
    William H. Crawford, Georgia, August 1, 1815
  Secretary of the Navy
    Paul Hamilton, South Carolina, March 7, 1809
    William Jones, Pennsylvania, January 12, 1813
    Benjamin W. Crowninshield, Massachusetts, De-
      cember 19, 1814

Attorney-General
    Cæsar A. Rodney, Pennsylvania, continued
    William Pinckney, Maryland, December 11, 1811
    Richard Rush, Pennsylvania, February 10, 1814
Postmaster-General
    Gideon Granger, Connecticut, continued
    Return J. Meigs, Ohio, March 17, 1814

James Monroe, 1817-1825
    Vice President
    Daniel D. Tompkins
    Secretary of State
    John Quincy Adams, Massachusetts, March 5, 1817
    Secretary of the Treasury
    William H. Crawford, Georgia, continued
    Secretary of War
    George Graham, Virginia, April 7, 1817
    John C. Calhoun, South Carolina, October 8, 1817
    Secretary of the Navy
    B. W. Crowninshield, Massachusetts, continued
    Smith Thompson, New York, November 9, 1818
    John Rogers, Massachusetts, September 1, 1823
    Samuel L. Southard, New Jersey, September 16, 1823
    Attorney-General
    Richard Rush, Pennsylvania, continued
    William Wirt, Virginia, November 13, 1817,
    Postmaster-General
    Return J. Meigs, Ohio, continued
    John McLean, Ohio, June 26, 1823

John Quincy Adams, 1825-1829
    Vice President
    John C. Calhoun

Secretary of State
  Henry Clay, Kentucky, March 7, 1825
Secretary of the Treasury
  Richard Rush, Pennsylvania, March 7, 1825
Secretary of War
  James Barbour, Virginia, March 7, 1825
  Peter B. Porter, New York, May 26, 1828
Secretary of the Navy
  Samuel L Southard, New Jersey, continued
Attorney-General
  William Wirt, Virginia, continued
Postmaster-General ·
  John McLean, Ohio, continued

Andrew Jackson, 1829-1837
  Vice President
    John C. Calhoun, 1829-1833
    Martin Van Buren, 1833-1837
  Secretary of State
    Martin Van Buren, New York, March 6, 1829
    Edward Livingston, Louisiana, May 24, 1831
    Louis McLane, Delaware, May 29, 1833
    John Forsyth, Georgia, June 27, 1834
  Secretary of the Treasury
    Samuel D. Ingham, Pennsylvania, March 6, 1829
    Louis McLane, Delaware, August 8, 1831
    William J. Duane, Pennsylvania, May 29, 1833
    Roger B. Taney, Maryland, September 23, 1833
    Levi Woodbury, New Hampshire, June 27, 1834
  Secretary of War
    John H. Eaton, Tennessee, March 9, 1829
    Lewis Cass, Michigan, August 1, 1831
    Benjamin F. Butler, New York, March 3, 1837

Secretary of the Navy
  John Branch, North Carolina, March 9, 1829
  Levi Woodbury, New Hampshire, May 23, 1831
  Mahlon Dickerson, New Jersey, June 30, 1834
Attorney-General
  John M. Berrien, Georgia, March 9, 1829
  Roger B. Taney, Maryland, July 20, 1831
  Benjamin F. Butler, New York, November 15, 1833
Postmaster-General
  William T. Barry, Kentucky, March 9, 1829
  Amos Kendall, Kentucky, May 1, 1835

Martin Van Buren, 1837-1841
  Vice President
    Richard M. Johnson
  Secretary of State
    John Forsyth, Georgia, continued
  Secretary of the Treasury
    Levi Woodbury, New Hampshire, continued
  Secretary of War
    Joel R. Poinsett, South Carolina, March 7, 1837
  Secretary of the Navy
    Mahlon Dickerson, New Jersey, continued
    James K. Paulding, New York, June 25, 1838
  Attorney-General
    Benjamin F. Butler, New York, continued
    Felix Grundy, Tennessee, July 5, 1838
    Henry D. Gilpin, Pennsylvania, January 11, 1840
  Postmaster-General
    Amos Kendall, Kentucky, continued
    John M. Niles, Connecticut, May 19, 1840

William Henry Harrison, March 4-April 4, 1841, and John
      Tyler, April 4, 1841-1845

Vice President
  John Tyler, March 4-April 4, 1841
Secretary of State
  Daniel Webster, Massachusetts, March 5, 1841
  Hugh S. Legaré, South Carolina, May 9, 1845
  A. P. Upshur, Virginia, July 24, 1843
  John C. Calhoun, South Carolina, March 6, 1844
Secretary of the Treasury
  Thomas Ewing, Ohio, March 5, 1841
  Walter Forward, Pennsylvania, September 13, 1841
  John C. Spencer, New York, March 3, 1843
  George M. Bibb, Kentucky, June 15, 1844
Secretary of War
  John Bell, Tennessee, March 5, 1841
  John McLean, Ohio, September 13, 1841
  John C. Spencer, New York, October 12, 1841
  James M. Porter, Pennsylvania, March 8, 1843
  William Wilkins, Pennsylvania, February 15, 1844
Secretary of the Navy
  G. E. Badger, North Carolina, March 5, 1841
  A. P. Upshur, Virginia, September 13, 1841
  David Henshaw, Massachusetts, July 24, 1843
  T. W. Gilmer, Virginia, February 15, 1844
  John Y. Mason, Virginia, March 14, 1844
Attorney-General
  John J. Crittenden, Kentucky, March 5, 1841
  Hugh S. Legaré, South Carolina, September 13, 1841
  John Nelson, Maryland, July 1, 1843
Postmaster-General
  Francis Granger, New York, March 6, 1841
  Charles A. Wickliffe, Kentucky, September 13, 1841

James K. Polk, 1845-1849

Vice President
  George M. Dallas
Secretary of State
  James Buchanan, Pennsylvania, March 6, 1845
Secretary of the Treasury
  Robert J. Walker, Mississippi, March 6, 1845
Secretary of War
  William L. Marcy, New York, March 6, 1845
Secretary of the Navy
  George Bancroft, Massachusetts, March 10, 1845
  John Y. Mason, Virginia, September 9, 1846
'Attorney-General
  John Y. Mason, Virginia, March 5, 1845
  Nathan Clifford, Maine, October 17, 1846
Postmaster-General
  Cave Johnson, Tennessee, March 6, 1845

Zachary Taylor, 1849-July 9, 1850, and Millard Fillmore,
    July 9, 1850-1853
Vice President
  Millard Fillmore, 1849-July 9, 1850
Secretary of State
  John M. Clayton, Delaware, March 7, 1849
  Daniel Webster, Massachusetts, December 6, 1852
Secretary of the Treasury
  W. M. Meredith, Pennsylvania, March 8, 1849
  Thomas Corwin, Ohio, July 23, 1850
Secretary of War
  George W. Crawford, Georgia, March 8, 1849
  Winfield Scott (ad interim), July 23, 1850
  Charles M. Conrad, Louisiana, August 15, 1850
Secretary of the Navy
  William B. Preston, North Carolina, July 22, 1850
  J. P. Kennedy, Maryland, July 22, 1852

Secretary of the Interior
    Thomas H. Ewing, Ohio, March 8, 1849
    A. H. H. Stuart, Virginia, September 12, 1850
Attorney-General
    Reverdy Johnson, Maryland, March 8, 1849
    John J. Crittenden, Kentucky, July 22, 1850
Postmaster-General
    Jacob Collamer, Vermont, March 8, 1849
    Nathan K. Hall, New York, July 23, 1850
    S. D. Hubbard, Connecticut, August 31, 1852

Franklin Pierce, 1853-1857,
    Vice President
        William R. King, March-April, 1853
    Secretary of State
        Wilham L. Marcy, New York, March 7, 1853
    Secretary of the Treasury
        James Guthrie, Kentucky, March 7, 1853
    Secretary of War
        Jefferson Davis, Mississippi, March 7, 1853
    Secretary of the Navy
        James C. Dobbin, North Carolina, March 7, 1853
    Secretary of the Interior
        Robert McClelland, Michigan, March 7, 1853
        Jacob Thompson, Missisippi, March 6, 1856
    Attorney-General
        Caleb Cushing, Massachusetts, March 7, 1853
    Postmaster-General
        James Campbell, Pennsylvania, March 7, 1853

James Buchanan, 1857-1861
    Vice President
        John C. Breckinridge

Secretary of State
  Lewis Cass, Michigan, March 6, 1857
  J. S. Black, Pennsylvania, December 17, 1860
Secretary of the Treasury
  Howell Cobb, Georgia, March 6, 1857
  Philip F. Thomas, Maryland, December 12, 1860
  John A. Dix, New York, January 11, 1861
Secretary of War
  John B. Floyd, Virginia, March 6, 1857
  Joseph Holt, Kentucky, January 18, 1861
Secretary of the Navy
  Isaac Toucey, Connecticut, March 6, 1857
Secretary of the Interior
  Jacob Thompson, Mississippi, March 6, 1857
Attorney-General
  J. S. Black, Pennsylvania, March 6, 1857
  E. M. Stanton, Pennsylvania, December 20, 1860
Postmaster-General
  Aaron V. Brown, Tennessee, March 6, 1857
  Joseph Holt, Kentucky, March 14, 1859
  Horatio King, Maine, February 12, 1861

Abraham Lincoln, 1861-April 15, 1865, and Andrew Johnson, April 15, 1865-1869
  Vice President
    Hannibal Hamlin, 1861-1865
    Andrew Johnson, March 4-April 15, 1865
  Secretary of State
    William H. Seward, New York, March 5, 1861
  Secretary of the Treasury
    Salmon P. Chase, Ohio, March 5, 1861
    W. P. Fessenden, Maine, July 1, 1864
    Hugh McCulloch, Indiana, March 7, 1865

Secretary of War
    Simon Cameron, Pennsylvania, March 5, 1861
    Edwin M. Stanton, Pennsylvania, January 15, 1862
    Ulysses S. Grant (*ad interim*), August 12, 1867
    Edwin M. Stanton (reinstated), January 14, 1868
    John McA. Schofield, New York, May 28, 1868
Secretary of the Navy
    Gideon Welles, Connecticut, March 5, 1861
Secretary of the Interior
    Caleb P. Smith, March 5, 1861
    John P. Usher, Indiana, January 8, 1863
    James Harlan, Iowa, May 15, 1865
    O. H. Browning, Illinois, July 27, 1866
Attorney-General
    Edward Bates, Missouri, March 5, 1861
    Titian J. Coffee, June 22, 1863
    James Speed, Kentucky, December 2, 1864
    Henry Stanbery, Ohio, July 23, 1866
    William M. Evarts, New York, July 15, 1868
Postmaster-General
    Montgomery Blair, Maryland, March 5, 1861
    William Dennison, Ohio, September 24, 1864
    Alexander W. Randall, Wisconsin, July 25, 1866

Ulysses S. Grant, 1869-1877
    Vice President
        Schuyler Colfax, 1869-1873
        Henry Wilson, 1873-November 22, 1875
    Secretary of State
        E. B. Washburne, Illinois, March 5, 1869
        Hamilton Fish, New York, March 11, 1869
    Secretary of the Treasury
        George S. Boutwell, Massachusetts, March 11, 1869

William A. Richardson, Massachusetts, March 17, 1873

Benjamin H. Bristow, Kentucky, June 2, 1874

Lot M. Morrill, Maine, June 21, 1876

Secretary of War

John A. Rawlins, Illinois, March 11, 1869

William T. Sherman, Ohio, September 9, 1869

William W. Belknap, Iowa, October 25, 1869

Alphonso Taft, Ohio, March 8, 1876

J. D. Cameron, Pennsylvania, May 22, 1876

Secretary of the Navy

Adolph E. Borie, Pennsylvania, March 5, 1869

George M. Robeson, New Jersey, June 25, 1869

Secretary of the Interior

Jacob D. Cox, Ohio, March 5, 1869

Columbus Delano, Ohio, November 1, 1870

Zachariah Chandler, Michigan, October 19, 1875

Attorney-General

E. R. Hoar, Massachusetts, March 5, 1869

Amos T. Akerman, Georgia, June 23, 1870

George H. Williams, Oregon, December 14, 1871

Edwards Pierrepont, New York, April 26, 1875

Alphonso Taft, Ohio, May 22, 1876

Postmaster-General

J. A. J. Creswell, Maryland, March 5, 1869

Marshall Jewell, Connecticut, August 24, 1874

James M. Tyner, Indiana, July 12, 1876

Rutherford B. Hayes, 1877-1881

Vice President

William A. Wheeler

Secretary of State

William M. Evarts, New York, March 12, 1877

Secretary of the Treasury
  John Sherman, Ohio, March 8, 1877
Secretary of War
  George W. McCrary, Iowa, March 12, 1877
  Alexander Ramsey, Minnesota, December 12, 1879
Secretary of the Navy
  Richard W. Thompson, Indiana, March 12, 1877
  Nathan Goff, Jr., West Virginia, January 6,
    1881
Secretary of the Interior
  Carl Schurz, Missouri, March 12, 1877
Attorney-General
  Charles Devons, Massachusetts, March 12, 1877
Postmaster-General
  David M. Key, Tennessee, March 12, 1877
  Horace Maynard, Tennessee, August 25, 1880

James A. Garfield, March 4-September 19, 1881, and Ches-
    ter A. Arthur, September 19, 1881-1885
Vice President
  Chester A. Arthur, March 4-September 19, 1881
Secretary of State
  James G. Blaine, Maine, March 5, 1881
  Frederick T. Frelinghuysen, New Jersey, December
    12, 1881
Secretary of the Treasury
  William H. Windom, Minnesota, March 5, 1881
  Charles J. Folger, New York, October 27, 1881
Secretary of War
  Robert T. Lincoln, Illinois, March 5, 1881
Secretary of the Navy
  W. H. Hunt, Louisiana, March 5, 1881
  William E. Chandler, New Hampshire, April 12,
    1882

Secretary of the Interior
  S. J. Kirkwood, Iowa, March 5, 1881
  Henry M. Teller, Colorado, April 6, 1882
Attorney-General
  Wayne McVeagh, Pennsylvania, March 5, 1881
  Benjamin H. Brewster, Pennsylvania, December 16, 1881
Postmaster-General
  Thomas L. James, New York, March 5, 1881
  Timothy O. Howe, Wisconsin, December 20, 1881
  W. Q. Gresham, Indiana, April 3, 1883
  Frank Hatton, Iowa, October 14, 1884

Grover Cleveland, 1885-1889
  Vice President
    Thomas A. Hendricks, March 4-November 25, 1885
  Secretary of State
    Thomas F. Bayard, Delaware, March 6, 1885
  Secretary of the Treasury
    Daniel Manning, New York, March 6, 1885
    Charles S. Fairchild, New York, April 1, 1887
  Secretary of War
    William C. Endicott, Massachusetts, March 6, 1885
  Secretary of the Navy
    William C. Whitney, New York, March 6, 1885
  Secretary of the Interior
    Lucius Q. C. Lamar, Mississippi, March 6, 1885
    William F. Vilas, Wisconsin, January 16, 1888
  Attorney-General
    Augustus H. Garland, Arkansas, March 6, 1885
  Postmaster-General
    William F. Vilas, Wisconsin, March 6, 1885
    Don M. Dickinson, Michigan, January 16, 1888

Benjamin Harrison, 1889-1893
   Vice President
      Levi P. Morton
   Secretary of State
      James G. Blaine, Maine, March 7, 1889
   Secretary of the Treasury
      William Windom, Minnesota, March 7, 1889
      Charles Foster, Ohio, February 21, 1891
   Secretary of War
      Redfield Proctor, Vermont, March 7, 1889
   Secretary of the Navy
      Benjamin F. Tracy, New York, March 7, 1889
   Secretary of the Interior
      John W. Noble, Missouri, March 7, 1889
   Secretary of Agriculture
      Jeremiah M. Rusk, Wisconsin, March 7, 1889
   Attorney-General
      W. H. H. Miller, Indiana, March 7, 1889
   Postmaster-General
      John Wanamaker, Pennsylvania, March 7, 1889

Grover Cleveland, 1893-1897
   Vice President
      Adlai E. Stevenson
   Secretary of State
      Walter Q. Gresham, Indiana, March 6, 1893
      Richard Olney, Massachusetts, June 10, 1895
   Secretary of the Treasury
      John G. Carlisle, Kentucky, March 6, 1893
   Secretary of War
      Daniel S. Lamont, New York, March 6, 1893
   Secretary of the Navy
      Hilary A. Herbert, Alabama, March 6, 1893

Secretary of the Interior
    Hoke Smith, Georgia, March 6, 1893
Secretary of Agriculture
    J. Sterling Morton, Nebraska, March 6, 1893
Attorney-General
    Richard Olney, Massachusetts, March 6, 1893
    Judson Harmon, Ohio, June 7, 1895
Postmaster-General
    Wilson S. Bissell, New York, March 6, 1893
    William L. Wilson, West Virginia, March 1, 1895
William McKinley, 1897-September 14, 1901, and Theodore
        Roosevelt, September 14, 1901——
Vice President
    Garret A. Hobart, 1897-November 21, 1899
    Theodore Roosevelt, March 4-September 14, 1901
    Charles Warren Fairbanks, 1905——
Secretary of State
    John Sherman, Ohio, March 5, 1897
    W. R. Day, Ohio, April 26, 1898
    John Hay, Ohio, September 30, 1898
    Elihu Root, New York, July 19, 1905
Secretary of the Treasury
    Lyman J. Gage, Illinois, March 5, 1897
    Leslie M. Shaw, Iowa, January 10, 1902
Secretary of War
    Russell A. Alger, Michigan, March 5, 1897
    Elihu Root, New York, July 22, 1899
    William H. Taft, Ohio, January 11, 1904
Secretary of the Navy
    John D. Long, Massachusetts, March 5, 1897
    William H. Moody, Massachusetts, April 29,
        1892
    Paul Morton, Illinois, July 1, 1904
    Charles J. Bonaparte, Maryland, July 1, 1905

Secretary of the Interior
   Cornelius N. Bliss, New York, March 5, 1897
   Ethan Allen Hitchcock, Missouri, December 21, 1898
Secretary of Agriculture
   James Wilson, Iowa, March 5, 1897
Secretary of Labor and Commerce
   George B. Cortelyou, New York, February, 1903
   Victor H. Metcalf, California, July 1, 1904
Attorney-General
   Joseph McKenna, California, March 5, 1897
   John William Griggs, New Jersey, January, 1898
   Philander C. Knox, Pennsylvania, April 5, 1901
   William H. Moody, Massachusetts, July 1, 1904
Postmaster-General
   James A. Gary, Maryland, March 5, 1897
   Charles Emory Smith, Pennsylvania, April 21, 1898
   Henry C. Payne, Wisconsin, January 10, 1902
   Robert J. Wynne, District of Columbia, October 10, 1904
   George B. Cortelyou, New York, March 6, 1905

PRESIDENT AND CABINETS OF THE CONFEDERATE STATES

Jefferson Davis, February 9, 1861-May 11, 1865
- Vice President
  - Alexander H. Stephens
- Secretary of State
  - Robert Toombs, Georgia, February 21, 1861
  - R. M. T. Hunter, Virginia, July 25, 1861
  - Judah P. Benjamin, Louisiana, March 18, 1862
- Secretary of the Treasury
  - Christopher G. Memminger, South Carolina, February 21, 1861
  - George A. Trenholm, South Carolina, July 18, 1864
- Secretary of War
  - LeRoy Pope Walker, Alabama, February 21, 1861
  - Judah P. Benjamin, Louisiana, September 17, 1861
  - George W. Randolph, Virginia, March 18, 1862
  - Gustavus A. Smith (acting), March 18, 1862
  - James A. Seddon, Virginia, November 21, 1862
  - John C. Breckinridge, Kentucky, February 6, 1865
- Secretary of the Navy
  - Stephen R. Mallory, March 1, 1861
- Attorney-General
  - Judah P. Benjamin, Louisiana, February 25, 1861
  - Thomas Bragg, North Carolina, November 21, 1861
  - T. N. Watts, Alabama, March 18, 1862
  - George Davis, North Carolina, January 2, 1864
- Postmaster-General
  - Henry T. Ellet, Mississippi, February 25, 1861
  - John H. Reagan, Texas, March 6, 1861

Milton Keynes UK
Ingram Content Group UK Ltd.
UKHW022145080923
428346UK00005B/109